A Few Wise Words

Amersham Publishing Limited
Buckinghamshire
England

First published by Amersham Publishing Limited 2020

A catalogue record of this book is available from the British Library.

ISBN 978-1-5272-6980-4

Front cover tree design by Charlotte Posner

Typesetting by RefineCatch Limited

Printed and bound in Great Britain by Clays Ltd, Elcograf S.p.A.

We are committed to helping ensure a sustainable future for our planet
so that future generations may continue to enjoy our wonderful natural
environment. This book has been printed on Forest Stewardship Council
(FSC) certified paper.

a
few
wise
words

volume one

stories of success and inspirational advice
from 22 extraordinary individuals

edited and compiled by
Peter Mukherjee

To Sebastian, for your journey, and with huge love.
Thank you for inspiring me to make this happen.

CONTENTS

CONTRIBUTOR CHAPTERS

FOREWORD

by Lord Mervyn Davies of Abersoch, CBE

As we all know, life is an interesting journey, full of ups and downs and lessons to be learnt. And from those that have already found success and purpose in their lives, there is so much knowledge and wisdom that can be passed down to help our future generations.

We are living through a period of extraordinary change, with many challenges, but for the bright, brave, and optimistic, it is also an exciting time. I often say when speaking to young people, that if they can discover what they are really good at, have a zest for life and an appetite to learn, then anything they may wish to achieve is possible.

So when Peter and I first discussed the idea he had for this book, I immediately recognised the potential it had to deliver something genuinely inspiring and impactful. But to create a special piece of art, music, or literature, takes time, energy, talent, and commitment. In preparing *A Few Wise Words*, Peter has shown all of those qualities to create this wonderful book, which will be the first of an international series.

We have worked together on this over the last few years and I am very proud of what has been achieved. The contributors have also given of their time freely and put a lot of thought into their material, with extraordinary stories of highs and lows. Their words of wisdom offer help and inspiration for anyone who is striving to become truly successful in life.

I hope you enjoy the read.

Introduction

I recall some years ago hearing a lovely anecdote on my local radio that went something like this:

A father is sitting next to his teenage daughter Chloe at the breakfast bar in their kitchen. Conversation is sparse and as patchy as usual – he is wondering how best to communicate with his daughter, while she keeps glancing at her phone, hoping for any message that might pop up and save her . . .

During a long moment of silence, her phone suddenly pings. After a pause, she says, with a slightly bemused expression on her face, 'It's a text from Mum . . .' She then holds the phone up so her dad can see it. He leans forward slightly and reads the message aloud: 'What do you want from Life?'

They look at one another for a few seconds, both slightly surprised at the uncharacteristically philosophical question being posed by Mum. But however unusual the message, it certainly does the trick; for the first time in ages, Chloe begins to relax and talks openly with her dad about what is, after all, a very important question. He responds gratefully, and they both embark on one of the most deeply interesting and fruitful conversations they have ever had before as father and daughter . . .

Twenty minutes into an amazing discussion, Chloe's phone pings again – it's another text from Mum. Both she and Dad look at the message: 'Sorry! Spellcheck! Meant to say, what do you want from Lidl?'

It is, of course, one of the most fundamentally important questions that any of us will ever ask of ourselves: 'What *do* we want from life?'

For many, the answer may be quite simple: 'To be successful, and to be happy'. But, while these are clearly wonderful aspirations for anyone to have, the older we get, the more we learn to appreciate how success is not something we are simply entitled to, and it is definitely *not* that easy to achieve. Because for any person, whatever their age, and whatever success might look like for them, getting from where they are now to where they may dream to be will usually require a long, arduous and often complex journey – the bigger one's aspirations, the more challenging it's likely to be.

Each journey is unique and a very personal experience, and to reach our destination successfully will always demand effort, focus and determination along the way. Careful preparation from the start and continuous learning throughout are also essential; acquiring the knowledge and skills we will need to navigate our way forward while getting ready to face the numerous challenges and obstacles that will inevitably lie ahead. But mastering how to find – and attract – opportunities and knowing how to make the most of them are also essential, especially the big ones that can take us up to the next level.

Whether we're a young person, a young adult or older, realising the potential we have will always remain largely in our hands. And while some journeys might seem destined to play out like a game of snakes and ladders, there are some enormously helpful things we can all do that can actually, load the dice significantly in our favour.

One of these is to study in depth what highly successful people the world over have done within their own lives to accomplish extraordinary things. This naturally leads us to ponder, 'How did they manage to achieve that?' and 'What can I learn from what they did?' There is a vast amount of knowledge and wisdom we can absorb from the lives of those who have enjoyed great success.

Some might be fortunate. They may already have connections to incredible people, whom they can talk to and from whom they can learn. But for the majority of us who do not, access to this knowledge is fortunately still entirely within our reach. It can all be found in literature – biographical and autobiographical books that detail the lives of countless amazing individuals are just a trip down the high street or a mouse click away. And for those who prefer to consume knowledge in bite-size chunks, modern media can also provide access to great material, with insights, quotes, speeches, interviews and articles about or from a vast range of super-successful men and women.

While these valuable resources may be widely available for anyone to access, we must be prepared to commit time to study them well, because self-education done properly will always demand quality time. But for those of us who are willing to make that investment, the rewards can be truly enormous; it can often take the import of just one or two good ideas, that applied to our journey, can transform a moderate trajectory into a stellar one.

Our extraordinary contributors . . .

Whatever your personal vision of success may be, *A Few Wise Words* has been crafted to be your ultimate travelling companion and guide. From the start of your journey all the way through to your eventual destination, this book offers special access to an extraordinary reservoir of knowledge and an invaluable source of inspiration, to help you press forward with confidence and purpose. It is jam-packed with wisdom and advice from twenty-two exceptional individuals, equally divided between men and women from a wide range of backgrounds. Each of our contributors has already achieved remarkable success in their own lives and is happy to share their knowledge with you, while articulating clearly what you will need to do if you want to be successful in yours. Their inclusion within this book recognises not only their extraordinary achievements, and the enormous respect that each has earned over the years, but also their generosity and a willingness to help others.

This book is *not* a third-party academic study of what these individuals have done. Each contributor presents their own unique chapter in which they speak directly to you, the reader. They begin by defining what 'success' means personally for them, what their own journey was like, and how they managed to conquer the many challenges they had to confront along the way. Each then conveys what they believe are the most important steps that *you* should take to enable you to successfully negotiate your own special journey. They will help you to reveal the amazing potential that you have, while understanding exactly what you need to do next to take full advantage of it.

A Few Wise Words conveys their knowledge and advice in a concentrated and digestible format; no fluff, no waffle, just straight-to-the-point, down-to-earth, neatly distilled, essential value. It is a book that you can dip in and out of at any time during your journey for advice and inspiration.

Over many generations, academics and educators have consistently expressed how laying the right foundations early in life can significantly increase the chances of any child performing well in their later years. Most of us will recognise the importance of this too. Our contributors therefore offer additional guidance especially for us, as parents. This covers the crucial role that we can play in preparing our children early, while enabling them to 'hit the ground running' when the serious part of their journey begins in earnest later on.

Who this book is intended to help . . .

Whether you have acquired *A Few Wise Words* for yourself, or whether someone has kindly gifted you a copy, this book aims to deliver practical answers to the key questions you may have about where you are now and what you need to do next.

From young person to older adult, every one of us will be at different stages along our own respective journeys:

Perhaps you are a *student still at secondary school* – you may or may not have any idea about where you are heading, what you want to do with your life, or where your talents really lie. You understand that your performance at school is hugely important and will help determine your future direction, whatever that may eventually be. But you also realise that there's a lot you can learn for yourself, outside of what you would normally expect to pick up from school, that can help you to develop early personal skills and to grow as an individual.

You may also be a *secondary school leaver* – you could be heading for university or some other form of further education, an apprenticeship even, or you may be going straight out to work. You might have chosen your career direction already, or you might have only an inkling about what you would ultimately like to do. You might, indeed, still have no clue at all just yet! You are always looking for inspiration and new ideas, and know how vitally important the next few years will be for you. Getting the right advice and guidance at an early stage can therefore be enormously helpful for your immediate and future development as a young adult.

You might be a *young adult embarking on a new career* – a hugely exciting time, a bit scary perhaps, but a wonderful challenge. It's a new world, full of possibilities, but there's a huge amount for you to learn. You know it's also a time for you to really optimise all of your skills and accomplishments, since the size of the impact you make early in your career can have a profound effect on your future success within it. The only thing you lack right now is experience and know-how. This is where other people, who already have that experience, can certainly help you.

You may be an *older adult in the middle of developing your career* – whatever career path you have chosen, to get ahead you will need to have an edge. To be noticed, you will also need to shine. If you can cultivate exceptional personal skills – also known as soft skills – and can arm yourself with the right knowledge and capabilities, there is no limit to what you can do. So, if your aspirations are big, you will need to do all you can from now on to create the very best version of you. This will take time and effort, but you know it's an important investment to make. It will enable you to move ahead positively, with confidence and self-belief, so you can be ready, when the time is right, to move up to the next level.

And for all of us who are *parents of young or older children* – we all naturally want to learn more about the role that we can play to help our children to really flourish, how to nurture their development, encourage and empower them, while ensuring they can have the best possible start in life. Having an intuitive understanding of what their journey might look like, and of the choices and the challenges they are likely to face, will enable us to be far more empathetic, helpful and supportive during the important years ahead.

How this book can help you . . .

For young people, young adults and older adults . . .

So, your journey might have just got started, or it may be well underway already, but whatever stage you are at right now, our contributors will be on hand and ready to support you. With insightful anecdotes and a broad spectrum of advice, they can help you to plan your journey purposefully, and then navigate it confidently, with a clear vision of where you want to go.

Here are some of the main areas covered by our contributors in this book:

When contemplating your future career (perhaps your initial career direction as a student, your first job, your first venture, a move up or even a change in direction), you will learn why our contributors consistently stress the importance of finding a purpose or a mission, a role or an activity that you feel genuinely *passionate* about, and why this is so fundamental. Most will explain how they found their own passion, and how crucial this was to their success, with practical advice on how you too can explore, both introspectively and externally, what that special something might be for you.

Good values are essential. Being led by them will always help you to stay on track, as Sir Roger Carr describes brilliantly in his chapter. You will also discover which disciplines are the most important ones to embrace and how they can substantially increase your chances of finding success. Our contributors will explore with you how to develop a great attitude and show how this will attract amazing people to you who will want to help you. You will learn why having a good mentor can be helpful too, with advice on how to find the right one(s) for you, how to approach them and when is the right time to do so.

Goals are always very personal and will, of course, vary, depending on your career and the nature of you as an individual. Our contributors explain how they approached their own goals, while some describe in more detail the science and logic behind truly productive goal-setting.

As you start to make good progress in your journey, you will naturally start thinking about ways to move up. Our contributors will guide you on how to look for the doors to open, that can lead you on to fabulous opportunities. They will also show you how to attract great opportunities, through making yourself more interesting as a person to those that matter around you.

Every journey is beset with challenges, and some of these will be big. You will learn not only how to face them when they occur but also how to plan for their possibility in advance, as expertly covered by Sir Clive Woodward in his chapter. Having moments of self-doubt is completely normal – you will discover how to manage them and even exploit them. You will find out as well why failure can actually be good for you, and how, when processed correctly, it can become a real opportunity to learn and move up.

And finally, while good fortune will doubtless play a significant role in any individual success story, the simple truth is that we are all far more in control over our own futures and our own fortunes than most of us actually realise. Our choices are quite clear-cut; we can either go with the flow and hope for the best, or we can take charge now and apply some hugely positive changes to our lives . . . We can either leave everything entirely to chance, or we can work hard to stack the odds substantially in our favour.

One of the key principles you will absorb naturally from this book is that you really *do* have the power to 'make luck work for you', and our contributors will show you how. As Declan Kelly fittingly states in his chapter, for example, 'If you cast a line in the water, you might catch a fish. If you cast fifty lines in the water, you are *going* to catch a fish.'

For parents . . .

A Few Wise Words can actually help a young person *before* they are old enough to read and appreciate this book for themselves . . . through helping their parents first.

As a parent, we naturally want to be the very best mum or dad that we can possibly be for our child. Many of our contributors describe how their parents played a crucial role in their journey and eventual success. They explain precisely what their parents did to help them, from childhood through to young adulthood, and often well beyond.

In the separate tinted sections that provide advice specifically for parents, but also within the main body of each chapter, we can find insightful advice on how to help our children to flourish at a young age, how to fire their imagination and curiosity, and why this is crucial. Our contributors explain why developing a curiosity for even the smallest of things can stimulate not only a healthy early desire to absorb knowledge about a particular subject but even a passion for it, and what a wonderful catalyst this can be, as recounted brilliantly by Stephen Fry in his chapter. They discuss the best way for us to engage with our child and how this can have a hugely positive impact on their outlook later, and how introducing the right values early on will help our children to develop their own moral compass and equip them fundamentally for their future.

Advice is also given on how we can instil confidence, self-belief and a healthy attitude at an early stage, and how to literally empower our kids so that they can learn for themselves and take responsibility for their actions. And, as Sir Ben Ainslie perfectly describes in his chapter, how this can stimulate initiative and motivation. We will also learn how to present choices to our children to help them explore different possibilities, one of which could even spark a passion for something significant that their future career may eventually revolve around.

The guidance offered to parents can also be helpful for grandparents, aunts, uncles, other caring relatives and, of course, godparents too.

A Few Wise Words has taken nearly four years as a project to assemble and complete. I am incredibly grateful to all of our wonderful contributors, and to everyone else who has supported me to make this book possible (please see the Acknowledgements).

I hope that the wisdom and advice conveyed by our contributors within these pages will help you to make the most of your journey, while providing the support you will need as you navigate your way positively and safely towards your dreams.

So whatever stage you are at on your own journey, may I wish you all the very best of good fortune, and I hope that you will go on to find your passion, your purpose, success, and ultimately, true happiness in your life.

And if you are a parent, I hope this book will provide the guidance you will need to help your child to prepare themselves for an amazing future, so that they too can reach their dreams.

Peter Mukherjee – *A Few Wise Words*

How to use this book

Young people, young adults and older adults . . .

Using the phrase 'our journey' has long been a popular way to describe what lies ahead of us, when we envisage the long process of moving towards a place that we may expect or hope to reach at some point later in life. It can also be a relatively positive way of depicting the future, evoking feelings of adventure, exploration and discovery, and with these, a sense that anything can happen along the way. While this may be true, one thing is for certain: no two journeys will ever be exactly the same – each will be as unique as we are as individuals.

This premise is perfectly illustrated when we witness the extraordinary array of different journeys that each of our contributors have experienced, and that they describe for us in this book.

And while one would expect there to be natural differences between the journey described by, say, an athlete compared with that of an actor, both will often stress the importance to them of the same values or disciplines, and how these have contributed substantially to their own success. 'Working hard' and 'having a positive outlook' are two good examples – you will see these expressed in various forms regularly across this book. But rather than seeing it as repetition, this should really be viewed as *reinforcement* of such important principles, underlining firmly the significant impact that they can have on the outcome of anyone's journey.

On the other hand, we will sometimes observe key differences in the approach that some of our contributors may have applied to particular aspects of their journey compared with others, where both will have still sought to achieve the same end. A good example is the way in which they might approach creating goals. Some describe how the only goal that they would ever set themselves was to perform any role or task that they had to complete today, to the *very best* of their ability. Others take a more structured approach: they might express the importance of setting long-term goals, while also breaking these down into smaller short-term goals. At first sight, such an apparent divergence in views may seem contradictory, or a little confusing at best, but each method was right for the individual concerned because it worked for them.

So, with this diversity in mind, it seems pointless (and it's certainly not our mission) to try to determine, from what all of our contributors have conveyed in their chapters, some narrow one-size-fits-all formula that can be applied to any person's individual journey. You will not, therefore, find any form of academic analysis or any 'conclusion' that attempts to do so at the end of this book.

A Few Wise Words aims instead to present a rich and varied collection of personal insights, knowledge and advice from our contributors, who are all willing to share their stories of success with you, and in their own words. It is ultimately for you to choose which pieces of advice you gather from them resonate the most with you or most closely align with your own plans for your journey.

Where you might have aspirations of becoming, say, an entrepreneur, then our contributors that have found success in the world of business will probably be of greatest interest to you to begin with. However, the views expressed by others – from the world of sport, for example – could be hugely inspiring and helpful for you too. Several contributors have expressed to me in conversation how they often find inspiration and help from people totally outside their field or profession, who may approach their own challenges in a completely different way.

The best way to use this book, when reading it for the first time, is to pick a single chapter from one of our contributors to study on a particular day. After reading and absorbing it, make notes about which points were especially interesting or helpful to you, so that you can reflect on these again later. Make a special note of any particular piece of advice that you feel could make a big difference to how you approach your journey, why you think it will help and how you should apply it. After reading a chapter, you may wish to let this rest with you for a little while before reading the next one.

You will notice areas of text within each chapter with a grey tint behind. These are sections that have been included especially for parents – you may choose to skip these if you wish.

As you work your way through this book, our contributors will help you to visualise how your own journey might look and how you can take more control of it. They will also help you to anticipate the challenges you are likely to face, and how to handle them. *A Few Wise Words* will help you to plan with clarity and purpose what you need to do next.

At any stage in the future, whenever you feel a need for inspiration or advice, or a reminder about how to do something, you can pick this book up again and re-read your favourite chapters. Each one is completely separate from the next and can be read independently.

As already described in the Introduction, *A Few Wise Words* aspires to be your perfect travelling companion and guide. Our amazing contributors will be on hand when you start thinking about your journey, and will remain by your side throughout, ready to offer advice and support, whenever you need it.

For parents . . .

The development of a young person will invariably be influenced by their childhood experiences, which can ultimately shape their character, confidence, resilience and outlook in later years. As parents, we naturally have an essential part to play here, and a considerable responsibility too, since much of what our children experience early in their lives will be in our hands, to introduce, share or to encourage.

A Few Wise Words, therefore, aims to support us in two important ways: first, to help us explore all the things that we can do as parents to nurture our children, from those critical early years, all the way through to young adulthood. Second, to help us attain a better understanding of what our children are likely to face on their journey ahead, and how they should best prepare for it.

It is, of course, virtually impossible for any young person, let alone their parents, to predict what the future is going to look like for them at a time when the world is evolving so quickly. The traditional 'career path' is no longer likely to be a single channel to pursue; the professions are transforming, trades are disappearing, while new occupations we never dreamt of are emerging. Many of our contributors suggest how futile it is for any young person to plan today for what their career may look like in ten years' time. The most they can realistically do now, as individuals, is prepare themselves fundamentally for their future, so they can handle with confidence whatever may arise.

As parents, we need to have a healthy understanding of what all of this will actually mean for our children, if we want to stand any chance of being relevant to them later on.

A Few Wise Words provides an opportunity for us to understand each stage of a young person's likely journey and what we can do to support them along the way. It starts with advice from our contributors on how to nurture a child's development, with the introduction of simple values, from when they are a toddler, all the way through their primary school years. As a child approaches secondary school age, we can begin to share helpful ideas from the book with them by reading it together. This can stimulate thinking about positive engagement and excelling at activities. As they move into their teenage years, we can encourage our children to read key sections of the book themselves, or to read whole chapters, whenever we feel that this might provide a helpful and positive intervention for them. As they transition through their teens into becoming young adults, we can eventually pass this book on for them to adopt and read for themselves, to continue to receive inspiration and support from our contributors throughout their journey ahead.

So while *A Few Wise Words* aims to inspire our young people, young adults and older adults in how to prepare for and then manage their journey, the same content is also highly relevant and important for us as parents. It can provide the insight we need to empathise with our children and their journey, while the additional tips and advice in the tinted sections of each chapter are also included specifically for parents.

And finally, all parents naturally want to see their children go on in life to achieve their full potential. Some will simply delegate much of the responsibility for developing their kids to 'the system'. They will leave everything to their schooling, their kid's own initiative and the influence of their peers, to help them negotiate their way ahead – and who knows, some might eventually find success for themselves. Alternatively, others may choose to take a far more responsible, sensitive and proactive approach as parents. *A Few Wise Words* has been crafted to enable us to do just that. Our contributors can not only help any young person or any young adult to create the best versions of themselves for their journey ahead, but they can also help us to become the *best version of parents* for them as well.

Covid-19

At the time of going to print, we are sadly still in the middle of a worldwide crisis.

A Few Wise Words was originally set to be published in the spring of 2020, but we decided to delay its release, in view of the pandemic that was beginning to unfold and the prevailing uncertainty.

All of the chapters in this book were completed a while before we began to learn about Covid-19. There is therefore no mention of the virus in any part of their content.

While the world has of course experienced enormous change since the virus first appeared, most of the advice contained within this book is still relevant. Many have suggested to us that it is even more pertinent now, and we have received considerable encouragement to publish *A Few Wise Words* this autumn, rather than delaying any further.

The world will hopefully emerge from this pandemic soon. In the meantime, we are naturally thinking about the many millions who have suffered directly from Covid-19 and the countless more that will have been severely affected in some way indirectly. We all feel a real sense of sadness and compassion towards those that have, and wish everyone a safe and positive recovery from this crisis.

Sir Ben Ainslie, CBE

From his silver medal at the 1996 Olympic Games in Atlanta when he was just nineteen, Ben Ainslie went on to become the most successful sailor in the history of the Games, winning medals (including four golds) at five consecutive Olympics. As a young competitor, he won four World Championships in the Laser class before moving up to the Finn class and winning a further seven World Championship gold medals, thereby becoming one of the most decorated sailors of all time. He has also competed at the highest levels of professional yacht racing, including challenging for the famous America's Cup, both as a team member and through his own team, Ben Ainslie Racing (competing as Land Rover BAR). He is currently leading the INEOS Team UK challenge for the cup, which will next be competed for in 2021. Ben was knighted in 2013 for his services to sailing.

'You absolutely have to find something you're passionate about. If you are not passionate about it, then it's not right for you.'

'I soon learned that it was always much better to be self-critical, to analyse what I did wrong and then work hard on it, rather than just blaming circumstances or other people, and then missing a clear opportunity for self-improvement.'

'There are lots of talented people in the world, in many different walks of life, but the *really* successful ones are those who genuinely apply themselves the most to whatever they are doing. It's hard work – and there are simply no shortcuts.'

'Parents should introduce their children to the sort of values that can help them to succeed at whatever they want to do later in life. The importance of hard work and dedication, preparation and focus are obvious examples.'

About success . . .

As a sportsman, my own view of success will, of course, be highly personal. It's about setting your goals and those key targets you want to reach as an individual, either short- or long-term, and then striving hard to achieve them. Measuring success in sport is relatively straightforward; you either reach your personal goal (to win a gold medal, for example) or you don't. To achieve something as big as that, however, will always require a *massive* amount of effort, sacrifice and many years of preparation. So, when you eventually do win and reach your ultimate goal, you will naturally enjoy a deep sense of fulfilment and pride in the success that you have achieved, but also a huge feeling of relief.

Until recently, my life has been driven primarily by individual success in a sporting environment. But now it's about the success of the team I've been leading to challenge for the America's Cup, which means setting goals for a large group of people rather than just for me personally.

From junior sailor to Olympic champion . . .

I first started sailing on my own when I was eight years old. My father was a wonderful man and my early inspiration, introducing me to the water at a very young age. He was always a keen sailor and had even taken part in the first Whitbread Round the World Race in 1973, four years before I was born. When he retired, we moved as a family to the coastal hamlet of Restronguet in Cornwall. I was soon invited to join a handful of kids at a local sailing group, where I learned how to sail in a small but competitive dinghy known as the Optimist, which is still favoured by junior sailors around the world today. In the end, I took to this type of boat so well that my father decided to get me one for Christmas. I can remember that my parents somehow managed to get the dinghy upstairs, rigged it up in my bedroom while I was asleep, so it was the first thing that I'd see when I woke up on Christmas morning!

As I learned to master my dinghy, I soon developed a love for the sport, and by the age of ten, I was already competing regularly at my local sailing club.

My early education was not particularly great, and I struggled a little at school. I wasn't really a natural student at that time, I suppose, so I didn't enjoy school as much as I could have done. I also suffered from a skin allergy – I had quite a conspicuous rash as a youngster and was often picked on by other kids because of it. But, from an early age, I was also developing my love affair with sailing. I would spend most of my time during class at school just daydreaming about sailboats and being on the water.

By the time I was thirteen, I had already been sailing and racing for a while, and was doing pretty well for my age group, competing nationally and also internationally (in the Optimist World Championships). My parents were always brilliant and completely supportive of my sailing activities and the competitions, regularly taking me to events at the weekends. My father was definitely a huge early influence on me. But, needless to say, my developing love of competitive sailing and the amount of travel this required to reach different events was also proving quite disruptive to normal family life.

There was one occasion when something significant happened that would ultimately become a really pivotal moment for me and my future sailing career. I was racing in a local club competition, but it was a difficult race and things didn't go that well. It seemed to me that the wind wasn't working in my favour and I was feeling quite hard-done-by. I slipped back several places and just gave up in the end, cruising home simply to finish the race while feeling rather sorry for myself.

I was at home that evening, having dinner with my parents, when my father asked, 'So, how did you get on in the race today?'

'Not that well, really,' I replied. 'I was a bit unlucky with the wind and didn't win.'

To my surprise, he then calmly said, 'Well, OK, that's interesting, because I was actually *there*, and I watched the race, and saw how you simply gave up . . .' It was an embarrassing moment for me, but I listened to my father as he continued: 'Look, as a family, it's a really big commitment for us to support you, and as you know, we're delighted to be able to do that. But, you have got to make a big decision here, Ben. We are, of course, more than happy to continue to back you completely, but only if you are willing to commit yourself *totally* to what you are doing and put *everything* into it! Now, you don't have to do that, of course, and if you decide not to, that's fine, but then you can't really expect us as a family to keep putting such a big commitment into you as well . . . So, you're going to have to think about all of this very seriously and decide whether or not you *really want to go for it!'*

When I look back now, many years later, to that crucial conversation, I remember thinking at the time how my dad was absolutely right. It was a hugely significant turning point for me, and perhaps one of the most important moments of my life. My father had really struck a chord, and from that point onwards I was to commit myself wholeheartedly to becoming *the very best* I could be. I was soon setting my goals around, quite literally, how to become the best sailor in the world. I found myself taking full responsibility for what I was doing, creating the self-determination needed to improve – and above all to win.

I remember seeing the 1992 Olympic Games on TV when I was fifteen. It was the first Olympics that I had watched properly, and I really got into it. Linford Christie won gold in the 100 metres and I thought that was seriously cool. At first, I thought how lovely it would be to go to the Olympics one day as a spectator, but that was soon to change into a real desire to attend the Games as a competitor, and to win a medal for sailing.

In the previous Olympic Games in Seoul in 1988, Mike McIntyre and Bryn Vaile won gold for Great Britain, sailing in the Star class. They became inspirational heroes of mine and for many other sailors of my generation who were coming through. But it was after the 1992 Olympic Games that a real opportunity opened up for me. The boat that I was beginning to sail in competitively (when coming out of the youth classes) was known as the Laser. The International Olympic Committee then announced that from 1993 a new Olympic class was to be created *for* the Laser. I remember thinking that because I was already one of the top guys in the world at junior level in this class of boat, a pathway had just opened up that made it possible for me to compete in a future Olympic Games. Perhaps I could even emulate the success of McIntyre and Vaile, and win gold . . .

I was also fortunate that one of my coaches was Jim Saltonstall, who first took an interest in me when I was around ten years old. He was the famously successful coach in charge at the time of the Royal Yachting Association youth programme. Historically, Great Britain had always performed reasonably well in Olympic sailing and also international dinghy sailing, but it was Jim who inspired a whole generation of young sailors to start *winning*, and he certainly helped the nation over three or four Olympic cycles to become a dominant force in Olympic sailing. His gift was to help instil a real passion in all of us, allied to a firm belief that there was *no reason* why we should not be winning World Championships or Olympic medals one day . . .

My family moved to Hampshire when I was fifteen. I was already taking a much more mature and responsible approach to my future, and I realised that my education was actually also important. School was starting to become enjoyable. The subjects were more interesting, and I also began to appreciate the value of self-learning. I would eventually go on to a really good sixth-form college in Winchester, but, after completing my first year of A-levels, I learned that I had qualified to represent Great Britain at the 1996 Olympic Games in Atlanta.

It was, of course, a dream come true, but it meant that I had a really important decision to make – do I leave school early and apply myself 100 per cent to training for the Olympic Games? Or, should I finish my A-levels now and train just part-time, while knowing that I wouldn't be giving the Games my best shot? My dilemma was that I simply did not know if I would ever again get the chance to participate in an Olympic Games. In Olympic sailing, you only get one spot for each discipline per nation – and with the UK's strong sailing tradition, actually winning that place to represent your country would always be very tough. I remember thinking that this was probably a once-in-a-lifetime opportunity for me, and in any case, I could always go back to complete my A-level studies at a later date. My father was easy to convince that this was the right thing to do but my mum was not so sure at first. She was naturally concerned that if I didn't finish my A-levels now, I might never do so.

I therefore made a deal with her and said, 'Look, I'll pursue the Olympics now, but as soon as I'm finished, I promise you that will go back and complete my A-level studies straightaway.' She agreed, and that is exactly what I eventually did.

While qualifying for the 1996 Olympics felt like a real privilege, it also followed many years of really hard work and a lot of competitive racing. I had already started to get some major titles under my belt, which included winning the 1993 Laser Radial World Championship and the 1995 ISAF Youth Sailing World Championship. I was nineteen years old when I won a silver medal at the Olympics Games in Atlanta, but, far from being elated about my achievement, I was actually hugely upset – the finals were *very* close, and I only just missed out on winning gold.

Preparation before the Games meant being away for twelve months of intensive training. I was part of a team and racing against people much older than me, so I grew up enormously during that time. When I returned home, I kept my promise to my mum and went straight back to complete the second year of my A-levels. But, within the first few days, I realised that half the lessons were being taken up unnecessarily by my teachers having to deal with disruptive students, some of whom had not completed their course-work. This immediately troubled me – when you prepare for something like the Olympics, you become acutely aware of how precious time is, and I certainly did not want to waste any of it now. I had, in the meantime, been fortunate enough to find a sponsor for the next Olympic Games. I decided to use part of the funding I received to pay for a tutorial college, where I could also conveniently work my studies around the training I would need to do.

I eventually won my first gold medal at the Olympic Games in Sydney in 2000. My overriding emotion was one of huge relief after so many years of working tremendously hard to win what was for me the ultimate sporting achievement. But I also look back now with some amusement at what went through my head at the time. For a day or two, I kept thinking that I had finally achieved everything that I had ever wanted, and it was an amazing feeling when it happened. But, because I had been so focused on that single end result, I had never really looked beyond 'the winning' and what to do next. After the initial euphoria, I realised that life was moving on and I began to think, 'Where do I go from here?' and 'What's going to be the next challenge for me?'

It had already become a real ambition of mine for some while to get into professional sailing, with a goal one day, of being part of an America's Cup-winning team. The America's Cup is simply the most historically significant and prestigious yacht-racing event in the world. It is also an enormously challenging competition for any team to participate in. An opportunity arose in 2001 for me to join the OneWorld Challenge team based in Seattle, and I was to spend a year working with them. It was quite difficult for me, however, to make the transition from a single-handed background to becoming one of the youngest members of a team with over a hundred people. I also wasn't *steering* the boat now, but was engaged in a role that I didn't really enjoy doing. So, after a year, I made the decision to leave the team and get back into Olympic sailing. I now look back at my time in Seattle as certainly an interesting experiment for me, both professionally and socially.

When I returned to single-handed competition, I soon moved up from the Laser to the Finn class, and won my first World Championship in Athens in 2002. Feeling very comfortable racing at this new level, I would eventually go on to win seven Finn World Championships in total and a further three Olympic Gold medals in the Finn class at the 2004, 2008 and 2012 Games.

During that time, while I was chasing World Championship and Olympic medals, there were two significant periods during which I again became involved in the America's Cup. The first was in 2005, when I helped the Emirates Team New Zealand in their challenge for the 2007 America's Cup. In the same year, Team Origin was launched, a new venture that set its sights on becoming the first British team to win the cup since 1851, with the next race scheduled for 2009. I was invited to join the aspiring team and eventually to skipper the boat.

Unforeseen problems and legal issues then arose that revolved around the organisation of the race schedule (which was completely outside of our control). With these came the threat that there might be a delay of at least two years before the race could take place. This would potentially conflict with my intention to take part in the 2012 Olympic Games, and I knew that I'd have to make a decision on whether to focus on Team Origin's challenge or to participate in the Olympics, because I couldn't do both. It was a real dilemma for me, but I eventually decided to commit myself to Team Origin. I remember telling Sir Keith Mills, who was the founder and inspiration behind the team, 'Look, you put a lot of faith in me to skipper the boat and I want to do the very best job that I can, but I can't do that *and* participate in the Olympic Games as well. So, I'm willing to forego the Olympics and just focus on the America's Cup . . .' In the end, however, because of uncertainty about rule changes and a number of other technical reasons, he decided to close the team down shortly afterwards. This gave me a clear opportunity to pursue the 2012 Olympics, and although I hadn't been sailing in the Olympic classes for a while, I still had enough time to prepare.

After the Olympic Games, having participated competitively in them for the last time and proudly won a fourth gold medal, my attention was once again drawn towards the America's Cup. It was now a new and very personal goal of mine to lead a winning team to regain the cup for Great Britain after so many years. But it would also be a hugely ambitious task. Competing at this level requires a large team and an enormous amount of resources to develop and race boats that are technically highly advanced. In addition, the competition's rules regularly change – a bit like the seasonal rule changes in Formula One.

In late 2012, I announced that I would be forming a new team, Ben Ainslie Racing, to take the challenge on. This would be a long-term project that would require raising investment, finding sponsorship and creating new facilities. In the meantime, I was also to participate as tactician during the last twelve races for the successful Oracle Team USA's defence of the America's Cup in San Francisco in 2013. This was an amazing time and also a hugely valuable experience for me.

With the help of our initial sponsors, our team – JP Morgan BAR – was to compete extremely well in the 2013 America's Cup World Series (the heats for the ultimate America's Cup races). For this, we had acquired an AC45 catamaran on loan, which enabled the team to gain experience for future events and attract the interest of potential sponsors. In the same year, we set a new multi-hull record for the Round the Island Race (Isle of Wight) and subsequently finished fifth overall in the 2014 Extreme Sailing Series.

It was in 2014 that everything really came together in establishing a world-class competitive team. With initial investment and the continued support of Sir Keith Mills, Chris Bake and Sir Charles Dunstone, we set about raising the £100 million that would be required to realistically compete for the 2017 America's Cup. With additional backing from the UK government, we established our brand-new headquarters and development centre in Portsmouth, building a truly state-of-the-art facility. We also teamed up with Red Bull Advanced Technologies, who were instrumental in helping us with simulation design. We ultimately attracted a new sponsor, and the team now became known as Land Rover BAR.

Despite winning the 2015-16 America's Cup World Series, which enabled us to compete for the right to challenge the previous America's Cup holder for the title, we were knocked out of the competition by New Zealand in the Challenger Semi-Final (they were ultimately to go on and win the cup). Whilst hugely disappointing for everyone involved, the momentum and experience we gained from competing in all the stages have been invaluable. We are now looking forward to leading the challenge for the 36th America's Cup, as part of the newly-formed INEOS Team UK.

Finding what I want to do . . .

I was very fortunate in being able to discover something early on in life that I enjoyed immensely and really wanted to do. I had no idea if I was going to be successful at it then, of course, but I was definitely developing a passion for both sailing and competing from a young age. By the time I was thirteen years old, and after having *that* conversation with my father, I became very clear about what my goals were and what I needed to do to turn my passion for sailing into a successful career.

My advice to any young person is that you absolutely have to find something you are passionate about. If you are not passionate about it, then it's not right for you. In order to be successful at something, you are going to have to work very hard at making it happen – and you're simply not going to commit the time or the energy to something for which you lack genuine enthusiasm. One of the keys to success, therefore, is to keep looking until you find *that thing*.

Until this happens, it's also vital for any young person to continue to work hard at their education. It was slightly different for me because I won my first World Championship when I was sixteen and already had a clear vocational path set at that stage. But I did also ensure that I made time for my education as well, which I saw as very important, especially if things had not gone so well for me for any reason in my sailing career.

In addition to having a passion for something, there are three things in my view that are essential when considering what you might want to do. The first is that you definitely need to have a natural talent for whatever it is that you are thinking of doing, whether it's in sport, the arts, business or whatever.

Second, you have to be ready to apply yourself fully. There are lots of talented people in the world, in many different walks of life, but the *really* successful ones are those who genuinely apply themselves the most to whatever they are doing. It's hard work – and there are simply *no* shortcuts.

Third, however talented an individual you may be, it is important to remain modest and avoid being arrogant or overconfident. Arrogance is one of the worst traits a human being can have, especially in sport. It can alienate the people whose support is most needed and can also lead to failure, because an arrogant individual is often simply not as good as they think they are, they fail to analyse themselves and their discipline properly, and they don't train as hard as they should because they think they don't have to. We all need help from others to develop our skills and to become successful. If you can portray a modest, determined and positive attitude, you are far more likely to attract the right people to you, the people that can help you.

Communication skills are key . . .

Once you've found something that you have a talent for, you have to be able to reach out to the resources that are available around you, in terms of the experience, knowledge and support from friends, family and contacts. Knowing exactly how to reach out is a skill in itself. It's about communicating, being confident to ask, and developing all-important people skills. It's also knowing how to look out for opportunities, how to build the right relationships and a community around you within the area that you're interested in.

Developing these skills takes time and effort. The best way to learn is to put yourself out there and get involved. Mix with people who are older and more experienced than you. Interacting with other people will help to build your confidence. When you're in a gathering or in a meeting, be prepared to contribute and speak up. If I'm self-critical about anything that I should have done better when I was younger, it was perhaps not pushing myself enough to develop those communication skills much earlier. I remember when I joined the America's Cup team in Seattle – it was a real struggle for me because it was the first time I had worked in a big team environment. I was a bright-eyed twenty-three-year-old thrown into the deep end, working with America's Cup winners who were mostly in their mid-thirties. I had no idea how to handle people – especially those with such strong personalities. It ended up being a big learning (if not a life-changing) experience for me because I was forced to interact. So I think it's really important for young people to work on developing their communication and people skills, but to start doing so early on.

When interacting with others, especially those that you would like to get behind you, always appear self-assured (but not arrogant!), convey the sense that you've got the determination to do what is necessary and demonstrate persistence. Once again, you will win their attention far more easily if you're humble and can show that you're able to communicate well. If you can do that at a young age, you will set yourself apart from everyone else and begin to attract opportunities to you.

Many of the relationships you will build and rely on when you are young will be carried forward with you into later life. It's a small world out there, and I'm still amazed how, twenty years down the road, I'm now working with people that I raced against in the 1996 or 2000 Olympics or whom I knew from other teams. It is all part of the amazing journey of life and how it plays out.

To parents . . .

When children have a talent for something, how their parents support and encourage them to develop is very important. If parents start having ambitions *for* their child and start pushing them too hard, it can often put them off doing something they might otherwise excel at. One sees that a lot in sport. When I look back, many of my peers who clearly had overbearing parents that continuously pushed them *weren't* the ones who kept going over the long term.

By contrast, both of my parents were amazing, and I certainly would not have been able to move forward in sailing without the support that they gave me when I was young. They took me everywhere, encouraged me to do well but without the pressure.

I still really appreciate my dad's honesty with me, so many years ago, and how he encouraged me to take responsibility at an early age for my future. It was such a key moment for me, being empowered and taking ownership of what I was doing. It was only when I started to really think about and analyse things for myself – rather than coaches or parents telling me what I did wrong or what I should do – that I started to make some big strides forward in my understanding of the sport, how to become better at it and what I needed to do to win.

So, where a child is developing a talent for something, I think parents should continue to provide support, encourage their children to work at it and even help them a little to make those important decisions about their future. But, it should ultimately always be their child's decision, which *they* can take responsibility for, since this will often be the catalyst to finding their self-motivation.

Another thing that can be counterproductive is when a young person feels pressured. It can either be pressure and expectations from their parents or the pressure that they put on themselves, often because they are fearful of letting their parents (or others) down if they fail or don't perform well at something. When things don't go well, parents can help by guiding their children in a measured way: 'Look, you didn't win that competition, but let's take a look at it and see what went wrong, and what you can do better next time.' I think this is really important, because in order to improve at what we are doing – especially in sport – we all need to learn to be good at self-analysis, to identify our strengths and be honest about our weaknesses. Where parents can, they should encourage their children to do this at a relatively early stage.

And finally, parents should introduce their children to the sort of values that can help them to succeed at whatever they want to do later in life. The importance of hard work and dedication, preparation and focus are obvious examples.

Attitude towards effort and failure . . .

I have always had a talent for sailing, but there are, of course, many talented sailors out there. So when I was young, I needed to work really hard at my training and go that extra mile. After a while, I developed perhaps my greatest strength, which is perseverance, and this attribute would help me enormously throughout my career. Having the right attitude is hugely important if you want to be successful in life. Excelling in sport is mostly about attitude, both as an individual sportsperson but also when working in a team environment.

From time to time we can all experience self-doubt. Sometimes we might even question if we are doing the right thing or whether we're really good enough. For me, I would use those moments as the impetus to go back to the drawing board, to work harder at getting back up to where I should be – and that has always been my approach to it.

There is a really good saying: 'Luck is what happens when preparation meets opportunity.' For me, you can be lucky by being in the right place at the right time, but it's mostly preparation that *puts* you in that place to begin with . . .

The only time I would ever be nervous about competing in a race was when I knew that for some reason I hadn't done the right preparation. But that would only ever happen because of an injury or some external circumstances, not from a lack of effort. I might still get a little anxious before a race, but when I know that I have done everything I possibly can to prepare for it, then after that I will simply look for any opportunity to 'ride my luck'. This is an important point – when an opportunity arises during a race, you can then really go for it. If you haven't prepared well enough, however, then you probably won't be able to maximise the benefit of the opportunity presented anyway.

My own attitude throughout my career has generally been very good. I have always been passionate about my sport, but there have been one or two occasions where that has boiled over in competition. One sees this a lot in sport, of course, where passions run high or even too high. It can be a fine line sometimes, because it's mostly passion that drives and motivates the individual, and also makes them unique. One wouldn't want to take that away from someone, but a sportsperson needs to learn how to control it, and how to channel it.

When you are young and things go wrong, there can be a tendency to make excuses to justify the reasons for one's failures. If you lose a race, it is easy to say, 'I was a bit unlucky' or 'I was doing well, but *this* happened . . .' As I grew older and more competitive, I realised that these were just excuses for not being good enough. There were times when I was probably a little too hard on myself, but I soon learned that it was always much better to be self-critical, to analyse what I did wrong and then work hard on it, rather than just blaming circumstances or other people, and then missing a clear opportunity for self-improvement.

Occasionally, however, things do happen that are completely out of your control, and *that* can certainly be much more frustrating because it's simply out of our hands. Once again, one has to analyse, limit any damage, assess the experience and move forward. In any case, whether out of our control or because of our own doing, I will always view failures or obstacles as real opportunities to learn!

Where it becomes a little more complicated is when you are racing as part of a team and not just competing on your own. When things go wrong in a team situation, it requires a different psyche because it may not be all your fault, but it may not be the rest of the team's fault either. You have to be able to analyse things together – as a collective – which can be difficult at times. One definitely needs to create a team environment where everyone can be honest and open. It's important for all members of the team to feel comfortable enough to admit and discuss their mistakes and any failings freely. No one should feel that they have to be defensive for fear of losing their place in a team.

When really big failures happen – because you fail, or your team fails – it can be very painful. The pain can often last for days. Once again, a good attitude can convert that pain into the driver to improve and do better next time. At Land Rover BAR, we failed as a team in our bid to challenge for the America's Cup in 2017. We didn't have enough speed and we simply failed to win. We were clear about the fact that we were unlikely to win anyway, being a first-time team and because of the way in which our preparation had gone, but, after four years of working so hard to put everything together, our goal was still *to win*! So, despite being a very tough challenge, it was nonetheless hugely disappointing, very painful for the whole team and probably the biggest single disappointment of my career. But today, all of that pain has been channelled into real motivation for our next campaign; we've used the disappointment and what we learned from it to drive us forward.

Finally, while it is possible for an individual sportsperson, or individuals in other walks of life, to sometimes get away with having an indifferent attitude, this doesn't really work in a team environment. You need to present yourself to the group with positivity and confidence, but without any arrogance. The team needs to feel from its leadership that it *can* be successful and if any big issues were to arise, that they can be dealt with in a clear and assured way. The same applies outwardly – how the leaders and members of the team present themselves to their opposition or to the outside world is also very important.

Goals . . .

Setting goals has certainly been a hugely important part of my own success in my career. In sport, it is perhaps easier to define goals compared with other walks of life. Some goals are, however, more attainable than others. For example, fitness goals might be all about pushing hard in the gym, where it should be a given that you'll be able to reach the targets you set, whereas competition goals are more outside of your control. In sailing, for example, your performance is often at the whim of Mother Nature.

I do still believe, however, that it's important for youngsters who are pursuing a sport to have those bigger competition goals to work towards – these are what motivate them to reach the next stage and to go on to compete at a higher level. It may be that they win a local competition and then a regional event. In time, it could be a national event or even a world championship. For sportsmen and sportswomen, winning an Olympic medal is usually the ultimate goal. But to get there, you have to set a range of short, medium and long-term goals and clear targets that can help you to improve, while also carefully measuring your improvement at each step.

Finding your space . . .

When you are young, and before you have any family commitments, it is easier to be 100 per cent focused on your sport or on your career. As you mature, and especially when you have a young family, establishing more of a balance becomes essential, although it can also be a real challenge to manage well. On the other hand, you cannot continue being absolutely focused and working flat out all of the time without suffering for it in other ways.

The older you get, the more you realise how important it is to find time away from what you are doing, to find that 'creative space'. In my role today, when I am at the office and with the team, it's invariably full-on and flat-out just dealing with stuff, and it's usually difficult to find the time and space for creative thinking. It is often only when I'm able to take myself out of that environment that I can get a clear head and things really fall into place more easily. I can then think much more clearly about important decisions or essential planning, such as strategy or setting long-term goals for the team.

While the intensity may change between when I'm at the office or at home, I'll still constantly think about my work, the team, our goals and the America's Cup. I will often consider different projects when at home and how we can do things differently. I'm not someone who gets to five o'clock on a Friday afternoon and then says, 'That's it, I'm not looking at my phone now until Monday morning.' But for me, while my work can be 24/7, I'm also naturally able to shut off when I'm spending time with my family so that I can focus my attention on them. Being with my family is *hugely* important for me. My home is my sanctuary, and this will always be an essential part of my balance. However, as my family knows well and understands, if something significant were to happen or an issue comes to mind that demands my attention, I can often be up and working on it in the middle of the night, or even through the weekend if necessary.

Physical and mental preparation . . .

For some sportspeople, it just seems to be in their DNA — they only have to look at a barbell and their biceps start expanding! Unfortunately, I'm not one of those people, and I've always had to work very hard at my fitness, which has included spending many hours in the gym.

Aside from training to be physically fit, which is naturally key for anyone competing in sports, it's also important to look after your body's health. For all of my adult life, I have had issues with my back, which are becoming increasingly more challenging as I get older. With the benefit of hindsight, I realise now that this was something I could probably have managed better when I was younger and perhaps should have paid more attention to and put more effort into.

From an early age, I was strongly encouraged to spend time with sports psychologists to help manage my mental approach to the sport. But, I remember resisting this and questioning at the time why it was necessary since I was already performing a lot of the processes anyway, such as centring and goal setting. I also used to feel that I was mentally quite adept and 'if it ain't broke, why try to fix it?' But, as I got older and more mature, I began to appreciate just how every decision you make comes down to your psychology. Today, I really value the importance of understanding, developing and fine-tuning the mental approach to your sport and the extent to which this can help you to excel.

Learning how to focus and to self-analyse, examining how you performed in a competition, the decisions you took and why, what's working and what is not working, how you could have done things better — these are all really important processes to assimilate and practise. I would highly recommend to any young person to take them seriously. For a sportsperson, this is really all part of maintaining good mental health. I'm not suggesting that you need to see a sports psychologist once a week, but be mindful of the importance of maintaining mental fitness and health. Invest time in learning about these things, and it can benefit you enormously throughout your career and life.

Frank Arnesen

After playing for his local club in Denmark, Frank Arnesen was scouted in 1975 when he was nineteen by AFC Ajax, one of the best football clubs in the world at that time. He was club captain at twenty-three and helped Ajax win three Dutch league titles. He later helped PSV Eindhoven to also win three league titles – and the European Cup. Frank was capped fifty-two times, scoring fourteen times for the Danish national team and participating in the 1984 European Championship and the 1986 World Cup. After retiring from playing, he has enjoyed a highly successful career in football management, first as assistant coach and then director of football back at PSV Eindhoven. He became sporting director for Tottenham Hotspur FC and later for Chelsea FC, then Hamburger SV. He is currently Technical Director of the leading Dutch football club Feyenoord Rotterdam.

'One's *ego* can easily stand in the way if you want to do something good or great – it should never be about *you*. When I think about success, it has always been *our* success as a team of people and not just me.'

'One of the main reasons why you *must* find something that you love doing is because it is impossible to find success in life at anything unless you really work hard at it. And, when you are working hard at something you really *love* doing, it doesn't *feel* like hard work!'

'I always recommend making time for keeping fit – it will enable you to prepare yourself better for life's challenges, give you stamina and help to keep you mentally agile.'

'A parent's key role in helping their children to find their way to enjoying a successful life is mainly encouragement – be positive, allow them room, help them to explore and give them lots of encouragement to be their best.'

On success . . .

My view of success and what it means to me has certainly changed as I've got older. When I was playing football professionally, it was all about winning as a player or what I could achieve with my club. It was also about being signed by great football clubs to play at the highest level and then being considered good enough to represent my country. Recognition from my peers was also an important measure of success for me.

But in later years, as my career in football developed from active playing into player management, my view of success has evolved. I now think about the positive *difference* I've been able to make to the clubs I have worked for and to the players and coaches I am working with, most especially where my work has been particularly challenging or has taken place under very difficult circumstances.

Success for me is also a continuous journey. It becomes more about what you want to achieve today and tomorrow – what has happened in the past is now done. What you take *from* the past, however, is your experience, and you apply this to what you have to do today, to help you to become even better at what you do professionally in the future.

But I've often said that success is not *just* about you. In professional football you can never have success entirely on your own – you will always rely on people around you for help, and people will depend on your help too.

My journey . . .

I have always loved football. I started very young and enjoyed playing with my father, who was extremely enthusiastic about the game. He would regularly gather boys from around where we lived, and we would go and play football for two or three hours in the park. My father taught me two key things when I was just seven years old: 'It's *as enjoyable* to make an assist for a goal as it is to actually score a goal,' and 'To be a great footballer, you must have great balance and you must be two-footed.' This second piece of advice made such an impression on me that every morning, when going from my home to school (around one and a half kilometres), I used to hop along on just my right leg for ages, and then just my left leg, to improve my balance. And at home, I would practise keeping the ball up in the air, kicking with just my left foot for literally hours, until I was as good with it as I was with my right . . .

As a young boy, I was soon playing regularly as an amateur player for Fremad Amager, my local football club in Denmark. I worked really hard and did my very best to improve and to become a good footballer. After a while, I was excelling as a youth player and eventually attracted the interest of the legendary Dutch football club AFC Ajax, who approached me to join them in 1975. I was just nineteen. It was, of course, an unbelievable opportunity for me, and one of the most important decisions of my life, although when the best club in the world comes and knocks on your door, you just cannot say 'No'!

I learned a huge amount at that club. You were expected to have the mentality that you *had to get better every day*. You are never satisfied when you're an Ajax player – if you win a game 5–0, then it should have been 7–0! From training two or three times a week as an amateur, I was now training hard twice a day. I put on ten kilos of muscle in just over a year. But it was very difficult for me, to join Ajax, as I had been the best player of my former club and I was now playing with (and against, in training) some of the best footballers in Europe.

I had always been good at dribbling the ball, but when I tried to do so during our training matches, the ball was taken off me *every* time, before I could pass it. My teammates would yell, 'Just *pass* the ball!' But I kept getting tackled and dispossessed every time before I had a chance to. In the end, they would scream at me, *'Play the ball! You keep losing the ball, Frank, all the time! We want to win!'* I was becoming increasingly demoralised by the criticism, and my confidence and self-esteem were also beginning to slip, which became a serious problem for me.

We then had a big team meeting. The club hadn't been playing at its best for a while, and our coach, Tomislav Ivić, wanted us to discuss why. He expected everyone, including the junior members, to speak out and contribute. He asked me, 'Frank, what do you think?'

I remember saying, 'It doesn't really help when my teammates are always so *negative* towards me every time I make a mistake – why can't you be more positive?'

After a moment of silence, with everyone looking at me, they started laughing. Soon everyone was laughing out loud. Ruud Krol, the Ajax captain, then turned to me and said, 'Frank, what are you talking about? Listen, we could say, "Will you please next time, kindly pass the ball left?" but instead we prefer to say [and he yelled], *"FRANK, YOU IDIOT!! PASS THE BLOODY BALL LEFT!!"* It's nothing personal. But the day where you make a mistake and we *don't* say anything, *then* you're in trouble, my friend, because that means you're not good enough to play for Ajax.'

It was a great lesson for me, but it was also a moment when I realised that it wasn't because they disliked me for any reason – my teammates *all* wanted to help me to become a better player. I also began to appreciate how you learn *far* more from defeat or during difficult times than you do from winning. I also understood that it was actually OK to make mistakes, provided you really learn from them and always try to avoid them in the future.

After two years at Ajax, I was training unbelievably hard and improving every day at my game. I wanted to achieve the very best that I could. I was also single-mindedly determined to become good enough to be recognised one day as the best player in the world. But then one morning, I woke up and the harsh reality suddenly hit me . . . Johan Cruyff (the legendary Dutch player, who is still widely regarded as one of the greatest footballers of all time) is *always* going to be better than me, and I'll *never* be able to catch him. I was actually completely devasted, and for four days I was deeply depressed, grappling with the realisation that I'd now probably *never* reach my goal of being the world's best player. On the fifth day, I woke up again, and I remember standing in front of the mirror and saying to myself, 'Frank, do you know what? You now have to set your sights on becoming the *second-best* player in the world!' And, that became my new goal . . .

One of my proudest moments was when I became captain of Ajax at the age of twenty-three, and only the second foreigner ever to captain the team in the club's history. Before eventually leaving the club in 1981, I helped Ajax to win three Dutch league titles. I then joined Valencia CF in Spain, followed by a spell with RSC Anderlecht in Belgium. I returned to Dutch football in 1985, joined PSV Eindhoven and went on to win three league titles with them, as well as the European Cup in 1988. My international debut, playing for the Danish national team, actually came in 1977, and I was eventually to participate in the 1984 European Championship and the 1986 World Cup.

After a wonderful time and a successful career as a player, I eventually retired from the field and took my first management position, as assistant coach under Bobby Robson at PSV Eindhoven. It was a great time for me. Bobby was a wonderful man and I still feel that I owe a lot to him – he was a huge influence, teaching me some great things that I would carry forward and apply throughout my management career.

One of the key things I learned from him was how to give people space and to empower them – to be more of a mentor to them and to give them room to develop. He did that with me throughout my time under him at PSV, and it was a philosophy that I was to successfully apply when I worked at Chelsea FC and Hamburger SV in years to come.

I remained at PSV Eindhoven and was director of football for ten years. It was a challenging but also an amazing time for me, during which I helped to bring through a number of exciting players into the game, including Brazil's Ronaldo, and Dutch players Jaap Stam, Ruud van Nistelrooy and Arjen Robben.

I eventually left the club to join Tottenham Hotspur as sporting director (I was to become the first sporting director in the Premier League) and to be in charge of their scouting and player transfers. I had a three-year contract and it was a great club to work for. But, after a year, I was to end my relationship with the club and became director of football for Chelsea FC. It was a controversial move for which Spurs were eventually compensated by Chelsea, but it also became a great opportunity for me to run the whole of Chelsea's scouting programme.

I had a truly fantastic time at Chelsea, especially in the early years. I built up the youth team, and it was also a great opportunity to train the coaches, who were all very responsive and would really listen. I had a lot of experience to bring to the club at that time, and they took it on board and accepted what I was trying to do, especially for the players.

I really loved my time developing the youth team. We were all young once, of course, and we've all had our dreams to be the best – it may be to become the best footballer at school, or the best in the world. Nobody can tell you that you *cannot* be the best, because you're still young. It's wonderful when you see kids at twelve, thirteen, fourteen or fifteen playing with enthusiasm and with such natural ability. But they all still make mistakes, and so you have to teach them. Soon, they're not making as many, they start to develop the mentality they need and begin to improve all the time. But also, everyone is different. Sometimes, you see young players with fantastic ability and you'd bet everything on them going really far, but they simply don't. They have a great opportunity, but they don't quite seize it, often because they're just that little bit lazy or their mentality is not quite right.

We actually enjoyed a lot of success at Chelsea. I had a fantastic team of coaches around me, all very knowledgeable, and they were all good team players. Having such a strong team meant that I could let them focus on structure while I concentrated on philosophy. When I first joined Chelsea, everyone wanted all the players to win whatever game they were playing in, across the club from the first team down to the youth teams. I remember getting all of the coaches together and saying to them, 'Look, there's only one team in the club whose number one goal is to win, and that's the first team. For the rest of the club, *our* number one goal is to develop the *individual* players and get them up to the very highest level possible.'

For me, it was important for all the junior players to learn to play a different sort of football. One of the rules I introduced was when we were playing eleven-a-side in our practice games. The goalkeeper would not be allowed to kick the ball out – they had to pass it short to one of their defenders every time. It put the whole of the defence under pressure, including the goalkeeper (who now had to learn to *play* football), and it taught the players how to move into good positions to help the man with the ball, and also how to receive the ball and keep possession.

I would say to my coaching team, 'Look, we're not a national football club, we are an *international* football club! We have to play and win against clubs like Real Madrid and Juventus. If a player moves up to the first team, they really *have* to understand how to play football at that level.' So, our goal for the first team was to win trophies, while in the youth team it was all about individual player development. It was great because Chelsea became a training ground not just for the players but also for the coaches, many of whom have since gone on to have great coaching careers.

I am proud of my time at Chelsea. I had a great relationship with its owner Roman Abramovich, and he allowed me to build a very strong youth academy for the club over six years.

After my time at Chelsea, I accepted an offer to join Hamburger SV in Germany as sporting director, and this was to prove one of the most challenging periods of my life. Hamburg was a fabulous club with a great history. They had never fallen out of the German Bundesliga, they had won the European Cup and the Cup Winners' Cup, and had been league champions six times. But the club was now in trouble. It was in the relegation zone, and when I was approached by its chief executive, I was told that they desperately needed to bounce back and they needed my help. I was also assured that I had a healthy budget to acquire new players. Before I left Chelsea to join them, however, the CEO was replaced. I was then told by the new management that the club had no money to spend on new players and that they actually needed to sell players in order to balance the club's finances.

It was, therefore, a totally different situation to the one I had expected when I was first approached by the club. I thought about it for a while and instead of turning the job down, I decided that it would actually be a great challenge and a real opportunity for me to make a *big* difference to this club. So I decided to continue with my plans to join them.

One of the biggest challenges I first had to deal with was that the club's players had an average age of thirty-one, which meant they were the third oldest squad in Europe. But I had left Chelsea on good terms and was able to bring a few young players over to Hamburg, together with some of my coaching team.

We ended up completely restructuring the squad, sold off a number of the club's biggest players and after a year we had the *third-youngest* team in the Bundesliga. I remember telling the club's supervisory board when I started that the only way to solve the club's problems was to acquire young players – they would be less expensive and more hungry to win, although they would also lack experience and would make mistakes. So we would not be able to win every week to begin with, and would have to be patient. In the first year, we ended up fourteenth out of eighteen clubs in the league. By the second year, we were seventh in the league.

Being a sporting director in Europe is much more high-profile than say, in Great Britain, where it's the managers who have to face the press and speak for the club. At Hamburg, I had to hold weekly press conferences, which was very hard in the first year, especially when we were still losing most weeks. I remember always trying to stage the post-match TV interviews outdoors – it was usually too cold for the journalists and films crews, and they didn't want to ask too many questions!

For me, I look at my time at Hamburg as very difficult and hugely challenging, but also as a very successful period and a fantastic experience. But it was a job I could never have done without the previous seventeen years of experience as a sporting director with PSV, Spurs and Chelsea. It was almost an impossible challenge, and I had to use every little piece of experience that I had previously acquired to make it work.

Today, I take pride in the fact that I've been able to make a positive impact on each of the clubs I have worked with over many years, either as a player or in management. At PSV Eindhoven alone, I have helped them to win the Dutch league title numerous times between 1985 and 2018, and each time while in a different role – I was either performing as a player or assistant coach (with three months as head coach, when I deputised for Bobby Robson during his illness), or as head scout, head of academy or technical director, and this year as a member of the Board.

Teamwork . . .

There are two things, in particular, that I have learned during my extensive management career in professional football. The first is how important it is to have the right team around you. I would always try to surround myself with people who are better than me. I might take responsibility for making decisions, but I would never do so without talking to my people first. It is also important to concentrate on the things you are good at, and then delegate, manage and mentor your team to handle the rest.

Second, one's *ego* can easily stand in the way if you want to do something good or great – it should never be about *you*. When I think about success, it has always been *our* success as a team of people and not just me.

I think both of these things apply not just to football but to any occupation. Always look for great people you can surround yourself with and think about what you can do as a team, not just what you can do yourself.

A few pointers to help you with your journey . . .

The key to achieving success in life is first of all to find something that you really *love* doing. This is relatively straightforward to do in sport, but can be more difficult in other occupations. For many young people, they may have a goal to do something when at school but end up pursuing a completely different career – perhaps studying to become a lawyer and ending up becoming a teacher. This is usually because they were not really passionate about what they first thought they wanted to do . . .

One of the main reasons why you *must* find something that you love doing is because it is impossible to find success in life at anything unless you really work hard at it. And, when you are working hard at something you really *love* doing, it doesn't *feel* like hard work! In fact, you are more likely to have to be pulled back than pushed to do something.

When you work hard, you also become good at what you are doing – and faster. You are then more likely to get noticed. In football, when a club loses a good player and is looking for a replacement, if you're playing in that same position at your club, are having a great season and are seen to be working hard, they are more likely to spot you and want to sign you up. You might be in the right place at the right time at that moment, but you will also have *put yourself there* through your hard work and desire to be the best you can be. I have always believed that luck follows those who work hard.

Always be prepared to push yourself outside of your normal comfort zone. Obviously, you don't want to pursue something you can't do, because it's not in your area, but don't be afraid to take a risk on something that stretches you. Be brave when making decisions. Sometimes you will get them wrong, but you'll gain useful experience anyway, which you will always take with you.

If you fail to solve a problem, or you are doing something wrong when you think you're doing the right thing, be prepared to listen to others and be honest with yourself. When you are criticised, don't just become defensive or make excuses. You sometimes have to look clearly at yourself in the mirror and admit that you are doing something wrong or that you're not working hard enough. I have often seen this with highly talented footballers who start to do things wrong, but they cannot take criticism and don't like to be confronted about what they're doing wrong or about what they can't do. They don't want to listen because they think they know better, and if they're not working hard enough, they don't want to be told. It usually ends badly, impacting on their whole career.

There are times in life when you can get distracted from what you really should be doing. It often happens during our teenage years – it is easy to go off track, but the time you actually lose might never be recovered again, especially in sport. And if you leave it too long before getting back on course, it can ruin any chance of succeeding at what you initially wanted to do. So there are times when you have to be brutally honest with yourself. You have to ask, 'What do I really want?' Sometimes, it can really hurt because you are seeing the truth – 'I'm simply *not* doing what I should be doing, so now I have to do *this.*' But it can still be very difficult to get back on track, so you will then have to be *very* determined about doing so and work *really* hard at it.

Keeping healthy and staying physically fit is very important for me – it's part of my life. I feel good when I'm fit, and I've always made time for exercising. Also, to be mentally fit, you do need to be physically fit, in my view. A lot of the time in my job I'm sitting down, because I'm either talking to people in meetings or watching a game. So I still try to train at least five times a week in the gym. Wherever I travel to, I always take my kit with me and find somewhere to work out. I will typically give myself a target to do sixty minutes on a cross-trainer. But, even if I'm dead after forty minutes, I'll still push myself to do sixty minutes – *not* fifty-nine, it has to be sixty! I always recommend making time for keeping fit – it will enable you to prepare yourself better for life's challenges, give you stamina and help to keep you mentally agile.

It is always good to have a positive attitude about life and to be able to enjoy things. I sometimes see people so focused on becoming successful that they forget how to live. This is not only bad for their life, it's also not good for what they're doing, which becomes counter-productive. Remember to avoid being negative about yourself and negative towards others. You can self-criticise or be critical of others but in a non-negative way. When you are critical in a positive way, you are then *building* something constructively.

Giving young people space to learn for themselves . . .

When kids are young, they need encouragement to pursue activities such as sport. At first, this comes from their parents, who naturally want the best for their children. Kids look up to their parents too, and it becomes an opportunity for parents to mentor their kids. But in football, this can also be a problem. Some parents have dreams *for their children* and imagine that they can become top football players and achieve fame and wealth, so they push their kids hard in a direction that may not be best or right for them. Others try to be coaches, and I often see this with young, talented kids whose parents are telling their children what to do in a match from the sidelines. Parents should be parents – they should offer encouragement, but leave the coaches to do the coaching.

I remember at PSV, we used to tell the parents of our academy players, 'Your children are only with us for two to three hours. We will dedicate everything we can to them, to teach them. We will hopefully bring them enjoyment, discipline, team spirit and the right mentality. They will win and lose together as a team. *We* will help them to learn from this, but *you* must remain as parents. When you take them home afterwards, don't talk about football. Don't talk about the way they played or what they should do.'

Something I have thought a lot about as a coach is not to 'over-nurture' young players. It's important for them to have the space to make their own decisions (especially split-second decisions) and not be told all of the time what they should do. We discussed this a great deal at Chelsea. We wanted our players to think more for themselves, to take responsibility for their actions both on and off the pitch. We would even encourage them to criticise their teammates, and to receive criticism and take it on board. As coaches, we would provide discipline but give them space to think and be creative. We'd tell the players what the training was going to consist of that day and then afterwards we'd ask, 'How did it go? What did we learn today?' We wouldn't try to *tell* them what to do but would ask them what *they thought they should do*. When training on Fridays, we'd let the players organise themselves – pick their own teams, select their own referee, and the coaches would just watch.

Mentoring in football has become very professional these days and is widely used. But for any young person, having a mentor at various stages in their development can be very helpful for them. It's not the same as asking someone casually and occasionally for advice. You need to find someone who is genuinely interested in you, that wants to help you to develop and who can offer constructive advice. They should be able to talk through with you from time to time what it is that you're doing and want to do, what interests you, and to also help you to make choices. When you are young, you will need a different type of mentor. To begin with, you will need someone who can help you to unlock your potential and encourage you. Later in life, as your career develops, a mentor should have more specific knowledge about your particular area and also be someone who can open doors for you.

Setting goals . . .

Goals are very important. In football, you have to have goals. When you start, you want to make it to the different levels within a club – it might be the under-sixteen squad or the under-seventeens, then the first team and so on. For me, my goals included to play for my country and, of course, to become the best player in the world. But there are lots of goals in between and targets to meet as a player.

Setting goals gives you something to aim for and a direction. If you don't have goals, it's difficult to know what you have to do next, because you don't know what you want to achieve. And then, when you look back, it's difficult to know how well you've done because you have nothing to measure against without goals.

Having support from home . . .

I believe that having the support of family and people around you outside of your work – people who are close to you – is very important. I have been extremely fortunate because my wife has always been highly enthusiastic and understanding about my career. Kate and I came together when we were both seventeen. She knew nothing about football, but I remember her willingness to watch me for the first time, in a league match when I was playing for Fremad Amager in Denmark – it was freezing cold, foggy and pouring with rain!

A couple of years later, I was signed up to join AFC Ajax and I told her that we had to move from our home in Denmark to Amsterdam. It was a big thing for her then because she was pregnant with our twin girls, she had to move away from her family and she didn't know a word of Dutch. But she said yes because she knew how important it was for me. We did not know anyone in Amsterdam. I had to work really hard at the club, and I would come home in the evenings and just spend time with Kate and the twins. It was a wonderful time for me. But we also never went out. It was two and a half years before a clubmate of mine and his girlfriend *insisted* that they came over to babysit for a few hours so that we could go out and have a nice dinner at a restaurant . . .

My wife took care of the house and the children while I worked on my career. She was fantastic and always totally supportive of what I was doing. It was also *very* important for me to have my family at home.

After my active playing career, when I was offered the job of becoming technical director for PSV Eindhoven, I remember saying to my wife, 'If I take this job, you'll probably not see me for three years.' But I told her that this is what I really wanted to do, and in order to build a successful career in football management, I needed to learn everything, work very hard and spend a lot of time at the job. Once again, she said, 'OK, no problem. I'll look after the children, you do what you need to do.'

In the end, it was *more* than a full-time job. I was up at six o'clock every morning to do my ten-kilometre run, then I'd go off to the office. I was working during the day and most evenings. Over the summer holidays, while most players and coaches were relaxing, I was busy with buying and selling players. It was therefore a hugely demanding time for me, but my wife gave me her blessing, and made sure that everything was organised and functioning at home. We have now been married for forty years, have four children and a growing set of grandchildren!

So for me, having good support from home is essential. This is in fact a major factor in the lives of most successful people.

Facing times of insecurity . . .

I have not yet met anyone in my life who has never had doubts or moments when they felt insecure. It's invariably all about self-belief – 'Am I able to do this thing or not?' or 'I haven't got there yet. Will I ever get there?'

I remember well my first few years at PSV Eindhoven, after I had retired from active football. Being assistant coach was great – I knew about *playing* football, so being a coach was natural. But when I became director of football, it was a completely different ball game. I was now often behind a desk, dealing with contracts and administrative stuff. I was also chief scout and head of the youth academy. It was an unbelievably crazy time for me.

I had a lot of problems to handle and different people to deal with, and the first two years were a real nightmare for me. Twenty-five per cent of it was enjoyable, but the rest was tough. I didn't yet have the knowledge or experience, and after a while, my self-esteem went down and down. And of course, the problem with football is that when other people sense you are feeling insecure, they're like wolves and they want to eat you! You get questioned by the media about the decisions you are making, and this makes the situation even worse. After a while, you concentrate only on the bad things you've done, and you forget about all the good things you are doing. You start digging yourself a hole.

At times like these, you *have* to be very strong. If you give up because it's too hard, it will be a disaster, and I was absolutely determined *not* to give up. I had to learn how to deal with the problems, learn from my mistakes and to fight on. You also have to have good people around you to support you, people who are honest with you, who want the best for you, who you can listen to and trust. My wife was fantastic at that time, hugely supportive, and this was very important for me. But it can also be friends or your mentors – you need that honesty and support around you.

I fought on, worked hard, learned as I went along – and after just a few years it got better. My experience grew, I built a great team around me and I became very good at my job. I now look back and think that they were probably my best years for developing character and for *real* learning. The experience of that time would help me enormously in the future to deal with all of the challenges I had to face later in my career and to excel.

Looking positively at failure . . .

When I was a player, I absolutely hated losing. At Ajax, when we lost a game, I didn't want to go out anywhere for at least two days. I felt bad for the club and also bad for the fans. All I wanted to do was to get back into training, work really hard to improve and be 100 per cent ready for the next game. It was part of my character and it helped to drive me. 'I could not fail!'

But I still had to learn how to deal with failures when they happened. Penalties were a case in point. I was actually very good at taking them, and would train very hard every day and practise my penalty kicks. For Ajax, for the Danish national team and for Valencia, I had a spell where I took twenty-four penalties in a row and scored twenty-four times. But then, during a very important game against Switzerland, I missed one . . . I could not believe it. I was devastated, and it was something that really haunted me for a long time afterwards. But I recalled at the time the advice from a former coach. He would say, 'If you take twelve penalties and you miss two, it doesn't matter! You scored ten! Don't look at the penalties you missed, think only about the ones that you scored, because they're the ones that really count.'

How parents can help . . .

As a parent, I think the number one role when helping our children to find their way is *encouragement*. Encourage your children to be their best and to work hard.

When one of my daughters was growing up, I would gently encourage her to do the things she felt insecure about. It might be making a speech at school – she'd say, 'I can't do that!' and I'd reply, 'Of course you *can* do it, and look, if you fail, it's just one failure . . . it doesn't really matter. Life goes on. The most important thing is that you do your best!' I'd then continue to encourage her to work hard at it so that she *could* do her best.

When she was twelve years old she went to secondary school, but she struggled for a while with maths. There were thirty-five kids in her class, so the teachers had no time to help her and she got left behind. Because maths was so important, it affected her assessments, and her self-esteem and confidence suffered. She began to feel that she was not good enough and would never be able to do well at school. But I made a promise to her that we would do everything we could to help, and just gave her loads of encouragement: 'Don't worry, we'll help you to be the best. You can do it – just keep fighting.' So we changed her school, and she ended up having a very good maths teacher who then really helped her to catch up. She worked hard, passed her exams, and went on to complete her undergraduate degree and then a master's degree. We always encouraged her as parents to do well, to fight her self-doubts and to be her best.

Whenever your child says that they want to do or become something as a career, parents should never say 'No!' if they don't agree with them or they think they should pursue something else. It is much better to say, 'OK, are you sure that's what you want?' You can suggest reasons why it may not be a good idea and what the alternatives may be but in a positive way. If they say, 'Yes, I'm sure!', then you should say, 'Fine, so what can we do to help you?' One should never dampen the enthusiasm that a child has about something – being enthusiastic about *anything* is very important in itself and is something to nurture in the young.

So for me, a parent's key role in helping their children to find their way to enjoying a successful life is mainly *encouragement* – be positive, allow them room, help them to explore and give them *lots* of encouragement to be their best.

Zak Brown

Born in Los Angeles but now residing in the UK, Zak Brown's career started at an early age as a professional racing driver, competing successfully in both the US and Europe. After seeing an opportunity to create a business around helping other drivers and race teams to raise sponsorship, he founded Just Marketing International (JMI), which was listed four times in the Inc. 500 Fastest- Growing Private Companies of the Year. JMI would ultimately become the largest motorsport marketing agency worldwide, successfully attracting many of the world's biggest brands into the world of motorsport. Zak joined McLaren in 2016 and is currently Chief Executive Officer of McLaren Racing, famous for its hugely successful F1 team.

'If you are fundamentally a good person with good intentions and high integrity, people will trust you and they'll want to help you.'

'Being an entrepreneur is a huge challenge for anyone. If you want to start a business, you really need to know what you are in for. You have to be pretty honest with yourself, and make sure that you possess the core skills and attitude required to succeed — or else you won't last very long.'

'You have to be motivated and you have to be prepared to work hard, really hard, in order to win and to succeed over the long term. If you work hard and you're pushing all the time, you actually create the opportunities that help you to move forward.'

'The most important thing that parents can provide their children is simply support and understanding. Parents need to appreciate how hard it can be to grow up and find your way as a young person today.'

On success . . .

People are naturally motivated by various things and will work for different reasons. How they measure success, though, will also vary – from fiscal to emotional, to lifestyle or other yardsticks. Sometimes they will work for all of these things, sometimes one or two . . .

For me, success has always been about winning and then winning more. It's about growing, because real success has to be viewed over the long term, not just seeing fleeting moments of success. It has to be based on *continuous improvement*, each and every day.

The journey . . .

Everyone starts their journey by figuring out what they may be good at, what they like doing and, ideally, discovering something that they can feel passionate about. But not everyone will find or have a real passion for their work. For many people, they'll see their work as just 'a job'. That will be good enough for them and they end up living perfectly happy, normal lives, while still doing something that's actually *not* their dream job. For those that want to achieve more and who are especially driven, then it really helps for them to find something that they can become genuinely passionate about – because when they do, opportunities to find *real* success will naturally open up for them.

My own journey revolved almost entirely around motor racing – it seemed like I was born into it. I enjoyed competing as a driver from a young age, and this naturally led me to turn what was fun for me into a career. My passion was simply following my love. I never really viewed motor racing as a Job; I was just pursuing something that I really loved doing and then figured out a way to turn it into a business.

Motor racing is expensive, so drivers and race teams need to find sponsors to support them. This is always a big challenge, but it is also something I became good at. It was when I saw the potential to help others find their own sponsors, rather than just do it for myself, that I visualised a great business opportunity. In 1995 I founded Just Marketing International, which I led and grew successfully for several years. JMI was to become a successful business, winning many awards and ultimately becoming the world's largest marketing agency in motorsport.

When I think back over my journey, I have been consistently critical of myself, a bit of a pessimist and have always had a slight fear of failure. I certainly believe that when someone wants to start their own business, if they have a naively optimistic outlook, just kidding themselves all the time that everything is going to 'turn out fine', they're more likely to go *out* of business in three months. I have always believed in anticipating and trying to solve those things that could go wrong, along the way, as opposed to just chasing what might feel like 'victory'.

When JMI was eventually bought out, eighteen years after I had started it, part of the due diligence from the acquiring business was to subject me to psychological analysis – they wanted to understand the mindset of the CEO that they were buying! As it was explained to me then, there are two types of business leaders: those that *want to win*, and this is what motivates that type of individual, and those that *don't want to lose*, and that's what motivates them (they'll probably both arrive at the same end point, but just get there in different ways).

So, I'm firmly in the 'I don't want to lose' camp – very self-critical – and I believe that if you're not going forwards then you're going backwards. So I push very hard every single day, and have been doing so for twenty-five years.

My experience as a racing driver was to prove very helpful to me when I was building my business. When you are competing in a race car, you have to make critical decisions every second. You have to concentrate hard, while constantly evaluating the condition of your car and the track. You can't sort of 'waffle' when making these decisions – when you see an opportunity to pass someone, you either go for it *now* or you don't. You need to know exactly when to step it up, when to pull back, when to make a left and when to make a right. There's a huge level of intensity involved when racing because if you get it wrong, the consequences can be fatal.

Teamwork is also critical — you've got to have great engineers and great mechanics. You really learn from motorsport just how important it is to build a good team and how much you end up relying on having good people around you. While running a business may not be quite as intense as racing a car, I have approached both challenges in a similar way, which has certainly proved very positive for me.

Preparing for success . . .

When you start up a business, the first few years are crucial and inevitably very difficult. In the early days you have no choice — you have got to wake up early and you've got to get out of the gate first, strong and fast. You have got to be prepared to work hard, very hard.

You will also have to face many issues early on. It's never fun dealing with these, but you have to learn to tackle any problem head-on, quickly and aggressively *before* it escalates, and you must be very critical of yourself if you fail to do that.

As your business develops, especially if it grows fast in the early stages, it can be hard to keep track and keep up with everything until you have built a solid foundation. As you push out, you get stretched and you don't always get the business running properly. It is easy to get into a bind early on. At times like these you have to be straight and honest with people, or they simply won't work with you. Even when giving people bad news, just be honest about it. I remember when I got my business going, I had to raise funds but was unable to repay people back by the time that I intended. So, I was just completely honest with them. I offered to pay them something towards the debt to show good intent and it worked — they could see I was genuine, serious and committed and that they could trust me. In the end, of course, everyone was paid back.

Unfortunately, some people want to shortcut their way to success or, worse still, scam their way there. Eventually, they get caught out, especially when they let people down. But if you are fundamentally a good person with good intentions and high integrity, people will trust you and they'll want to help you.

Having the right attitude is crucial. Racing and winning are largely about attitude, of course, but as my sports-marketing career developed, I found myself working increasingly in the 'people business'. I was handling clients directly on a one-to-one basis, and this depends heavily on your possessing a good, positive attitude – people naturally like to engage with, support and be around positive individuals.

Being a good communicator is very important too. In my business, I manage a lot of projects and continuously push out a lot of boats. You have to make sure that everyone knows who captains all the boats, and this requires good, frequent and clear communication.

When you are in business, you have to learn to multi-task. To push forwards as quickly as you can, you have to get as many projects as possible going at one time. This might seem to contradict the idea that you should focus on one thing at a time, but if you are highly organised and disciplined, you *can* focus on more than one thing at one time. I have seen some pretty messy desks over the years, but that's definitely not me! When you look at my desk, every project has a different coloured folder. You have to be good at compartmentalising your work, and you also have to learn how to set priorities.

Being an entrepreneur is a huge challenge for anyone. If you want to start a business, you really need to know what you are in for. You have to be pretty honest with yourself, and make sure that you possess the core skills and attitude required to succeed – or else you won't last very long. If you don't like hard work or find it hard to get out of bed in the morning, you might want to think about doing something else . . .

Finding good mentors . . .

When you start out in business, you need to surround yourself with good people. I was fortunate in the early stages of my career as a racing driver because I had a lot of very successful people around me at a young age. I watched them a lot and engaged with them whenever I could – many of them were happy to support me and are still friends of mine today.

Over time, I managed to bring on board various people to help me more as mentors, and I've had quite a few over the years. I will still call some of them today, depending on what the topic is.

Finding a mentor should be more of a natural process rather than something prearranged. Typically, you might meet someone, perhaps in the business environment in which you circulate. You hit it off, you get along with them, and they develop a special interest in *you* and what you are doing. They're in a position to help you and they really want to as well.

As we develop over the years, we will need different types of mentors. The people I may turn to now are at a completely different layer of sophistication and level of advice compared with the more basic stuff of twenty years ago. It has to be real mentorship, though, someone you can talk to when you are challenged by something or to seek advice from on matters that can enhance your development as a business person.

A good mentor can help you to create new business and also introduce you to the right people. There definitely has to be a high degree of relevance and empathy, however. If they like you or like the business environment in which you operate, they will be more likely to put the time and effort in to help you. If they're neither particularly interested in your business, nor have any real experience or knowledge of it, then that's no good to you.

Hard work actually creates good luck . . .

I have always been highly driven. I was born that way I think – very competitive and with a strong desire to win, whilst seeking to continually grow and get better at whatever I'm doing.

I really believe that you make your own luck, and that comes almost entirely from hard work. I have yet to meet a successful entrepreneur who is lazy. That's one of the reasons why being an entrepreneur is *not* for everyone. You have to be motivated and you have to be prepared to work hard, really hard, in order to win and to succeed over the long term. If you work hard and you are pushing all the time, you actually create the opportunities that help you to move forward.

Looking back over my business career, I can probably chart its progress as a sequence of deals where each one has taken the business up to another level. But my *biggest* deal might not necessarily be the most important one – I would never have got *that* deal if it wasn't for an earlier deal. So, was it then the first deal or the fiftieth deal that I won that was more important? In reality, one can look at a succession of 'deal milestones' along my journey from day one that have all contributed ultimately, and in a sustained way, to the success of the business.

You don't win every deal, of course, but the point here is that if you keep working hard at it, apply your passion, keep looking for opportunities, you *will* make your own luck, and eventually get the next deal and then the next one, and you will by sheer persistence continue to move onwards and upwards in your journey.

Failures and fears . . .

One of my biggest motivators has always been fear of failure. In the early stages of running my business it was, 'What if I don't get the next deal?' or 'How am I going to make the payroll next week?' As the business grew it became, 'How am I going to make it to the end of the month?' Your telescope then gets longer, and the numbers get bigger, and soon, running out of cash in six months feels like a luxury when it was previously one week at a time. But the bigger the numbers, the greater the anxiety and stress, and it was this that constantly motivated me. In the end, I learned to manage the pressures, and you soon get to the stage when you realise that 'if it all went wrong tomorrow, I'll still be fine,' which certainly removes much of the stress . . .

Everyone makes mistakes. When you do, you have to be able to get over things quickly – ideally within twenty-four hours. You cannot be down for a week, otherwise you're just compounding the problem.

There are lots of mistakes that I have made over the years that I wish I hadn't. But I probably would have still made them at some point, so I am glad that I made them then and not now – they would probably be far more catastrophic today. When you make mistakes, you have to treat them all as a practical learning experience. You can't just say, 'Yeah, I made a mistake' and move on. You have to learn not to make the same mistake twice. One mistake is fine – but never the same one twice, especially if it's what I call a 'stupid mistake', something that could easily have been avoided. It is something I rarely do now, but it does still happen every once in a while. But my self-critical attitude has always been, 'You're an idiot if you make the same mistake twice and don't learn the first time.' That is how I've learned over the years, and I certainly make fewer mistakes now.

When you make mistakes, it's not just recognising that you've made one and trying to remember for the next time. You have to be analytical and go back as far as to when you think the mistake first began – 'I didn't jump on that quickly enough 'or 'I said the wrong thing' or 'I didn't get that done on time.' You need to rewind, and see where and when you went off course to understand how not to do the same thing again.

Setting goals . . .

Goals for me are very important and always have been. I have, throughout my life, 'lived large', and have usually been driven by things that I want, that are material, but not because I am necessarily a materialistic person. I would set myself one goal at a time, normally on the things I wanted, and would then go out to create enough business to be able to get them. But it was never about 'Look what I've got'; it was always more to do with setting my sights on something big, often biting off more than I could chew, and then figuring out how to digest it. It might be planes, homes, cars or race cars, but I'd then work my socks off to go out and get them.

I didn't need to write my goals down because they came one at a time and I'd keep thinking about them 24/7. I didn't need any reminder notices either. I would just focus on what I needed to do in order to achieve the things I wanted. This helped to fuel my desire to work hard, to remain focused and to do and be my very best. I have thought like this from day one.

Finding that balance . . .

When you start out in your career, especially building a business, the first phase takes up virtually every hour of every day of every week. Your 'house is on fire' when you start out in business, unless you have a tonne of cash to start off with, which I did not. I started with nothing, and so had no choice but to work hard all of the time. If you're sleeping, you're not working. When you're working, you can then kick the ball up the field and make progress. Your objective in the early days is to reach a point of stability and build a team of people around you. As you become established, you can find a better balance, because with others to help you, you can better manage your time and focus.

Part of that eventual balance is finding time for relaxation and other activities to recharge your batteries and take your mind away from work. I play golf to help me to switch off and I still race occasionally when I can, but now it's just for pleasure.

Making time for your family can be very difficult when you are working so hard, particularly in the early stages of your career, but it's hugely important. The problem is, when you get home from working you often carry the stresses of the business with you and your mind can still be at work. It's a really hard one, but you must learn to manage it. Having the support of your family is really important.

How parents can help . . .

The most important thing that parents can provide their children is simply support and understanding. Parents need to appreciate how hard it can be to grow up and find your way as a young person today.

It is also important that parents do not interfere too much in what their children are doing with their careers and just remain as Mom and Dad. My parents knew nothing really about business, so they just let me get on with it and were just there to support me. Unless you are in the restaurant business, I'm not a big fan of family getting involved anyway. If your child wants to pursue something entrepreneurial, don't try to be a business partner.

If a child is finding it difficult to decide what they want to do as a career, parents can try to find opportunities for them through their own network where possible, open a few doors for them or even help them to find internships. But it should be limited to just opening the doors. Then it's up to kids to find their way – this is all a part of growing up and learning.

It's very difficult for parents to instil 'motivation' in their children. This is something that they need to develop or acquire for themselves. If they're fundamentally lazy and don't like hard work, then they should not really think about doing anything entrepreneurial because you need a certain drive and attitude to make your career work. As I mentioned earlier, I have never met a successful lazy entrepreneur!

Ursula Burns

From joining Xerox as an intern in 1980, Ursula Burns moved steadily through the company to become chief executive officer in 2009, and chairwoman until her retirement in 2017. She remains one of the most successful women in US corporate history and the first black woman to lead a Fortune 500 company. Forbes ranked her as the twenty-second most powerful woman in the world in 2014. She was adviser to President Barack Obama, led the Whitehouse STEM programme from 2009 until 2016, and also served as vice chair of the President's Export Council. She has held numerous board positions for some of the world's largest multinational companies, and is widely respected for her contribution to community, educational and non-profit organisations over many years.

'If you are really passionate about 'this thing' that you are doing, and you work really, really hard at it, and you put all of your energy into it, then you *will* find success and you *will* find happiness.'

'I was once told that I had three strikes against me – I was black, I was a girl and I was poor. But I was also raised to believe that I *could do* whatever I wanted and whatever I set my mind to achieve. My mother would tell me, 'There are lots of possibilities out there. Just go out and try!''

'It's about working hard, being bold, speaking up, taking initiative and taking responsibility about *your* future. The more you do this, and the more you put yourself out there, the further you increase the chances of good things happening for you, and the more you make your own luck.'

'Help your children to see what they *can* do rather than tell them what they *can't* do.'

About success . . .

I like to define success in a much broader sense than just *striving to reach a particular place* and then simply getting there and settling there . . . I look at what I call 'complete person success' based on a 360-degree view of an individual's life. Career success is just one part of it, family is another, and also the positive impact you have on your community and the world. These are all important measures of success for me.

When you start your career journey, especially working in a large organisation as I did, you will probably think of success initially in terms of how many people you get to manage or how much money you get to earn. As I progressed through my career, earning increasingly more money and achieving greater power, I began to realise just how much less those things actually mattered to me.

After a while, success becomes significantly more than just salary or your status in a company. You start to think about the things that aren't so easily measured – how much you are able to impact a community while still delivering business results, how good a team you can build, how you can influence strategy and affect how well your company is regarded by its customers and the wider community.

As you get older, the second thing you begin to realise is that being successful goes beyond your career; it's also about your family and others who are close to you. Your children are naturally especially important – how happy they are and how successful they will become. But there are people around you too that you can help, and whose lives you can also positively impact. In my family, we seek to do this through what we like to call our 'extended family'. It was an idea first started by my mother many years ago, where each of us would take on *one* additional person to look out for. They can be a family member or someone from outside of the family, but the aim is, through regular contact and support, to help them with their aspirations and shepherd them to a good place.

The third measure of success for me is what I call 'making yourself be heard'. There will be worldly issues that one feels passionate about

– these could be environmental, social, humanitarian and so on. Being able to use your wealth and your influence to speak out and try to move things along to a better place, this is personally very important to me. I just love it when I hear the statement, 'I wish *somebody* would do something about it!' and you ask, 'Who exactly?' and you hear, 'The government!' when fundamentally that's, of course, all of us. So being able to contribute something significant back to the world and the degree to which you can make a positive difference are, in my view, all part of this broad definition of success.

But there is another significant point here: you can also be very successful in life without necessarily achieving a 'certain status' or having made a lot of money. My mother was a remarkable woman. She raised three kids by herself in the most difficult circumstances. We were incredibly poor as a family, living in a New York public housing project, and yet our house was incredibly clean and well organised, we had reasonable food to eat, she dressed us well, sent us to a good school and taught us impeccable manners. She was very much in control of the family. We had, in a way, everything any 'successful' family would normally have, but without the money. And her aim was simple – to raise her children into well-rounded, educated individuals who could flourish. She dedicated her life solely to this ambition and in the end, she successfully created three impactful, kind, intelligent and reasonable kids who would each go on to build great careers and ultimately be able to contribute back to society.

It's quite ironic to me, the fact that I have on a number of occasions made it onto various 'power lists' that popularly depict how successful you're seen to be – the '*n*th' most influential woman in the US or the world or whatever . . . My mother, who was very successful in her own way, would never have made it onto any of these lists, and her own success was completely unrecognised by the world. She literally lived and died on this Earth, and nobody, apart from her family, gave a hoot. But she managed to achieve her goals and was very successful in doing so. Hopefully, society will be judging her favourably now, in recognising what her children have since gone on to achieve.

Finding your passion . . .

When you are young, you have to be open to try to explore many possibilities. Some of these may end up being dry holes, but you have to keep exploring. What tends to happen these days is that kids are 'assigned' choices early – they are tracked into something that perhaps their parents have done or want them to do, or their school seems to channel them into something that may be 'relevant'. The point here is that there's this *narrowing* that seems to happen really early on for kids. They end up exploring only a few options, from which they are expected to make big choices, career choices, that will impact the rest of their lives. It seems really crazy to me to ask a teenager to pick what they want to major in and decide what they want to do for the rest of their lives, at such an early stage. But that is literally what's expected . . .

So I think it's essential for a young person to explore and try lots of things, and be flexible. You have to find that 'something' you may really like, that you can eventually love and become passionate about – something that you are willing to dedicate your time to and become really good at. If you can find it, then I say, *go after it*! Because (and this is one thing that I would happily bet all my money on!), I can assure you that if you are really passionate about 'this thing' that you are doing, and you work really, really hard at it, and you put all of your energy into it, then you *will* find success and you *will* find happiness . . .

Developing your career . . .

Once you have found something that you are really good at and have chosen as a career, the more you work at it, the more you learn, you eventually begin to 'ground yourself' in it. Ultimately, it becomes what I call your 'mental rest space'. As you become an expert in something and develop a broad understanding of your subject, your brain can relax a little because it's 'at home'. When you are speaking on your subject, it's something you know inside-out and can feel confident that you have authority to speak about. It becomes your validation and credibility, both to yourself and the people around you. When you're then asked to participate and contribute to something else that you do not have any experience in at all, your brain can still remain in its mental rest space while helping you to focus on something completely different, but without feeling inadequate in any way.

As you grow, and your career develops, you have to realise that this is actually not about *you*. It's about the people around you – your teammates, the company you work for, your customers and so on. If you can look at your work like that, in a selfless way, not only is this the right way to approach things anyway, but your peers will also appreciate this as a quality in you and recognise your values.

While there may be some shortcuts, there are very few worthwhile ones. You simply have to work really hard at it. There is no substitute for hard work. Those that do work hard have a real shot at finding success, while those that don't very rarely do.

Apart from working hard, you need direction – and that includes setting goals for yourself. I set goals for literally everything I do, at work and also at home for my family. Some are short term, some medium and others long term. Some may be softer goals – when I was in my twenties I needed to force myself to go out and socialise with people who would not be within my natural circle, as I was always fussy about people I would mix with and would prefer to be by myself rather than spend time with those I did not especially like. But that was also limiting for me, so I set myself a goal to expand my circle and to push myself out there, which in the end was really helpful for me.

My own journey . . .

My mother was hugely influential for me when I was young, and her example was amazing. One thing that I will always love and respect her for was her unerring pursuit of one simple goal: her three kids were *all* going to get to college and they were *all* going to be successful. And that was it – everything else was always secondary to that.

She was unbelievably passionate about this, her goal, and as far as she was concerned that was her job. But, it was also a *huge* struggle for her. We had a really tough life growing up, living in a basic apartment in this awful building in the middle of a bad neighbourhood in Lower East Manhattan – half of the time we couldn't even go out because it wasn't safe. She had to raise three kids, by herself, in this very small place, and we all drove her crazy! But she never once wavered. She worked incredibly hard to keep us secure and to feed us every day, and my brother, my sister and I had really no idea just how hard it was for her at the time. It was only when I got to around sixteen, when my mental awareness started to mature, that I began to realise how physically tired, sick and completely worn down she actually was.

She would consistently scrape together the money needed so that I could go to a Catholic school, and she had to work hard and do side jobs just to keep everything together. She used to say to us, 'Just get to college, and then I'll be OK.' As I got older, I remember asking, 'But who is going to pay for that?' and she would say to me, 'Just worry about your grades and I'll worry about how we pay for college!' But the fact was that she didn't have a clue how she was going to pay for it – her hope was that we might piece it together with a scholarship here and a loan there, and in the end, that's exactly what happened. But in the meantime, she never gave up and she never once said, 'This is too hard.'

As we got older, whenever we used to despair about our difficulties or question our future, my mother would say, 'Don't let *where* you are define *who* you are.' She assured us that although it was really tough right now, there were much bigger things for us to understand – 'You can't have the world happen to you, you have to happen to the world!' Her grammar wasn't great, but the message was clear: 'Just go out there and take it! Do it!' She would also make lots of other *big statements* that made no real sense to us as kids at the time, but which mean so much to me now. One of the things she'd say all the time was, 'You know that you have been successful in life when you have left behind more than you have taken.' When you think about it, that is a very powerful statement and one that I often speak about today as a principle and a value.

I was to make two decisions in my young life, each of which was to have a profound impact on my future career. At school, I was being prepared for one of three career paths: nun, teacher or nurse. But none of these options appealed to me. I started dreaming of becoming an engineer. The cool thing was that there were precious few female engineers and certainly no black women engineers at that time. It was also an area that was in high demand and would continue to be so for a long time. I was offered a place by the Brooklyn Polytechnic Institute, and I studied chemical engineering to begin with. Later on, I decided to switch over to mechanical engineering, a subject that I was to learn to love, become very good at and that would be the foundation for my future success.

After I finished my Bachelor of science degree, I made a second hugely significant decision; I applied for a position as a summer intern for this big company called Xerox. It was an experience I enjoyed, so I decided that I'd join them permanently once I obtained a master's degree in mechanical engineering from Columbia University.

When I first started working for Xerox at their Rochester headquarters, I was definitely a bit rough. I was straight out of New York City – the nearest thing to the 'country' I had ever been to was perhaps Queens or Long Island and the closest thing to 'business' I'd seen was the corner bodega near home. I had lots of hair, didn't dress the way they did or speak anything like the way they spoke, but at Xerox they didn't seem to mind. They thought I was smart, and just asked me to work in different places and do different things, without spending a whole lot of time trying to have me fit in.

I was intrigued when someone would tell me that I was 'smart', because there were definitely a lot of very smart men and women working around me at Xerox. But I learned later that it was partly the academic field I was working in, but also because I was known to speak up about things that I had a keen interest in (I had an opinion, right or wrong, on just about anything!) I was kind of assigned this additional 'level of intelligence' by my peers. They were definitely very interested in my mind at Xerox and I received a huge amount of support. People took care of me and allowed me to flourish while I became good at something that I really enjoyed doing.

Early in my career, I was working hard and diligently in my role as an engineer. I would arrive in the morning, go straight to the lab, do my work, and then go home. One day, a scientist working on the same floor mentioned to me that he had been observing my comings and goings each day for the last six months. He suggested that I should probably engage a little bit more with the company and invited me along to this 'work quality of work life council meeting'. His name was Lloyd and I did not know it then, but he would eventually become my husband. He was one of the first people at Xerox to 'find me', take an interest in me, and he also became one of my early mentors.

So I attended this meeting, and a senior-looking guy was leading a communications session during which he would also take questions. At one point, someone in the room asked a question about women and minorities. It was actually a rude and disrespectful question in my mind, but I was even more troubled by the way in which this guy tried to handle and answer it in a very 'politically correct' way. I took issue with him straightaway, and we got into a pretty heated debate right in the middle of this meeting. I told him that he should have immediately dismissed the question as 'ridiculous', and how dare he answer it in the way he did. We argued, and I firmly stood my ground. In hindsight, I was wrong to have made such an issue during this meeting in the way I did, but he was a little bit wrong too! After the meeting had finished, Lloyd said to me, 'Do you know who that was that you were arguing with?' I said that I didn't have a clue, and he said, 'Well, that was actually Wayland Hicks. He is only the second-most powerful person in Xerox, but don't worry, the worst thing that can possibly happen is that you'll have to look for another job!'

Two days later I got a call from Wayland Hicks's secretary asking me to come down to his office. I remember nervously calling Lloyd up straightaway (we weren't even dating at that time) and recall him saying to me, 'I told you!'

So, I went down to see Wayland, expecting the worst . . . But we ended up talking, discussing what had happened, and it was to be the start of a great friendship. What is interesting, when looking back, was how we were both completely polar in our views – he was a staunch white Middle American Republican, and I was this black, female, edge-of-the-country Liberal Democrat! Everything he believed in I didn't, and everything I believed in he didn't! Over the years we would have these great discussions and perhaps met at the middle in just a couple of places. The fact that I could argue my case, even on issues that I really knew nothing about, clearly intrigued and impressed him. He was another person at the company that told me I was smart, and he became one of my early and most influential mentors.

It was a few years later that Wayland asked me to become his executive assistant. I remember saying to him at the time, 'Really? I've got a master's degree in Engineering – I'm not going to become anybody's darn secretary!' He told me in a polite but firm way, 'You should *learn* before you speak.' So, I had a good look at what the job would be like, and I was completely blown over – this was an incredible role and a great opportunity to learn something new. I decided to take the job, and it was to be a huge turning point for me in my career. I would become visible to the entire C-Suite of the company and often the board. They would see me organising everything for Wayland – managing his calendar, checking his speeches and a whole bunch of other stuff. I also travelled with him extensively to all these crazy places. It was, for me, one of the coolest jobs in the world.

After nine months – and shortly following my marriage to Lloyd – the chairman of Xerox, Paul Allaire, then asked me to be *his* executive assistant. I would have to leave Wayland to work for him. I remember Paul calling me in; he offered me the role and said, 'You should think about a transition period and when you're going to start.' But I was actually really concerned about taking on this further role. My time with Wayland had been very demanding and I managed to 'pass', but why would I want to take the risk of another two years with someone else who was also completely different? There was a huge contrast in personality and style between Wayland and Paul. So I said, 'I'm sorry, Paul, but I really don't want to do this – you are going to have to give me a very good reason why I should.' And I recall him saying to me, 'Because, Ursula, I'm the chairman and CEO, and I have asked you – *that's* the reason why you should do it.'

So I took the job in 1991, and it was to be among the best and most important two years of my career. I learned a huge amount about the company. It taught me a lot about the senior management, a lot about boards and board directors, how you set a good agenda, how to keep a high-level meeting going, how to 'read a room' a little bit and understand when you might be 'losing them over there', how it's really important to get 'this thing' across and being able to kind of tell when they don't quite get it.

When I look back now, I realise that I was being prepared for a top job in Xerox. Wayland Hicks was already convinced early on that I had the ability to run the company one day. I was barely six years into my career at Xerox when he was saying, 'This is what we are going to do: we're going to keep pushing you *hard*, and you're either going to get there or you'll bomb out.'

After my two years with Paul Allaire, I was placed in various roles, heading business teams in different parts of the organisation. These were all crazy, challenging roles that really tested me: 'I don't even know what the hell this part of the organisation is! I've never been here before! Who *are* these people?' I was simply told each time, 'Don't worry, you'll figure it out.' But I was never left out to just dangle.

The experiences I gained and the challenges I met would prove invaluable to me in my eventual corporate career. Just ten years after I first become Wayland Hicks's executive assistant, I was appointed senior vice president of Corporate Strategic Services. This was to bring me into contact with Anne Mulcahy, with whom I worked very closely for two years before she became CEO. After I spent a two-year spell as president of Xerox, I was to succeed Anne in July 2009 to become the first black American woman CEO to head a Fortune 500 company.

It shouldn't be all about money . . .

When I look back at my career path at Xerox, my journey had nothing to do with chasing a promotion or choosing something that would pay me more money. I was offered opportunities to pursue and often simply told what I was going to do, but I never asked, 'Well, how much am I going to get paid then?' and never said 'no' because of money or because I wasn't going to get a promotion out of it. In fact, had I been more calculating about money or about my career path, I probably would have turned down some options – perhaps the very ones that were to enable me to move up to the next level in my career.

Unfortunately, in the United States – and probably elsewhere in the modern world too – we're really burrowing into this 'money is the only solution to the problem' thing. I go to schools to speak and talk to kids, and I often hear them say that after they get their degree, they want to become an entrepreneur and develop some app that's going to make them a millionaire . . .

It goes beyond individual choice, it's also cultural. In the world today, we have some huge challenges: we can't get water from point A to point B, we have lots of water here but no water there. It's a global problem. It's the same with food; food distribution is very difficult and yet we have starving people over here and over there. These are *real* problems, but also great problems to solve. How about working on something like that? The reason is because there is no career in that. The 'market' exists, but it's just not paid. There are countless highly qualified and incredibly capable people who would be very willing to work hard to solve these issues, but there is simply no remuneration model for it. We have the people but not the incentives – it seems quite perverse to me. So we end up with this totally ridiculous path where people have to say, 'First, I'm going make it and then I'll be able to help.'

Parenting . . .

Parenting is real work, it's a full-time job. It demands more brain time and more physical energy than most people realise. Parenting cannot be outsourced to anyone else and you have to accept that it's *the* biggest, most important thing that you will have to do.

If you get it wrong, it can be a disaster. I know people who have messed up kids and their lives become hell. They're always worried and can never get settled. But of course, it's never easy. Occasionally you get this child who is totally compliant and reasonable and easy to raise, but more often they can be very difficult and very hard work. Both types of kids have a different way of expressing their value to the world, but they are both still worth the effort.

It's important for kids to know from their parents what the boundaries are, and these have to be very clear. My kids always knew what my husband and I expected from them. If they didn't do it, they knew that they would disappoint us, plain and simple. It's all part of good parenting in my view, and it's what we used to do a long time ago. My mother was very good at it, and we all knew clearly the difference between right and wrong.

With modern parenting, it's almost like we don't want our kids to fail at all. We even reward them with parties when they graduate from kindergarten . . . Really?

Children also have to learn not to take their parent's support for granted; it has to be earned by showing the right attitude towards something. Parents have to understand how to instil these values in them too. 'Do you love doing this? Are you willing to work hard at it? Well, let's go then . . . We're willing to put as much time and energy supporting you at this thing, but you have to show commitment. We can't want it more than you want it.'

My children have been unbelievably successful at school, and both are studying for PhDs. When people say to me, 'You must be so proud of your kids,' I say that I'm happy for my kids and yes, proud of them too, but this is just the start of their journey. They have been good students and it has been easy for them, but they'll soon be facing the wider world and all its challenges . . .

Fortune . . .

I was very fortunate when I was young. My mother was totally committed to her children, while encouraging and supporting us through school, even though we had no money. I was also very fortunate to have selected a great field to study, to major in and choose as a career, and then to pick such a great company to work for.

I had so much help when I was young. I went through college and got my master's degree with the help of fellowships, scholarships and work studies, and ended up with no more than a $5,000 debt. So, right from the beginning, I was very fortunate.

Success has an unbelievable amount to do with luck. That fateful meeting where I had my exchange with Wayland Hicks – he was to become a hugely important mentor to me and instrumental in my progress through the company. Who knows where I would have ended up had I not gone to that meeting and met him in the first place.

Had I been five years older, or had Anne Mulcahy decided to stay five years longer, I would probably have never been made CEO of Xerox. I was ready for it and she was ready to retire. It was great timing, and I was certainly in the right place. But, I also had to *be* ready. When people looked at me, they had to recognise something in me that *said* I was ready for the job. All the experience I had accumulated, all the opportunities I had taken advantage of, all the time and hard work I had put in . . . All of these things are essentially where you can 'make your own luck'.

And part of making your own luck is also about being flexible and open. It's also about being fearless (not reckless) and being prepared to speak up. If you have an opinion about something or you don't agree with somebody, express it! Be willing to engage. I love it when someone says to me. 'But nobody told me to do that!' So when you get out of bed in the morning, does somebody need to tell you to take a shower? You get on with it and do it because it leads to something. You don't always need to wait for direction or for someone's permission to do something – be bold and use your initiative, because luck certainly favours those that do.

When I'm sitting around the table with my management team, I expect everyone to speak up and to throw out ideas so that we can talk about them. If you are a lawyer and part of the team, you're not managing your law department at that moment, you're there because of your legal expertise and as part of a *leadership* team. The same applies if you have your engineering hat on or your finance hat on – I want them all to be 'good CEOs', and that's the point of sitting around the table. I don't want them to sit quietly and just wait for me to say something. I have often said, 'If I have to do all the work, all of you are going to be fired and I'm going to take all your pay! Because, what is the point of having you all sitting here if I have to think of everything?'

So, it's about working hard, being bold, speaking up, taking initiative and taking responsibility about *your* future. The more you do this, and the more you put yourself out there, the further you increase the chances of good things happening for you, and the more you make your own luck.

Self-doubt and failure . . .

I'm the least confident successful person you're ever likely to run into. I wake up with self-doubt and I go home with self-doubt every day! I'm naturally optimistic but also naturally negative and highly cautious. Self-doubt is this mental thing that happens but should not be dismissed. It's part of being alive and part of being human, and is also how you process a decision, how you analyse it 'outside of your body' in a way, and is an essential part of how we learn.

I look back at things that have gone wrong – and also when they've gone well. I will question if I did the right things and could I have done them any better, but I will not dwell on things for long.

On reflection, I have certainly made many mistakes and have a lot of regrets. But, it always intrigues me when I hear someone say that they have *none*. I recall one of our past US presidents being asked during an interview if there was anything that he would have done differently, and he said, 'Not a thing.' And, I remember thinking, 'Really? That's *not* good – that means that you actually haven't learned anything!'

We all fail, it's part of life and we learn from it. Most of my failures have been where I have got the timing wrong on a decision or made bad decisions about people, and often where I have not trusted my own instincts. I call this 'instinct override' – hiring someone where it has not turned out well, for example, after my instinct initially told me that something just wasn't quite right but I decided to ignore it.

I'm very confident in my abilities to get things done. But this usually requires me to rely on people to do things, sometimes really challenging things. I have more confidence in people when I know that they have experienced failure, that they've learned to grit their way through stuff – people who actually push more than those who are purely talented.

Some decisions you make today for all the right reasons will end up being a failure, and later on you look back and think, 'That was a stupid decision!' But, at the time, everything looked right – all the data, the facts and the input supported it. Your intentions were good, the decision seemed reasonable, but it went wrong. I call these 'honest mistakes', and we all make them.

As a chief executive, you have to make decisions all the time. But we cannot always get it right, any more than anyone else can. We are not this oracle on high with a crystal ball and able to call the right decision every time. And, because we have to make so many decisions, we probably have more black dots or crosses on our scorecards than most. Anyone who thinks that a successful CEO has got there with a perfect record of no mistakes is naïve. Most often, because you are at the lead, you get pegged with the decisions made, especially when they go wrong! You decided to buy this company, you decided to launch this project, you decided to invest in this thing. Out of a hundred decisions you have to make, fifty-one are going to be good and forty-nine are going to be bad, and that's about the batting average. The key is, and I say this all the time, the forty-nine that are bad, cannot be huge. If they are, then you are incompetent. The fifty-one that are good have to be really good and have to be relatively big! Out of the forty-nine bad ones, you can probably have one really big bad one in there . . . But you can also get fired for that one big mistake too!

So be prepared to fail in your journey. That's life. But when failures happen, don't dwell on them too much. Learn from them and move on. Trust your instincts and remember that self-doubt is normal too; it's all part of being human and helps us make better decisions.

Attitude . . .

Having a positive attitude and being resilient are both important attributes. We all have periods in our lives when nothing seems to be going right, and you often hear that 'bad things come in threes'. However, the second and third bad things often happen *because* of our attitude after experiencing the first bad thing, which virtually invites or forces the next ones to happen!

For me, resilience is more than just enduring the torture of punishing schedules, excessive travel, a lack of sleep or whatever. It's about keeping a clear mind and a good perspective on matters – having a truly multi-faceted view about things and understanding that there are probably other ways to get things done when under pressure.

An essential component of resilience is rooted in life outside of work. There are elements of your life that are quite separate, such as your family (especially when your kids are young) and your social life with non-work friends. It's very important that you keep these areas functioning properly and in a way that's really positive for you. When all of these things are going well, it helps to build and maintain your resilience. If bad things happen on this side of your life, they can severely chisel away at your resilience.

So having a complete life is important. You need to have a strong foundation of *something* outside of work to support you. If it's not family or social, it could be another activity such as sport or a hobby. If you do not have a foundation, it can be very difficult to handle your work life and it will be virtually impossible to become a good leader.

I strongly believe that the best way to cultivate positivity and to build resilience is to find something to begin with that you are good at doing and can be passionate about. Invest your time there, and you will always be able to look at even a failure and say, 'Yeah, but at least I'm doing something that I love.' And you will always be able to make it through the bad times.

Don't let anyone limit you . . .

In the workplace, I don't believe that there is a significant difference between men and women. From a cognitive point of view, women might approach things a little differently compared with men because we are not quite wired in the same way, but in the end, the results are much the same.

However, the system has certainly been tuned, not in favour of men, but *against* women and *against* ethnic minorities, in the United States, for sure, and certainly elsewhere in the world. It's as though everything says we need to have a set of 'second-class citizens' in order for society to function.

For me, this is especially obvious in the corporate environment. Why is it always *me* that seems to get singled out and lauded for my success? It's because there are simply very few of me – there are precious few black women business leaders in the Fortune 500. But why? Because the corporate status quo *doesn't* look for people like me. An institutional structure literally exists that prefers to have people like me out of it rather than in it – they prefer not to have women and they prefer not to have ethnic minorities within the system or inside the club.

I regularly come across senior corporate guys who look at me with bemusement when I start to present or discuss the maths – because women are not supposed to be good at maths. I'm a qualified engineer with many years of schooling behind me, of course I can do the maths! 'What exactly did you think I would walk into the room with today? Exactly the same skills that you walked into the room with!' And when they start to praise me for being something 'exceptional', it is simply because they fail to see me like they see themselves and as an equal. All of this has got to change, and hopefully it will soon.

For young women at the start of your journey, and for young people from ethnic minorities too, do not let others impose limitations on you or on what you are able to achieve in life. And to parents as well, help your children to see what they *can* do rather than tell them what they *can't* do. It's sadly quite commonplace (for many complex reasons) in African-American families for kids to be told, 'Why do you want to do *that*? You'll never be able to succeed at it, so why the hell bother?'

I was once told that I had three strikes against me – I was black, I was a girl and I was poor. But I was also raised to believe that I *could do* whatever I wanted and whatever I set my mind to achieve. My mother would tell me, 'There are lots of possibilities out there. Just go out and try!'

I have since found major success in my life and have even got to the very top in corporate America. And why? Because I always believed that I *could*, and I never listened to those who said I couldn't.

Sir Roger Carr

As one of the City of London's best-known and most respected business executives, Sir Roger has built an enviable reputation over many years for leading the boards of numerous large corporations. Today, he remains a highly sought-after chairman and non-executive director. Positions have included CEO of Williams plc, chairman of Centrica plc, Cadbury plc, Chubb plc, Mitchells & Butlers plc and Thames Water plc. He has also held positions as vice-chairman of the BBC Trust, deputy chairman of the Bank of England, president of the Confederation of British Industry (CBI) and senior adviser to KKR, the world's largest private equity company. In 2014 he was appointed chairman of BAE Systems plc. He was knighted for services to business in the Queen's New Year Honours list in 2011.

'It is important to recognise that it isn't just our ability to work, but it's our enthusiasm, our energy, our engagement with others, that will attract ongoing opportunities.'

'For all young people, before deciding on the direction of further education and career, you must first apply yourself and work hard to become equipped with the best school qualifications you can possibly achieve. A gram of effort made today will save you a kilo of effort in later life.'

'While performance and commitment are important, values will help to keep things on track. A young person's journey should be performance-driven but values-led.'

'One of the most important roles for a parent is to provide the bedrock on which their children can start to build and develop themselves. Part of this foundation is learning fundamental values and developing a personal value system.'

On success . . .

At its most elemental, I think success can be defined as liberating your full potential and ultimately, becoming the person that you want to be.

However, I do not think that success should ever be viewed as a destination. It is a continuing journey throughout life, and as you advance, your ambitions will change, and in your own mind your personal definition of success will evolve too.

Preparing for your journey . . .

While it's sensible to have a plan for our journey, success is not built on straight lines and there will be many twists and turns along the way.

A young person should recognise that one of the biggest influencers on their eventual success will be *other people* and that luck will certainly be as important as judgement (and potentially more important). In reality, it is most often a chance meeting with a significant individual that provides a trigger for change. A relationship is established with someone who often believes in us more than we believe in ourselves at that time. They see the potential in us and provide an opportunity for us to go in a certain direction. If we can reach out, take the opportunity and make the most of it, that can give us the springboard to leap forward and step up to another level.

Change-moments like these have helped propel me over the years towards my own career success, and I can think of at least six key individuals that have been utterly fundamental to what I have ultimately achieved – each of whom I met invariably by chance.

I took a train journey once on the Eurostar. By sheer luck, I happened to sit next to a man whom I had known previously but had not seen for ten years. He was chairing a large company at the time and in conversation he mentioned that they were looking for a new non-executive director. Our discussion subsequently triggered a formal search into my potential involvement, and it was a company for which

I would eventually become chairman. It was simply pure chance – and on a train journey! Who would have thought that? But I believe it's the same for most people: a chance encounter, an opportunity provided and an opportunity to be seized . . .

The ultimate direction of our own personal journey will normally have its roots in very early life, with our family and the environment in which we were brought up. What we are given by nature is the starting point. This can then be nurtured by other people, the first of whom of course are our parents. If they are engaged, involved and want us to 'succeed', then that's the first stimulus. The second is taking advantage of whatever educational opportunities we are given and the quality of our teachers. Thereafter, it's a mixture of picking the right opportunities that suit our journey, in areas that are appropriate to our own skill set and mindset. It is then engaging with those people we meet at the start of our career and pursuing the opportunities with which we are continually presented.

So, some of it will be luck, some will be judgement – it's a little of both most of the time, but whatever we do at any level, whatever opportunities are presented to us, *hard work* will always be the foundation of any success that we may ultimately have.

When we are young and beginning to think about what we would like to do in life, the starting point is really self-examination. What naturally are our interests? What instinctively are we good at? It's about understanding first of all in our own minds what we would most like to do and what we are most *equipped* to do. Once we have established that, we can then focus our energy on developing these skills through education, life-learning and networking, and doing it all with *real* commitment – there is no substitute for that.

From then, it is important to recognise that it is not just our ability to work, but it's our enthusiasm, our energy, our engagement with others, that will attract ongoing opportunities. Opportunities that can fulfil our potential by doing that which we both excel in and enjoy – an important combination.

Education . . .

My own education provided a good opportunity for me, a firm foundation for life. I enjoyed activities like sport, the Cadet Force and pursuing things that were broader than simply academic work. The learning process continued, however, well beyond schooling, and I often think, 'When does education really ever stop?' I have done many different things throughout my career which have required much additional learning, especially when allied to new opportunities. So, for me, education is very important, but it is also a continuous process and one that is necessary to maintain throughout life.

For all young people, before deciding on the direction of further education and career, you must first apply yourself and work hard to become equipped with the best school qualifications you can possibly achieve. A gram of effort made today will save you a kilo of effort in later life.

If you are looking to align yourself academically with where the future is going, you may wish to focus on the STEM subjects (Science, Technology, Engineering and Mathematics), since they really form the basis for the most-required skills of today and will probably be fundamental to the most secure jobs of tomorrow, and this applies to both girls and boys.

Looking back in time, there were once many routes that one could follow to develop a career – an apprenticeship, a technical college or university. A young person would work out what the most appropriate route was for them, based on the person they were and the skills that they had at that time.

More recently, we have seen a period in the UK where from 5 per cent of school leavers going to university, this has grown to 40 per cent, and technical colleges have closed. Alongside this, a perception has unfortunately also developed that university is really the *only* route to achieve your end goal and success. Over twenty years or so, a kind of status has emerged that those who have been to university are at one level, and those who have not are at a different level. As a consequence, perhaps a whole generation of young people – who could have developed important skills and talents through apprenticeships that would have been very valuable to the country – have simply not been encouraged to do so.

University is not for everyone and it is simply *not* a prerequisite for success. In today's world, I would say there are plenty of examples where people go to university to pursue a subject that may be of interest, but it has limited career value, as opposed to those who take on a real apprenticeship and emerge fully qualified and capable. Individuals can even develop from apprenticeship to go on to university with the help of company sponsorship – but it is the apprenticeship itself that delivers the person who can ultimately become a huge added value to the community.

I am really pleased to see that balance is coming back into the working community and for young people in this country. An awareness is growing once again around the options a young person has beyond schooling, options that are not focused entirely on academia. Opening the mind and opening the door to young people so that they can see what awaits them beyond the first phase of learning is very important.

To parents . . .

Not all parents can offer their children knowledge or specific relevant experience, but they can offer interest and engagement, while providing support and encouragement. This is a very important starting point. Children need encouragement from home to learn. The more knowledgeable parents are, the more they can impart to their children while avoiding becoming tutor or lecturer (which can be counter-productive). But one of the most important roles for a parent is to provide the bedrock on which their children can start to build and develop themselves.

Part of this foundation is learning fundamental values and developing a personal value system. Integrity, truth, honesty, openness, transparency, recognition of doing to others what you would have liked done to yourself – all the basic things that we are all taught. And they are basic for a good reason. These are essential life-foundation stones that have stood the test of time. Many of these values are acquired naturally by children from observation of how their parents behave and how they live their lives. This is important because without a set of values to follow, and a moral compass to guide them, life may not end up going the right way. While performance and commitment are important, values will help to keep things on track. A young person's journey should be performance-driven but values-led.

Parents can also help their children to understand that success is not necessarily always defined in terms of money or status. It may be that way for some but certainly not for everyone. Young people who are ambitious and capable can still be encouraged to achieve and realise their potential, but they need to be mindful that pursuing material or hierarchical achievement is not the only purpose in life.

Fortune . . .

Life for all of us at the end of the day is a balance sheet that reflects how much good luck and how much bad luck we have had. The reality is, while you can do all the right things, work hard and have the right value system, if you are not favoured by luck, your efforts will not translate into the end result that you may have wished for.

I am a strong believer in the idea that one should never discount the importance of luck (when I speak at schools, I always make this point). But first, you have to 'put yourself in a place' where you have the chance of being lucky. If somebody then provides a piece of good luck, you have got to seize it and take full advantage of it. So it's what you do with the opportunity that ultimately counts, but being given the opportunity in the first place is hugely significant.

Your life starts with the luck of the draw. Where you were born and in what circumstances, what your parents are like, how you look, how you sound – all of these things are about the luck of the card we are given when we start off in life. Whatever your hand, it's then down to how you play it. But it's an ongoing process that never stops. It's a journey of discovery, where 'timing' becomes everything.

In my own career, I was fortunate to discover the computer industry in the 1960s when it was in its infancy and expanding rapidly. At that time, if you were good enough, you were old enough. You didn't have to serve fifteen years in a job to get promoted – you just had to demonstrate that you had the technical ability and willingness, and you were given the opportunity.

I was given considerable responsibility when I was quite young. I was fortunate in that I had an aptitude for computers, being blessed with an analytical and logical mind, but most importantly, having that mind at a time when computers were just starting to change the world. When I look back, I can see how this was a huge piece of good fortune for me, but it was also the catalyst that provided a series of opportunities for me, culminating in my senior roles later in life.

For young people, it is important to recognise that they *can influence* their chances of being lucky. Luck favours those who possess the right values, who can demonstrate they have some abilities, who are keen to find opportunities and who can communicate. It's about networking, getting to know people, being open-minded; it's walking through doors that are half-open rather than constantly looking to see if they're half-shut. No one can expect good luck – you are entitled to nothing and must earn everything.

When things go wrong . . .

Whatever happens in life, things are never as bad or as good as they may seem at first sight. Maintaining the right perspective is very important. When you are in difficulty, getting out of it is largely about mindset and character.

Whatever your make-up, resilience is vital because nobody has a smooth journey. Without it, you may be knocked off course permanently. So that is why I feel perspective and resilience are two vitally important elements for managing the good luck and bad luck that come your way.

Dealing properly with failures when they happen is part of recognising that life is made up of a mixture of events, some good and some bad. It is the way in which you can learn from these events that helps to equip you to do better the next time around. This will often be defined as 'seasoned experience'. Things go right and wrong for everybody. You should never be overly excited by triumph or unreasonably depressed by failure.

Attitude and self-discipline . . .

Attitude and character are naturally linked, and for me are as important and sometimes more important than raw ability. I believe fundamentally that average ability, applied enthusiastically with energy, will beat pedestrian brilliance most days of the week. It's wonderful when people are very clever but, if by being so, they are also a little complacent, then that will work against them in a business environment and will certainly not be a way forward for them in their career.

Academic credentials are Important – but the will to win and the self-discipline to work through adversity are the real drivers of success.

Goals . . .

While setting them is important, goals should be more broad than overly prescriptive, particularly in the age we live in now. Whatever we may believe we may want to do in ten years' time, by the time we get there it may not be there to do. The old days of having a long-term plan for a life in the work environment have gone.

So one needs to recognise that whatever your personal definition of success is now, it will inevitably change and evolve as the world changes.

For everyone, the principal goal should really be to become the best version of yourself you can possibly be. That involves focusing on the task in front of you *today* rather than constantly looking ahead at a goal for tomorrow. If you only look ahead, you may not be able deliver now what's actually needed to make 'the ahead' come true. There is a lot of good fortune in life, but opportunities are invariably presented to those who are *delivering today*. So have a plan, be ambitious, be flexible, be realistic – all of those things – but focus on the task of today, and if you do so, and do it well, then somebody will invariably give you a task for tomorrow.

Attributes of successful people . . .

I have worked with many successful individuals over the years. These include very intelligent people at the Bank of England, hugely dedicated people at the BBC, highly engaged people at British Gas, hugely principled people at Cadbury and highly skilled people at BAE Systems.

When looking for 'common denominators' among these people, there are certain attributes that most of them seem to possess. Any of these, adopted by a young person, can help them enormously in their own journey to becoming a successful individual:

Confidence – being confident but without arrogance. Possessing self-assurance, while knowing what you are good at doing and recognising what you're not so good at. Having the courage to surround yourself with people who are better than you and understanding that great team members make a team leader look even better.

Courage – to take a decision and then live with the consequences. Being able to stay on course and remain persistent. Even when everything seems lost, still having that will to win.

Integrity – being honest with others and yourself. Being fair in your dealings and knowing that 'doing the right thing is the right thing to do'.

Authenticity – being true to yourself and faithful to your values.

Flexibility – having a plan but being adaptable to change. Being prepared to adjust your route without changing the goal.

Humility – enjoying your success while learning from your failures. Valuing praise for your achievements but remembering that good fortune is often the true architect of great success.

Enthusiasm – strong engagement with the right attitude, while remembering that hard work is *the* cornerstone for anyone who wants to succeed.

In summary, a CV will get you the interview, but your personality will get you the job. Hard work will get you recognised for promotion, but a good network will keep you on the radar for selection. Your track record will win you a following, and 'people-skills' will make you a leader.

So when thinking about your future, focus on performance and values, qualifications and character. These are within your power as an individual to develop and will serve as key determinants for your eventual success.

Health and energy . . .

Some people are fortunate and blessed with good physical health, they're robust and have strong constitutions. Some also seem to have more energy, and it often radiates from them. It depends, of course, on what career you are following, but in today's corporate environment involving mental challenge and international travel, having energy is helpful. Energy is contagious. People are energised by others who are energetic.

Having good health is not a right – you have to invest in it. A sensible diet and regular exercise are on the agenda of most of today's successful people.

Getting the balance right . . .

It's sensible to think about having the right balance between work and a life outside of work. Most of us do, but I have yet to meet anyone who can look back over their life and say honestly that they have managed to maintain the right balance at every stage.

I believe that it's important to continue to seek a balance, however difficult, to respect the fact that there are times when it's never going to happen, but aim to bring the needle back to the middle wherever possible. This means, especially when it comes to your family, giving as much engagement and energy to them as you give to your job, whenever the opportunity arises. Having the foundation and support of your family and your partner is vital and has been mission-critical for me – if you have got a strong marriage and a good home life, you can manage whatever else may come your way.

Sherry Coutu CBE

Canadian-born Sherry Coutu is a serial entrepreneur and angel investor, and has worked with hundreds of entrepreneurs over the years, mostly in technology. She sits on the boards of numerous companies, including the London Stock Exchange and Raspberry Pi, and chairs Founders4Schools, the Financial Strategy Advisory Group for the University of Cambridge and the ScaleUp Institute (having authored the famous *Scale-Up Report* for the UK government in 2014). She also supports the Prince's Trust, the Crick Institute and serves on the Harvard Business School European Advisory Council. Sherry is widely held to be one of the world's most influential women in technology, and has received a string of accolades and awards over several years, recognising her contribution to entrepreneurship, including a CBE in 2013.

'Opportunities certainly come to people who are open to them, and that means you have to be *out there* and willing to put yourself in circulation to receive them.'

'Whatever you aim for in life, pursue things you genuinely care about! It is really critical that you are engaged only in activities that you find really interesting and worthwhile.'

'In terms of being successful, I work *very* hard, and I *like* working hard and will always try to do my very best at anything I apply myself to. Is that creating luck? I think it is.'

'Parents should always allow their children to explore and try lots of things. Let them fail so that they can learn from it. Parents should not be fearful that if they fail, they may never get up again. We need to help them to build resilience.'

On success . . .

I think of success as making a difference and having an impact. When you don't make a difference, it's not necessarily failure, but it's not what I would call success either. So it's really important that every day one should strive to achieve things and move things forward. If you truly make an effort to have an impact and to make a difference, then you will be successful.

I have a very busy working life, but I've also chosen to have a family. I have three children, and it is important for me that I can spend quality time with them. A successful week for me includes having sufficient time at home with my kids. So, twenty out of thirty days a year, I aim to be at home by six o'clock, which means leaving my office in London two hours earlier than normal on those days.

Being able to achieve a balance between my work life and home life is vital for me, and a major part of how I perceive my own personal success.

Making your choices . . .

Whatever you aim for in life, pursue things you genuinely care about! It is really critical that you are engaged only in activities that you find really interesting and worthwhile. Should you find yourself doing something that you actually *don't* care about, then try to find your way out of that, so you can be chasing something you feel passionate about.

I've known people who have taken jobs in sectors that pay very well, such as financial services, but they simply don't like what they're doing. Some have ended up feeling bitter, miserable and full of regrets. There is absolutely *no* point in pursuing something just because the money is good but where you end up being unhappy. After starting your career, you have to be disciplined. Ask yourself regularly, 'Am I really enjoying what I'm doing?' and 'Do I think what I'm doing is actually worthwhile?'

I often say to young people that they should not be fearful of moving on if they find that what they're doing is not enjoyable. It's important never to remain stuck in a place that's not right for you. Over my career, whenever I have changed from something that I wasn't enjoying as much anymore, to something new, this has always been rewarded with liking my new role a lot more. Many people are fearful of moving on, because of the risk that they might not find something better or that they like more. But for me, it's *far* riskier for you to stick at something you *dislike* than it is to move on.

While it may be conventional to think in terms of 'what I want to become' later in life when considering your future career options, I would say, 'Don't try to choose *what you want to be*, because what you think your role might be now will probably not exist in just a few years' time!' The world is changing incredibly fast, and it can be really dangerous setting your mind on something too specific – heaven forbid that you choose a career that disappears entirely. Where will you be then? So, I would always choose instead a set of skills and frameworks that allow you to continue to evolve.

One of my favourite quotes, which appeared recently in *The Economist* magazine, is that over the next ten years, one billion children will enter the global labour market and only 40 per cent will find themselves in jobs that currently exist. In other words, 60 per cent will be in types of jobs that have not even yet been created! According to LinkedIn, the average person is now likely to have twenty-five jobs between graduating and retiring, with six different identifiable career streams. When you look at how fast industries are today restructuring, all of this leaves me quite fearful of the idea that *anyone* can reasonably tell a young person what they should *do* when they grow up!

One clear route for any young person would be to start with a real determination to have an impact and to solve problems that are worth solving. But that, of course, is not a 'role' as such; it's more of an attitude or a mindset which helps them to be more open and hopeful of doing things that are more interesting and more worthwhile or that have a mission.

Even being in a profession like medicine, it's impossible for any student to realistically predict exactly what they'll be doing once they've qualified, because everything is evolving and moving so fast. I know of one successful individual who started his medical career in clinical pathology and eventually became a professor of pathology. Today, he is responsible for the entire teaching faculty at his hospital, and while he started out as someone who was deeply involved in pathology research, he doesn't go near that type of work any longer. He is, of course, still engaged *within* the medical profession, but he's now working at things that are completely different to what he originally thought he'd be doing.

The importance of your network . . .

My network has always been hugely important to me and has certainly been very helpful during my career. It has grown significantly over the years, mostly because of those times when I have been trying to make something important happen. But, I have never set out with the specific aim of building a network, and I don't try to *network* for the sake of networking either.

I have generally listened, been curious, been willing to learn and been open to suggestions from my network (and, of course, from other people too) when looking for answers to problems. I have also never been shy about saying that I can't figure something out, especially if it's stopping me from having an impact. But whenever I *have* asked people for help, it has always been for a good reason. In order to receive advice from your network, and also for people in your network to be willing and happy to give you advice, you must be really clear and know exactly why you want it. It should never just be, 'I'm wondering about this for academic reasons . . .'; it should be, 'I have this problem I'm trying to solve, which I think is *really* worth solving. Can you please help me think it through?'

Sometimes I have been fortunate because the issue that I've been trying to figure out is the very same thing that other people have also been trying to figure out. But mostly, I have found people really generous and happy to help where they can see a good reason for doing so, even if they don't necessarily have anything to gain from it. Where someone does not have a definitive answer for me, they might still say, 'I'm not quite sure, but why don't you *try this . . .* or think it through *this way.'*

If you have a problem to solve as an individual, you can research it by yourself or even google it, but if you have a good network available to you and can ask three or four people that have already faced the same challenges before or have experience in the area in which your problem lies, you're going to sort out the issue far sooner than someone who doesn't approach it in a *team* or *network* way.

It works both ways, of course, because people in my network will sometimes need help too. I find most weeks that I will spend time having conversations with people who want advice or need to talk something through. I may also have nothing specifically to gain from such conversations, but I'm more than happy to participate in them, simply because others have helped me in the past when I may have been in a similar situation myself.

When someone from my network has been of help to me, I'll always thank them afterwards and let them know what I did and what the outcome was – and I do that quite meticulously. I always provide them with feedback and the extent to which their taking the time has helped me to resolve a particular issue. This naturally encourages a willingness to help me again in the future, too. But I mainly do so because I like it when other people do the same to me: 'Thank you for your time – this is now the way I'm thinking, and this is what I've done differently as a result.'

Mentors and role models . . .

When I ask someone in my network for help with something, it's usually for a piece of open advice that will come just once. There are those I will refer to, however, that I would regard more as mentors to me. These are people whom I'll turn to for advice over and over again, or who may have mentored me through a whole series of decision points. Some of these have been phenomenal individuals who have had a hugely positive impact on my life and career.

Role models can also be really important people that may inspire you to think differently about what paths you might take, without necessarily being a mentor. I can recall individuals I observed when I was a teenager, and teachers at university, who really helped me to see things in a different way and who were to help fundamentally change the way in which I would eventually approach life.

Having the support from mentors early on was actually very helpful to me. I'm the first person in my family that went to university. My family never really encouraged me to go because it wasn't part of what they were used to. After my master's degree, when I told them that I had been accepted into Harvard Business School, they said, 'Why would you want to do that?' I had to convince them that I hadn't lost my sanity, and not only that 'It was actually a really good place to go!' but also something I really wanted to do. Moreover, it wasn't going to financially hurt them in any way if I went because I could get financial aid . . . So while I didn't receive much advice or encouragement from home, those who mentored me at the time and helped me to see my future were especially important for me.

When I was studying for my master's degree at the London School of Economics, a fellow student encouraged me to become an entrepreneur and not the lawyer I was planning to be (he convinced me that I would be bored doing that!). He was eventually to become a very significant mentor for me and later invested in two of the companies I became involved with. He mentored me through twelve years or so, from near bankruptcy to flotation, subsequent acquisition and then eventual management buy-out.

I still have many mentoring relationships. Some are with men and some with women. I also spend time mentoring people myself, but never as many as may ask, unfortunately, because I would not be able to achieve anything if I were to say 'yes' to everyone that asked me to be their mentor – there are simply not enough hours in the day! But I do try my best to be available to those that I can help.

Something I try to convey to anyone that I'm mentoring is what questions they should ask (rather than asking me about everything). This is based on good advice I received from some of my own mentors over the years. I recall being told on one occasion, 'Sometimes you ask me about stuff I don't care about that much – you should really just ask me about *these* sorts of things.' This was very helpful, because I then knew which areas and what questions a particular mentor would be able to help me with, and our discussions could be more focused.

Mentoring is really about helping, if not challenging someone to make decisions. That person may be ploughing a furrow that actually isn't very sensible, or they may be wondering what to do about something and are struck with indecision and inaction. Sometimes they need someone to tell them to get off the fence and decide to go one way or the other. A mentor is not a cheerleader, but someone that can help an individual weigh up and evaluate decisions and then take action themselves.

To parents . . .

If you've *chosen* to have children, then you *should* spend time with them . . .

Some people have very busy lives and busy careers, and find it hard to make that time. Some choose to have two or three years of nannies because they're so busy. We had nannies to begin with, but then I realised that spending time with my children and being able to make it *quality time* for them, was simply too important to miss.

One of the main reasons I decided to give up being the CEO of a large company and become an angel investor instead, was to achieve the right balance. I had actually gone through decades of imbalance (which I don't recommend!) and wanted now to build-in the right equilibrium, because of my children. When you have some sort of equilibrium, it will actually *help* you with your work – you can make better decisions through virtue of your thinking being more reasoned and fresh. If you simply accept a decade of imbalance, under the belief that you will one day *have* balance, it may never happen. I feel today that it's essential to build balance into your schedule from the outset.

While I believe that we owe it to our children to spend time with them, we owe it to *ourselves* as parents as well. If we don't spend quality time with our kids, which is an essential value, then this part of our value system will not live on in them, because we won't have practised it or demonstrated it to them – we therefore won't have imparted it and our *impact* will be less.

I feel that all parents need to understand the real importance of *curiosity* for children. It's an attribute, and something we should all encourage and support. I love science, and in my house, we're forever exploring how things work. When one of our children asks, 'How does this work?' you will never hear us say, 'We don't know.' It will always be, 'Well, let's figure it out by exploring this together.' If we don't as parents know the answer, and even if we do know, it's more about *figuring it out together*, because developing curiosity (rather than just depending on others to provide the answers) will always stand them in good stead, and the idea of working it out *with* others collaboratively is actually really important.

Heaven knows, we do not have all of the answers to what the world will face in the future . . . So our children's curiosity, and having faith in themselves that they, along with others, can get to the answers of *any* question that they or anyone else may face in the future, will be very important for all of us.

Life is also mostly about collaboration. If a problem is worth solving, it's mostly *not* going to be solved by a single person – we always work better at solving problems working together in teams. This process of nurturing curiosity teaches our children that it's actually OK *not* to know the answer, and that the best way to resolve a problem is most often by working with other people to figure it out. This instils a value set of being happy to explore things with others in a team (especially where issues are of joint interest). I think that's far better than having someone that always tries to do things alone or becomes a 'know-it-all' or perhaps is not curious at all and always accepts the status quo.

And finally, parents should always allow their children to explore and try lots of things. Let them fail so that they can learn from it. Parents should not be fearful that if they fail, they may never get up again. We need to help them to build resilience. We all need resilience, and I think children will need more of it as they begin to chart their own pathway in life.

Education . . .

The provision of good education is hugely important for our young people. My education was certainly extremely important to me. I grew up in a lumber town in Canada and went to a state school. The system was healthy – it would generally turn out children who believed in themselves, where the teachers had enough time and were actually motivated to *be* teachers.

When issues exist within an education system, where there are teacher shortages because of poor incentivisation, or where teachers are too exhausted and stressed because of class sizes and constant changes in policy, then it's ultimately our children that are let down.

Poor education affects the world we live in and is responsible, I believe, for quite a few of the problems that occur in society today. Many of these could be solved by simply addressing some of the fundamental issues that exist within those education systems.

A university education can be very helpful and rewarding, but at present in many parts of the world there definitely seems to be a cultural bias in favour of the academic route. We will often say to our kids, 'You must go to university.' In reality, however, there are many children that simply aren't suited to academia. If, for example, they were to choose film production or data science or something else technical, or go through the apprentice route – or indeed some other route – they might end up being a lot happier. These alternatives may be better for them than being forced into an academic route to pursue a subject they are not really interested in – it might be that for reasons of attention-span, learning capacity or other circumstances, they have difficulties studying.

I really believe in the developing idea of 'T-Levels' in the United Kingdom, which would combine a technical route with a year's work placement. There is a lot of current evidence that work-experience placements have a really high transformational capacity for young people, in their aspiration, attainment, resilience and belief in themselves.

Fortune and luck . . .

I have heard myself say before, 'Life is entirely and exactly what you make it.' For me, what that really means, I suppose, is that *hard work pays off*. Being in the right place at the right time also suggests to me that you are looking at all the information and making judgements. I often like to quote the great Canadian ice hockey player Wayne Gretzky, who said, 'I skate to where the puck is going to be, not to where it has been.' In other words, it's all about timing and getting your timing right.

For me, if it's a business I'm interested in, this means analysing its structure, thinking on almost a macroeconomic level about all of the trends, and being clear about where it's likely to be in the future – which is definitely *not* where it is now. One then tries to bet on those things that are moving it to the place that you predict it's going to end up at.

I've been told that I'm a *very lucky* investor. But when I'm investing, I'm always thinking about things very carefully – 'What is the world going to look like?', 'What is the incumbent doing?', 'Which of *these* things are going to push you in *that* direction?' There is invariably much intellectual work and rigour required in figuring out where you think the puck is going to be . . .

And, in terms of being successful, I work *very* hard, and I *like* working hard and will always try to do my very best at anything I apply myself to. Is that creating luck? I think it is. But then it also means that I'm very lucky in *lots* of ways because I always look to mitigate risk – I will study all of the possible outcomes and what might happen. 'It could be *this*, but then possibly *that* . . . but *this* might not have to happen if we did *that*, so let's do *this* and it should lower the risk of *that* . . .'

There is not a moment of the day that goes by without me being worried about something. So trying to decrease the chance of whatever the thing is that I'm worried about happening is a natural preoccupation for me. I also believe that you can de-risk things by methodically breaking them down and trying to understand as much as you can about them.

For young people, creating your own luck also means putting effort into finding opportunities to pursue and people to meet. If you're in your room gaming on your computer, you will have less opportunity available to you than by going to lectures or extracurricular activities and mixing with people there, while at the same time feeding your mind, and building your energy and enthusiasm. Opportunities certainly come to people who are open to them, and that means you have to be *out there* and willing to put yourself in circulation to receive them.

Ups and downs and dealing with 'failure' . . .

I don't have utterly confident days every day! I still have ups and downs. But if something isn't going well, I try to be objective about it and very often will simply refer to my network and find someone positive to talk to. We all know people who are consistently positive (and some who are generally negative, of course!), so, if I'm having a bad day, I'll probably call someone and share something like, 'It seems like things aren't really going according to plan at the moment'. I will then try to balance the good against the bad.

I am by tendency someone who thinks the glass is always *half full*, if not *brimming*. While most people will usually see this as a good attribute to have, for me, I often see it as a bit of an impediment – I can be a bit too much of an optimist at times! What I have generally done to counter this is to look for *naysayers* and get them on to my team. I think this has practical advantages, because they will naturally look out for things that I might not have seen, things that might be negative but real. Having sceptics around you can, of course, be quite annoying at times, but it is important to have people with you who don't always see things quite as rosy as one might think they are. It has always been a conscious decision of mine to include them, and it's a good way of curbing some of my overoptimism and my natural belief that we're always going to win through.

I don't particularly like the word 'failure'. I love science, and as a part of that discipline, one routinely tests many hypotheses. From time to time, some of the assumptions you make mean that not all of your hypotheses will work in the way you first thought they would, but I wouldn't necessarily call that a failure. Whenever I don't get the outcome I thought I would get, I try to analyse the assumptions that I made and narrow down the ones that didn't pan out. It's more of an intellectual approach, really, that does not really consider *failure*: 'We thought this would happen and it didn't, why is that?' or 'OK, what else could we have done that would have achieved the outcome we expected?'

Sometimes we might hit a roadblock where something just stops working – 'We thought *this* would happen but it's not happening. That's OK, let's just break it down and understand *what* has happened and look again at our assumptions'. The point here is that whenever I have had a 'failure', it was invariably because I've *assumed* something that, in the end, wasn't true, or I've *assumed* that someone knew how to do something when they actually could not, and I didn't check first.

For parents . . . when children fail

With children, when they 'fail' at something, we should really help them to work out *why* they thought the desired outcome would happen in the first place. If one defines the outcome as a success, then when it doesn't happen for some reason, what *could* they have done to *see* that it actually wasn't going to happen. We can then help them to understand that if they had spotted potential issues earlier, they might have been able to pivot around and change direction. It's almost a way of turning things round and saying, 'It's not *failure*, it's just that you *failed* to see something coming.' Children should be encouraged to recognise that when they make an assumption about how something works and then it doesn't work out for whatever reason, it's mostly the wrong assumption that has been made that actually causes the wrong outcome to happen.

For example, a child takes an exam and they don't do as well as they had hoped or expected. So rather than talking about it as a 'failure', one should ask, 'Do you think you studied enough for it?' or 'Do you think you studied more or less for it than your other classmates did?' If the child replies that they studied less than their classmates, one might say to them, 'So you assumed that you didn't have to study more for it and your classmates *didn't* assume that they *didn't* have to study for it – they *did* study more for it and you did less well than them. So, do you think the real lesson here is that if you study *more* next time, you'll then do better?'

By looking at something that has gone wrong in a more rational way, it becomes a lot easier than dealing with the emotion of 'It's a failure!' And when a child thinks, 'It didn't work for me, life is random, it's not fair,' the answer is actually that it didn't work because life is *not* random – it will always be our decisions and the assumptions we make that determine whether a desired outcome is achieved or not.

Disciplines, attitude and goals . . .

To any young person, I would say that discipline and having routines are very important to help you improve and to excel. Doing your homework is good! Participating in sport is really important too, because it helps you to build mental resilience. Staying fit and eating healthily are vital, and also sleeping well. Above all, however, *hard work* and focusing on being your *very best* at anything that you do will be the most helpful disciplines to follow if you really want to achieve success in life.

My advice to young people would also be, to understand that the world is what *you* are going to make it. Things don't just happen . . . *you* need to make things happen.

For example, our children are going to inherit some issues they don't like, such as climate change. But, instead of feeling hopeless about that, they could study science and understand what they need to do to help us get out of this mess that we've landed them in. Initiating this kind of attitude in the young is really just showing them a pathway, while trying to make them feel positive about the impact that they can have *if* they take action – I think that sort of attitude builds resilience, because they're not just depending on somebody else to do something about it.

I think I'm unusually resilient and I'm definitely positive. I believe that these attributes are certainly fundamental for anyone aspiring to be successful in life. For me, resilience is about knowing that even when you cannot see your way out of something, there is *always* a way through – you've just got to find it. I personally will *never* accept hearing that there isn't a way through!

I have never been a goal-orientated person. But a kind of goal that I *have* followed is to make sure that I always find and do things that I am genuinely excited about. Throughout my career, there has been a succession of opportunities presented to me, largely because I have been open to them. Sometimes it has been thinking opportunistically – 'Oh, I'd really like to pursue that' – but for the most part it has been an ongoing process of evaluation of things being offered, deciding if I'm ready now to do something next, would I enjoy doing *this* more than doing *that*, am I still enjoying everything I'm doing right now and what capacity have I got to do anything else? Recently, there have been too many choices to be able to even consider them all, and little capacity for anything else new. It's a good position to be in, really.

Another very strong desire (if not a goal) I have always had is to be financially independent. I was naturally dependent on my parents when I was a child, but I wanted to ensure that later in life I could make my own decisions that would lead to some sort of financial independence. I never wanted to have to rely on my husband's salary or his decisions, for example, or to be dependent on anyone else.

Above all, I have always been motivated to do my absolute best at anything that needs to be done. It does my head in if I think that I didn't do something well. I don't like letting people down and I also don't like letting *myself* down.

Paul 'Pablo' Ettinger

Entrepreneur, investor and business angel, Pablo Ettinger has enjoyed a hugely successful career, creating and developing businesses, some of which have gone on to become highly respected brands. He is best known for being a founding partner of Caffè Nero, the growing high-street success story that now has over one thousand continental-style cafés in the UK and overseas. Today, Pablo spends much of his time helping start-ups as an investor and mentor. He is also a huge advocate of building your network as a route to finding success. His love of music has led him to co-found Talentbanq.com and also, more recently, as a founder investor in MusicGurus.com.

'I think that opportunities are in a way far greater than they were before, and often much more interesting. But you have to have a good education first — that's the foundation on which you build those opportunities.'

'I have been incredibly lucky in my life, but I have also worked hard at it — and that includes actively building my network. In my view, this is one of *the* most effective ways in which you can cultivate opportunities for the future and 'make your own luck'.'

'For young entrepreneurs, it's very important to remain absolutely focused on what you're trying to achieve. Part of being focused is to work hard to make things happen. Make your list of things that have to be done this week, and just get them done.'

'A child's attitude and confidence is something that becomes instilled at a very early age. As parents, we have a huge responsibility here since children are so impressionable when they are very young.'

On success . . .

I think for me, success is really about the ability to achieve stability in one's life. The concept of stability has been an important part of my life from an early age and is undoubtedly rooted in my background as a second-generation immigrant to this country. My parents were both refugees, forced to flee Nazi Germany and Austria in the late 1930s. It was really my father who originally instilled in me a sense of 'need' to find stability, because that was something he never had. He moved from country to country for many years, eventually settling in the UK, where he raised his family and subsequently built a very successful business.

For me, my physical home has always been a very important part of this. Having that stability, where I can buy a house with no mortgage that no one can ever kick me out of, was a huge driver in my earlier years. Overall financial security is naturally also an important part. I am not talking about 'wealth' for its own sake but simply having sufficient resources. It is not about money, but the stability that having sufficient finances can provide.

There is also a spiritual form of stability that comes from feeling completely at ease with myself and the world around me. For me, having that feeling is also an essential part of success.

The importance of education . . .

My parents brought me up within a very liberal and open-minded environment. I went to a grammar school, not a private school. I remember my father telling me that he had a decision to make when we were young, to send us to grammar school and have lots of great family holidays together, or to private school, which would naturally restrict our ability to go away regularly. So it was grammar school in the end, and we enjoyed lots of wonderful holidays abroad, and skiing in particular.

Travelling was very important for me when I was young. It gave me a chance to get to know different cultures and that's when I started to develop an interest in food – something that would later become an important part of what I do today.

After grammar school, I took a degree in high-energy physics, which in itself was not that useful, but learning to think like an engineer, and being able to analyse as an evidence-based scientist, would be very helpful tools later on in my business life. After a two-year spell working on a project in the Sahara Desert, an incredible experience, I then enrolled at INSEAD in France to study for my MBA. This opened up a completely new world to me – a global-opportunities world – together with giving me a world-class business education, all of which was to have a profound impact on my future career.

My education was absolutely critical for me. For all young people, getting their education up to the right level is so important. We live in a different world today, and with it, different types of opportunities. Jobs for life simply don't exist anymore. The great thing is that today it's no longer just about joining a big company. Even when I did my MBA, most of my classmates dreamed of becoming a consultant or a merchant banker, post-graduation. Today, most MBA graduates dream of being entrepreneurs. Thanks to technology, it's much easier today – young people can now start something up in their garage, and they do so all the time (I know this because I work with a lot of them). So I think that opportunities are in a way far greater than they were before, and often much more interesting. But you have to have a good education first – that's the foundation on which you build those opportunities.

Building your network . . .

If there is such a thing as a formula for success, for me it's about building your network.

Although I was brought up in England, my family background meant that I felt different to others in some way, and at school I started to really discover my European heritage. It was a natural step for me to go to INSEAD, and from there I became really a sort of global person and started to build my network of friends and contacts around the world. This was to become very, very important for me in everything that I've done since, and critical for Caffè Nero and even Streetlife, an online social community network business that I helped to build and which we sold recently.

My advice to young people is to actively create that network! Friends, and friends of friends – be nice to people, and keep building and growing your network. You never know when you are going to need someone for something and if there is one thing that I've relied on and used throughout my career, it has been my network. Even fairly recently, when I was looking for a strategic partner for Streetlife, I went to an INSEAD networking evening and met someone for the first time (I just happened to be standing next to him, overheard a conversation and introduced myself). He became both a friend and a strategic investor in the project. It was serendipitous, yes, but I was also at that event to build my network.

Be prepared to take risks . . .

I was running a chemical business in Germany, but frankly, I wasn't really enjoying it. The company was part of a multinational global business and with it came all of the usual corporate politics, which I've never been particularly good at. And then, by chance, a friend called me up. He was a guy I knew from INSEAD and was part of my network. He asked for my help to start a coffee-bar business. I was basically the only person he knew who had both an MBA business background and who also knew a lot about food. During my time in France, I had spent a lot of time cooking and getting to know food in some depth. I remember him saying to me, 'Look, you do all the food!'

I immediately thought that this could be great fun. It was a crazy idea, though, because it meant leaving a big company and a well-paid job to create a start-up, effectively, and with no money. But I had already developed a real passion for food, and so this side really interested me. We then brought together some friends, acquired five coffee bars, and that's basically how the whole Caffè Nero business got started.

At first, I was happy to help out on a non-executive director basis and to support the business for the first twelve weeks of getting it turned around. I then became more and more immersed in the buying, improving and distribution of the food for the business, which I really enjoyed. The problem was that prior to starting Caffè Nero, I had already committed myself to a new CEO role for another chemical company. I kept putting off starting my new job because I was having so much fun, but I had given my word and already signed a contract. So, just before Christmas of 1998, I left Caffè Nero to go and run this company, which I really did not want to do at that stage.

I spent my first day with the company's owner, who was also a friend. We went through all the numbers and looked at everything in detail. I soon realised that the business was actually in deep trouble and I had to tell him, 'You're going bust!' I told him that he had to make one-third of the workforce redundant immediately. I remember him saying, 'You're absolutely right, that's what we really need to do.' I then said to him, '. . . and I'm afraid I'm one of them!'

So I made myself redundant and came home to my wife, and she naturally said, 'Hi darling, how was your first day at the office?' I told her it was 'interesting' and that I had to make a third of the workforce redundant . . . She said, 'Oh, that's terrible. What an awful way to start a new job!' I then had to tell her, 'Well, actually, that's not the worst of it . . .'. She was very distressed, of course, and understandably so! 'You just want to get on with your *food* and Caffè Nero!' she said. But we then thought about it carefully and worked out that even if Café Nero were to go under, which was a real possibility at the time for a fledgling start-up, we could just about survive financially, with her career to support us. It was nonetheless a huge risk to take, but I was really loving it and my wife knew that too. So I went back to Caffè Nero to pursue what I *really* wanted to do. And from five coffee shops to begin with, we're now past eight hundred and counting.

Look out for those opportunities . . .

As a young person, if you can find something that you have a real interest in, that you can become passionate about, then you will probably be good at it. I regularly mentor young people and am also involved with Founders for Schools. I will often say, 'Be realistic, but try and do something that you really enjoy.'

Sometimes it may not be obvious what opportunities are available to you, and that is why I also tell young people to 'be open' and make sure that doors are always open to you. Talk to people, network all the time and be open to new ideas.

This is precisely how I became involved with Streetlife. I was attending a luxury goods conference and decided to go to a lecture on 'tribalism' – how tribes have evolved over time and how we still have tribes today. I became totally inspired by the idea of tribes and how, in modern societies and communities, people have lost their 'village tribe', they've lost their 'work tribe' and they've nothing to belong to anymore. It got me thinking naturally about Caffè Nero and the idea of creating communities. I would often say to people, 'We don't sell coffee ... We sell gathering spaces where people can collect for one reason or another and they buy coffee while they're there.'

At the same time, there was a journalist I got to know whom I'd regularly see at Caffè Nero in Clapham High Street. One day, as I walked in, he said, 'Hey, Pablo, come over here. Let me introduce you to John, who runs our local printing company – you two should speak.' What this journalist guy had actually done was to create an incredible community within this particular Caffè Nero bar, a wonderful community, and I thought immediately, 'Wouldn't it be great to be able to replicate what he's done and create "tribes" within coffee bars across the country?' I could see a really huge opportunity to rebuild communities using the internet, and I started a new project that I called 'meet-me-for-a-coffee.com'.

Then by pure chance, I came across a leaflet from another new venture named Streetlife, and I remember thinking, 'But that's what I'm doing!' So I decided to give them a call, and arranged a meeting. When we met, it did not take long for me to become impressed by the people involved – they clearly had the platform and a good tech team, and straightaway, I felt that I wanted to join forces with them. After half an hour, I made an offer to partner with them . . . By 2015 we had over a million registered members, and we eventually sold the business to Nextdoor, the US social networking service.

So, my advice to young people is always to look out for opportunities, but at the same time be realistic about what you want to pursue and be prepared to take some risks. Also, the harder you work, the luckier you get. I have been incredibly lucky in my life, but I have also worked hard at it – and that includes actively building my network. In my view, this is one of *the* most effective ways in which you can cultivate opportunities for the future and 'make your own luck'.

Deal with setbacks and find your way through . . .

If we are really honest with ourselves, all of us have doubts at times and we all have our own weaknesses and strengths. I think one has to try to forget the setbacks when they happen. Fortunately, the human brain has a wonderful capacity to generally forget the bad things while remembering the good things, which is really useful.

This is very important because you can't reflect on the past, you have to constantly look forward, and for me, one of the most important attributes for an entrepreneur is to be optimistic. The glasses are *always* 'half full', not 'half empty'. Even if there is only a 1 per cent chance that you'll get that funding at the very last moment, you still keep believing that it will happen – because there is always still a chance . . . You have to have that determination and conviction to keep going.

You must be realistic and honest with yourself, and know what you're good at and what you're not so good at. This is very important. However, when things do go wrong, it is always good to talk to and listen to those that you respect. They can help to pick you up and get back on track if required.

You often hear amazing stories about incredible founders of great businesses. When you look closely at what they have done and how they've done it, there has invariably been a strong team of people around them. They may be the great businessperson or salesperson that fronts their businesses, but behind them there's going to be a bunch of people who are filling in all those gaps. If you can become good at building that team and knowing where your gaps are, you will stand a much greater chance of creating a successful business.

When you experience failures or serious setbacks, you have to be thick-skinned and battle through. At Caffè Nero we have had some really serious setbacks – we had some very powerful competitors who have made life really difficult for us at times. On a couple of occasions, they actually attacked us in various ways and we had to just pick ourselves up, battle on and find a way through.

I recall one situation when we were busy building the Caffè Nero business. We had around eighty shops at the time and were having real difficulties in scaling our supply-chain network. I then found a new single supplier for all of our fresh goods, sandwiches, salads and everything. We agreed a deal with them, reorganised everything, and then, out of the blue on a Friday (we were due to go live on the Monday), I received a call from the owner saying, 'I'm sorry, but I can't supply you.' He then explained that our two biggest competitors had forbidden him from becoming a supplier to Caffè Nero. He was supplying them too, and they were also much, much bigger than us at the time. He said, 'I'm really sorry, but I just can't afford to lose their business.'

This was a very serious problem for Caffè Nero and could have killed us. But rather than dwelling on what should have happened, I spent a very busy weekend looking for a way through. Fortunately, one of our previous suppliers, who had also become a good friend, agreed to carry on and step up for a few months to allow me to find another solution. And that's exactly what he did, and somehow we managed to keep in supply. The irony was that the supplier who said that he couldn't supply us was, in turn, let down by one of the two major competitors a couple of years later, and he went out of business.

Stimulating activities, physical and mental health . . .

When you love what you're doing, it's hard to see the division between work and play, so the concept of a 'work-life balance' is a difficult one for me to comprehend. At the weekends, my wife and I are often working at home, and when we're out talking to people or at a dinner party, I'm often thinking about business and perhaps how *that* person might be a useful contact. The idea that you leave work at five o'clock and then suddenly you have this other life is unthinkable.

But it's important to find time for activities that you enjoy and that can also help you. Maintaining my mental and physical health is critically important for me. I'm at the gym doing some kind of sport virtually every day. If I've been sitting in an office all day long, I have to do something. For years, I used to regularly run half-marathons. Running was fantastic for me – the brain is being oxygenated and is therefore working really effectively. My wife and I go walking in the mountains in the summer. High-altitude trekking is a wonderful opportunity to think for hours in the fresh air.

Today, I am still a competitive skier and race regularly. Although I learned to ski when I was five, I didn't start racing until I was at university, which is far too late to become a professional competitor. But now I train and race through the winter. I enjoy everything about skiing – the adrenaline, the competitiveness and the social nature of it. Although I'm getting older, I'm still trying to get better, and I'm not going to give up! Around three years ago I discovered yoga, which I love doing now. It covers the mental and the physical side of things for me, and I have found it a wonderful way to make up for less running.

While sport has kept me mentally and physically fit, I also enjoy the spiritual and fun side of playing music. I'm a jazz musician and love playing the piano. I also sponsor young musicians and music festivals while looking out for new talent for Caffè Nero's music programme.

Reading is important for me, especially newspapers, which I have always avidly read every day. I think it's important as a businessman to have a broad knowledge of geopolitical affairs and to understand the big picture. I have always found this very useful for my work.

Have a dream and remain focused . . .

Whenever I hear a young person say something like, 'My goal is to become a millionaire by the age of twenty-one,' my first thought is, 'What complete nonsense.' For me, it's important to *have* a dream, but it must be based realistically on something that's within your power to achieve.

When Caffè Nero was first started, I remember talking about our dream with my partners. Our dream was to create a global company of continental Italian-style coffee bars that would have a certain ambience and would feel like home. That was our dream from the outset, and it has never faded or changed one iota since then.

In a similar way, with Streetlife, our dream was to create this global myriad of communities where we could help bring people closer together within their community to talk to each other, exchange information and meet in real life as well. That was our dream, and once again it never changed. It was just a matter of how we actually got there.

For young entrepreneurs, it is very important to remain absolutely focused on what you are trying to achieve. The thing that most young people tend to do, which is understandable, is to get distracted and pulled around in many different directions. You may have a great business that's doing *one* thing really well, and you think, 'Oh, maybe I can do that too,' thinking it might somehow add something else. But no, just stick to what you are doing now. See it through first with laser focus, and later on you will have time to do the other things.

With Caffè Nero, we were an international bunch of guys, so it was natural to plan for a global business. Every year at our board meeting, we would discuss whether we were now ready to go 'international', and every time we would invariably agree, 'Yes, we should probably look at other countries now.' But I remember for the first seven years our chairman saying, 'Yes, I think we should go international, but let's do it next year.' So each time it became next year, and the next, and then finally we did it, of course, but by that time we had hundreds of coffee bars – we were now a big organisation and, by then, ready to do it.

Part of being focused is to *work hard to make things happen*. Make your list of things that have to be done this week, and just get them done. This is so important. At the end of the week, you want to be able to go, 'Tick, tick, tick . . .' I've done all of that. I'm sure that it's in the nature of most entrepreneurs to organise themselves in this way, but if you can't make things happen, then you shouldn't be an entrepreneur because you'll probably never make it.

Our role and responsibility as parents . . .

I believe that a child's attitude and confidence is something that becomes instilled at a very early age. As parents, we have a huge responsibility here since children are so impressionable when they are very young. We shouldn't be overprotective – let them explore, and give them that confidence to do things by themselves.

I recall an extraordinary but lovely moment when my son Alex was just a toddler. We were all together, enjoying a picnic in the grounds of the Royal Hospital in Chelsea. I was chatting away to my wife, when all of a sudden, he got up and wandered off! Christine and I looked at each other, and our first reaction was to want to grab him. But we bravely decided to let him go, and just watched. Alex toddled up to some people and looked at them for a moment, tried to say something, and then simply carried on walking. He was exploring. It was wonderful – and also frightening! – to know how much confidence our kid had to just get up like that and start wandering around. The thing that really shocked us, though, and which will always remain ingrained in my memory, was how he never looked back, not once! I remember, I was so proud of him at that moment. He was so tiny and we both went,

'Wow!' But the amazing thing is that if you see him today as an adult, he's exactly the same kid. He has the confidence to walk into any situation and it doesn't faze him – he doesn't even have to think about it . . .

As children eventually become young adults, we as parents are there to encourage and gently push them out of the nest. But at some point, they are going to have to start flapping. Parents can continue to have a big influence on their children in all sorts of ways, even when they're ready to fly. I have always encouraged my kids in whatever direction they want to go. My daughter is leaving university this year and she enjoys branding, marketing and events. I naturally meet a lot of people in those areas, and when I came across a fascinating company just recently I made the introduction. Now, it's up to my daughter if she wants to meet them or even ends up working for them. That's entirely her decision. What I have done as a parent is simply opened another door for her. For me, this is an essential role for all parents – to encourage their children and then help them further by opening doors.

At the same time, however, we should neither be overprotective nor should we 'nanny' our kids too much. Encourage them to learn and help them to have a great education. If possible, they should learn at least one other language, and where possible, introduce them to travel early on.

Mikhail Fridman

As one of Russia's most successful entrepreneurs, Mikhail Fridman has earned enormous respect throughout the world as a leading businessman, investor and philanthropist. When he was just twenty-six he co-founded Alfa Bank, which is today Russia's largest private banking group. At present, he heads the international investment corporation LetterOne. In 2017 *Forbes* ranked him as Russia's second-wealthiest citizen, while BNE IntelliNews named him Russia's most important businessman. He is an active supporter of various cultural initiatives, and co-founded the Russian Jewish Congress and the Genesis Philanthropy Group.

'For young people, I think it's very important to search constantly and tirelessly until you find the thing that interests you, that you can develop a passion for and makes you happy.'

'In my case, I'm happy and I'm successful because for me my job is really my passion. I love starting work on Monday, and when Friday is finished I'm already looking forward to the next week with great enthusiasm.'

'If you are 100 per cent focused on your work or career, with no balance, you are taking a big risk that if something goes wrong, you will have nothing else around you to support you. One needs to build other areas of support or stability in your life – family, friends, hobbies and so on.'

'The fundamental values that we can give to our children today may help them maintain a true path through this changing world. But it's also important that we give our children room to make their own decisions and be responsible for what they decide to do.'

About success . . .

In my view, success is achieving a feeling of balance and harmony, inside. Every individual will have their own personal or subjective assessment of what this means for them, but I think it's an intuitive, conscious feeling about how happy you are with your life and whether all the different 'proportions' are balanced – your material circumstances, your work, your family and so on.

In a way, success is a synonym for happiness. If you are happy, you are probably successful. Now, I have seen many people who are very poor but who are also very happy. I have also seen many people who may be materially wealthy (whom others may view as successful), who are very unhappy. Again, it's a question of balance – you may be satisfied with your career, your financial status, your social status, but if you have issues with your family, for example, that result in a deep feeling of disappointment or frustration, then this can lead to unhappiness and disharmony.

For some people, happiness or a feeling of success comes from different areas altogether. Their goal might, for example, be only to achieve public recognition, approval or public endorsements. I know of a very famous mathematician, Grigori Perelman, from St Petersburg. He lived a very humble life in a small flat, eating only simple food and was totally 'plugged in' to mathematics. He was then awarded one of the world's most prestigious prizes in mathematics, having solved a Millennium Prize Problem set by the Clay Mathematics Institute. He was awarded a huge amount of money, but he rejected both this and the award. In the eyes of most people, he's a strange guy, refusing such a big prize, which could have completely changed his life. But he was very happy. He was a recognized and acclaimed mathematician, who was satisfied with his life. He was happy, and arguably, therefore, successful.

Life, of course, has its ups and downs, and you cannot feel happy every single moment of every day. But if, for the vast majority of your time, you can personally 'feel' this harmony, then for me, that is success.

Making the most of opportunities . . .

While I know that I have achieved pretty good success at business in my life, I frankly did not expect it when I was young. When I was eighteen years old, 'business' as we know it today simply didn't exist in the USSR, the country in which I grew up. It was *impossible* to even imagine at that time the magnitude of everything that I was going to be able to achieve later on.

During the late 1980s, fundamental changes – tectonic in nature – occurred in the Soviet Union. It was the collapse of an empire (which historically does not happen very often), and the complete reshaping and reforming of the whole of society; not just economic and political changes, but also mental and social changes. It was this unique set of factors that provided the ground and opportunity on which I could build my business success.

The epicentre for most of these changes was Moscow. Russia is a huge country, and Moscow is just a little dot on the map, so I was very lucky to have been located in Moscow at that time. I was also lucky to have been at the right age and in the right circumstances. I was twenty-four years old and had already graduated from university in Moscow as a metallurgic engineer, but I wasn't really committed to any particular career as yet. I had always dreamed of a career in a scientific area, but because of my ethnic roots, there were lots of institutional barriers, prejudices and obstacles that made it very difficult to pursue this.

With *perestroika*, the country's borders started to open and with it the opportunity to travel abroad. In parallel to these changes, so-called 'Private Initiative Cooperatives' were also being allowed and I was therefore presented with a clear choice: I could either travel to Israel or the United States, where many of my relatives lived at that time, or I could try to do something within this newly created environment at home in Moscow. I didn't have my own family yet, and I had nothing really to lose or to risk – I hadn't started a career at say, a research institute, which would have been difficult then to leave. So in 1988, with some friends of mine, we created our first cooperative. Our first business was washing windows – we began to employ a lot of students, and after a few months we were already making a huge amount of money.

I remember my mother, who was still living in Lviv in western Ukraine, came to visit me in Moscow. I was working in a state-run company as an engineer but at the same time, we had already established our first cooperatives. She was at the small flat I had rented and heard me speaking with my colleagues and to the students we employed, and began to ask what I was doing. She was curious because she thought that my engineering position was my principal job. I didn't want to tell her anything, because I was concerned that it would worry her. She was a very Soviet-type of person and thought – and probably still thinks – that it's much better to work just for a state-run company – no risk, just work . . . She was always very cautious and very careful.

She became increasingly curious about my other activities and asked me, 'How much are you making?' Now an average salary at the time in Moscow was around 150 rubles a month – everyone earned much the same compensation almost everywhere at that time. But, after just three to four months since we started the cooperative, I was making 10,000 rubles a month – an unbelievable amount of money! But I decided not to tell her the full truth, so I said I was earning 1,000 rubles a month. She turned as white as a sheet . . . She didn't even ask what we were doing. She just said, 'Please, Mikhail, I beg you, stop doing this immediately – it's far too dangerous.' She believed that if you were earning 1,000 rubles a month that it just couldn't be legal! 'You are definitely doing something illegal!' she said. I tried to convince her not to worry, that what we were doing was quite legal and we were doing nothing wrong, but it was almost impossible to convince her. My mother had spent her whole life with this concept that to make big money *has* to be illegal and is also ethically wrong. She was convinced that sooner or later I would be punished and sent to jail!

In fact, it was not just my mother who expressed concerns. I remember conversations with many smart people at the time, young people who also thought what we were doing was very dangerous – but who could *know* how everything was going to turn out? Many thought that it would become illegal sooner or later. And of course, in Moscow during those days there was a high level of crime and numerous criminal rackets. It was actually a dangerous and risky environment, and you could even be assassinated. But for me, it was a pretty clear choice — either to pursue this or to leave the country. For me, the interesting thing is that had I been, say, thirty years old rather than twenty-four, I would have been in different shoes. I probably would not have taken those risks. I would probably have had a family and a safe job, maybe not very well paid but stable.

When I look back, I would say that it was a combination of my individual circumstances together with my age and just being in the right place, in Moscow, at the right time, when Gorbachev's ideals of reshaping the whole system, the whole country, a big part of the world, were being played out. A major part of my future success started with factors that were outside of my control. But I made certain decisions and did certain things at the time that took advantage of the opportunities around me, while accepting the risks.

I am sure that my father and others I knew in the USSR at that time could have been more financially accomplished than they were, given the opportunity, but we lived in a different time. They were still balanced people, nonetheless, happy with their families, their careers and their achievements, and, therefore, successful in their own way.

Finding something that makes you happy . . .

I think it's too difficult to describe so profound an issue as finding success in life in terms of a simple formula. It is very important for young people to understand and discover what kind of things they enjoy doing, what is fun for them and makes them interested.

For me, it is a pretty simple sequence of events. If you like to do something and are interested in it, you will probably be good at it. So you pursue it and enjoy it, and sooner or later you become better and better at it, and people will start to recognise what you can do and how good you are. And then, people who actually know about what you are doing can assess you fairly and tell you that you are doing well, and that makes your confidence and aspirations grow even higher. You become committed and end up pursuing a career or profession in an area you like.

Everyone has a talent to do something. It might be a talent for more sophisticated areas such as science or it can be something as simple, perhaps, as carpentry. It is therefore important for a young person to find something that uses their talent and that can also develop their talent.

If you have a passion for something you will probably be successful at it. It may even be a pretty decent job in an area you're passionate about and you could be fairly compensated for it, let's say – it may not necessarily make you *a lot* of money, but you find happiness and fulfilment in doing it. But if you are doing something – even if you are getting well compensated for it – and you don't enjoy it, that for me is very sad.

In my case, I am happy, and I am successful because for me my job is really my passion. I love starting work on Monday, and when Friday is finished, I'm already looking forward to the next week with great enthusiasm. I have seen people counting down the days to the weekend or to their next vacation. They say, 'Oh! The weekend seems to have only just started and now its Sunday evening already.' It's very sad because their life is not pleasant – they're enduring a kind of torture because they're sitting perhaps in an office and doing something that's completely uninteresting to them. They have to do it because they have to pay the bills, of course, but it's a sad situation.

Some people say that to be successful, you have to work hard. But this is really an extension of what I'm saying. If you enjoy your career and the work you are doing, it doesn't seem like 'hard work'. I don't believe that you have to do crazy things like working eighteen hours a day – everyone has to find their own balance between work, family, relaxation and sleeping. But if you really like your work and are happy with your family or your social life, then you can naturally find the right balance.

So, for young people, I think it's very important to search constantly and tirelessly until you find the thing that interests you, that you can develop a passion for and makes you happy.

Dealing with mistakes . . .

When things go wrong, I always try to understand the core problem. Occasionally, it may be due to forces out of your control – historical changes that affect everyone, the markets and so on – but in the majority of cases, it's down to mistakes that you have made. I can become emotionally upset if I have made a mistake. If I have made a bad decision, not paid enough attention to something or not put enough time and effort into understanding something in detail and it goes wrong, or triggers something else that goes wrong, that can make me very frustrated. I will always take responsibility for my mistake, and even artificially generate internally a feeling of guilt because, if it becomes painful for me, then I will remember my mistake and learn from it. I want to ensure that I do not make the same mistake again.

Some people will try to shift the responsibility for a mistake onto others because they don't want to admit they were wrong. They don't want to accept responsibility or feel guilty for their mistake, and this is unhelpful to everyone and is also unfair. The Latin expression *'mea culpa'* helps us to acknowledge that it was through *my* fault or *my* mistake that something has gone wrong. This is very important if you want to be able to learn from your mistakes.

Sometimes the opposite occurs – mistakes are made that happen for reasons over which you have absolutely no control. In these circumstances, you should not become upset; you need to be more philosophical. For example, you sell something today at the market price and a week later the price has doubled. If that happens to me, it's not a problem. I take it with an easy heart. It was a mistake to sell a week before but who would know? It was because of the market, which no one could predict, so why be upset? I decided to sell at that time because of different reasons, but it was also a fair price then. Nobody deceived me. The fact is that the market is driven by thousands of factors – I could not have predicted what the price would be in a week's time because nobody knows what will happen in the markets. I have seen many people in such circumstances, however, becoming very upset and disappointed that they sold early. There is no point. It is not constructive, and it can become an obstacle to rational thinking.

Set your goals carefully . . .

When setting goals, I think it's important to very carefully consider what you are trying to achieve. One needs to create goals that you can realistically achieve, and then work consistently towards reaching them. If you set goals that are unrealistic, or practically impossible to achieve, then you're setting yourself up for disappointment. It's hard to work towards something that you have no real possibility of achieving and where you'll have little chance of finding success. But it can be difficult sometimes to understand what is really achievable and what is not.

For example, a sprinter may want to become a world-class athlete. If they set a goal to run 100 metres in 5 seconds, they will always be disappointed because it's impossible for a human being to run that fast. But if their goal was to run the distance in 9.8 seconds, then this would be a more realistic and achievable goal to set but still an extremely challenging one. In other words, a goal can be set high, but it must be well conceived.

Finding a balance . . .

For most people, their job is among the most important things in their lives. Their job or their career is their self-realisation, and understandably comes first. But in most work, not least in jobs like mine, you have to deal with problems and trouble all of the time. Pressures and stresses are just part of what you have to do, and in my view it's therefore very important to compensate for this by having some activity or hobby that can help attain balance. It might be music, theatre, art or going to watch football. Doing something else you enjoy outside of work helps you mentally to handle the problems and pressures you have to deal with in your job.

If you are 100 per cent focused on your work or career, with no balance, you are taking a big risk that if something goes wrong, you will have nothing else around you to support you. One needs to build other areas of support or stability in your life – family, friends, hobbies and so on. It's like a chair with one leg or perhaps two. Not very stable. But with three or even four legs, that's a lot better and provides the stability you need!

Mentors and free will . . .

It may sound a little arrogant, but I have never really had to rely too much on mentors. There have been a lot of people in my life that I respect and who have given me advice, but I have at the same time always felt quite comfortable with forming my own independent views. Whenever I have been given advice, I've always looked at it critically and made my own decisions. Even when my own views ran against the common view on something, I would always tend to rely on my own intuition and instincts.

I do think it can be valuable and important for someone to have a mentor, to have people around them that they respect and can listen to and learn from. But I also feel it's important to retain a sense of personal perspective and not to feel pressured to just go along with the advice of others. The notion of free will is a fundamental principle in Judaism – everything is in our own hands. Every single day you face a wide variety of choices to make and everything depends on you. Developing this sense of having an independent view and being in possession of free will can help you to learn how to make the right choices and decisions in later life.

To parents . . .

We live in a fast and rapidly changing world. For example, when I was young – which is not that long ago, really – I could not even dream of travelling abroad. I thought that I would never be able to leave the Soviet Union because it would be just impossible. But now I live in England and I travel, and I take my children everywhere too. This gives them a good understanding and knowledge of the world, but I would never have imagined then that it would be possible today.

Centuries ago, life was in many ways more predictable. Parents had a better understanding of life and it was an easier task for them to help their children to anticipate and prepare for the future. When I talk to my kids now, I find it difficult to explain to them how the world might change in the future because we simply do not know. Nobody does. It is impossible to forecast anything accurately today, and who could have even predicted all the recent political changes? All around us, the world is changing.

So for parents, rather than trying to prepare them for what they must do in the future, I think we should concentrate mostly on giving our kids advice on basic, important values, and guidance on principles that they can take forward with them into later life. To illustrate this, the Ten Commandments represent fundamental values that were written a long time ago, but even though the world has changed completely over more than two thousand years, these values are still applicable and still have relevance today. In the same way, the fundamental values that we can give to our children today may help them maintain a true path through this changing world. But it's also important that we give our children room to make their own decisions and be responsible for what they decide to do.

Parents should therefore always be at their children's disposal and be ready to discuss any issues they may have, to examine the pros and cons of the choices they might make, and what values should be applied to help with their challenges. At the end of the day, however, one should underline that it is *their* decision and that 'It's up to you.' It's their life – they must take responsibility for it and make their own choices.

Stephen Fry

One of the best-known and most widely appreciated English personalities, Stephen Fry is an award-winning actor, comedian, TV and radio presenter, narrator, voice-over artist, writer, film director, BAFTA host and mental health ambassador. His multi-talented versatility and intellect, together with his distinctive voice, quick wit and narration skills, have won him respect across the globe, while television programmes such as *Blackadder*, *A Bit of Fry & Laurie*, *QI* and *Stephen Fry in America* have become international hits. Recent best-selling books from him include *Mythos* and *Heroes*. After enjoying an extraordinarily prolific career, Stephen remains a much sought-after personality and presenter worldwide.

'Curiosity and a desire to try things out are where it starts for a young person. These help them to explore what they're good at doing, what comes naturally, easily and what they enjoy.'

'Almost everyone I have known that has found fulfilment in life (and I include myself) was invariably shocked to discover that hard work is actually what they *want* to do and is an extraordinary pleasure and the most fulfilling of all things.'

'Failure is important and it's natural. You just have to look at a baby trying to walk – the reason it can walk is because he or she has fallen over so many times. All the things we can do later on, all the multitasking, all the amazing processes, these are a result of the failures we experience earlier in life. We're continuously learning from failure.'

'When you light a fire, you start with lighting the kindling material. But it's not the kindling material that's important, it's the fire itself. It's the furnace that builds which matters, and it's precisely this that can make anyone capable of astonishing things later in life.'

Success . . .

I expect that my own views about success have nothing to do with how the world might normally regard success to be. For me, it's something completely *internal*. The closest English word that I can think of that describes success is perhaps 'fulfilment', and 'happiness' is, of course, a word that comes close to being contained within fulfilment too.

Fulfilment obviously denotes a sense of satisfaction, but for me it has more to do with a sense of personal contentment and a feeling that one may have come close to achieving the things that either in an objective sense, you feel you were put on this Earth to achieve (through your genes, or through your opportunities), or through a personal sense of ambition. Fulfilment comes from achieving the best you can be in the fields in which you have striven to be good.

Curiosity and desire . . .

At school, it was clear what I was *not* good at. I was just appalling at sport — I couldn't catch or throw or run without being laughed at. It's ironic, really, because while my pride made me despise sport so much then, I adore it now. I also couldn't sing, except flat, so music was also closed to me, and I couldn't really draw either.

The only thing I found out that I had any skill or empathy with was language. I loved words and I loved to play with words and alter their meaning. I remember telling my teacher excitedly, 'It's orchestra!' when she wrote the word 'carthorse' on the blackboard because I could immediately see 'carthorse' was an anagram of 'orchestra'. I also adored acrostic poems and cryptic crosswords, from a very early age.

Whilst my city friends enjoyed cycling around and going to cafés and having playdates, I lived deep in the country in a big house and had quite a lonely childhood. I also had terrible asthma and awful insomnia, and my parents didn't like television, so all I could do was read. A mobile library came around once every two weeks and I just consumed books at an extraordinary rate. I became passionate about reading, because language was clearly my thing. While everyone else enjoyed sports personalities and 'rock and roll' stars, I had my writers. I started with children's and popular books, and then moved up to what would today be called literary writers.

After a very difficult childhood and adolescence (which included being expelled from three schools and a short spell in prison), I picked myself up determinedly from my lowest point and resolved that I should go to university. From an early age, I had already set my sights on Cambridge, which I saw as the most romantic and inspiring place for study in the world. I achieved a scholarship, despite my troublesome record, and from that point everything opened up for me in the most marvellous way.

If you look at someone whom you might regard as having achieved a lot, there is only one way they could have done it – through an energy to do so, through a desire, a compulsion, and that applies to the body of knowledge one acquires over one's life. For me, it was a hunger for knowledge, a form of intellectual greed. I've always been fired by the desire to know, curiosity in other words, but also a desire to try things out. Curiosity is one of the most important qualities a human being can ever possess. Those who don't know things often bemoan their lack of knowledge, but it's only because they were not curious to know. When I was at school, there were people who ended up knowing nothing. They didn't listen, and they didn't pick up anything the teacher said because they simply weren't curious. I absorbed knowledge like a sponge because I was greedy. Now I don't know how I became greedy or why I'm greedy, but it's just a fact that I am. I would argue that it comes from an inner compulsion to know and to do and to strive.

Curiosity and a desire to try things out are where it starts for a young person. These help them to explore what they're good at doing, what comes naturally, easily and what they enjoy. They also help them to eliminate the things that are not really for them. I love music, but I never ended up performing music or writing music because I just knew that it would take me infinitely more time and care and expertise than I had been naturally given.

Education, too, should be about empowering and nurturing curiosity. Education, in its literal sense, is not about 'putting in', it's about 'drawing out'. In other words, drawing out a child's talent and getting them to think and to work things out and find their innate abilities. That is why education can be so valuable. It shouldn't be just about training, feeding in lots of facts and just building this 'citadel of information'.

To parents . . .

When it comes to the important subject of a child's personality and individuality, there is one inescapable truth: you cannot channel a child to be other than what it is and you cannot change its character. Years of research and many significant studies have shown that parents, beyond obvious genetic influence, have almost no influence whatsoever over their children in terms of their future behaviour. What has been discovered is that it's the influence of their peers that makes all the difference to 'who they are' and 'who they become'.

A child is an organic living thing that has its own personality well before any parent has any chance to change it. Children are fundamentally good, they're honourable, they're virtuous, they have what philosophers call a kind of deontic sense, a sense of morality . . . a compass that's already there. It's one that is, of course, reinforced by the group morality, and while there can be bad influences, bullying and so on (there's a dark side to almost everything that humans do), most children still propel towards the good and towards fun.

So parents should resist the urge to interfere, and give their children space to learn and develop. Obviously, they have to convey rules about things like using the internet, and parents will have legitimate fears about the modern world and its perils, but no reasonable parent would want their child to feel imprisoned by those fears either.

When I was young, the word 'discipline' made me shudder. I hated it. It was important for me to escape. I'm not very, very disciplined but self-discipline is the only kind that really counts — focus, concentration and a *need* to work and fulfil whatever I think of to be my full potential. These are words not far from what my school teachers and parents tried to instil in me, and from which I flinched and reacted very badly to then. But the further I ran, the more I found these weird principles lived inside me. Whether they've been put there or whether they're inborn is the subject of much philosophical debate.

Parents are children too, and most of them these days have both their parents living at the same time that they're bringing up their own children. Being a parent isn't a vocation, profession or career. It's something very, very well done by humans in the Amazon, the forests of Madagascar and the jungles of Borneo. No training, no books on the subject, just common sense and *no fuss*.

Just as children sleep best when there is a lot of noise and bustle going on around them, so they flourish best when there isn't too much attention and fuss made of them. Self-consciousness in parenting, as in all aspects of life, is destructive and damaging in my view. Don't pretend to be angry when you aren't or suppress anger when you are. Children can spot a false emotion quicker than a dog can scent aniseed. Be yourself, and your children will be themselves too. It's their siblings, friends and peer group who are responsible for almost everything they are.

Let them be, and simply trust, trust, trust. If you keep opening the oven and checking on the soufflé it will sag and be ruined.

Lighting fires and empowering children . . .

There almost isn't a child anywhere who is not enthused by something. It starts with curiosity and can lead naturally to a real passion for something. It's all about lighting fires, and a fire can be lit in any direction, it doesn't matter . . . it can be sport or fashion or anything. In the case of the slightly lonely, it can be a more obvious path to success because, although it can make them a lonelier and less happy child (it might be that they prefer less popular things like polishing pebbles or looking for fossils or doing small things that don't make them a great hit on the playground), by the time they get to fourteen, fifteen or sixteen, they've got other friends who enjoy the same sort of activities and clubs, and on it goes.

When you light a fire, you start with lighting the kindling material. But it's not the kindling material that's important, it's the fire itself. It's the furnace that builds which matters, and it's precisely this that can make anyone capable of astonishing things later in life.

It is fascinating how some kids, who might be regarded as intellectually poor by some, when you ask them about a subject they love, such as football, they can give you the names and details and transfer prices of Premier League footballers in the most bewildering detail. It can be the equivalent of a doctor talking about anatomy or a Shakespearean scholar talking about the cast of *All's Well That Ends Well*. It's the same brain that's being used – and it's achieving, it's connecting facts and it's thinking and aware of the tactical and strategic aspects of football. To some, this might seem irrelevant or trivial, but the point is that their way of thinking and connecting and absorbing facts and knowledge about something they love is the thing that's being lit, be it about football, fashion, pop music, fossils or anything. It stimulates their curiosity about something, and children instinctively and almost against their will start to absorb knowledge about these things because of their passion. If they can transfer this to more useful life skills later on, then *that* surely is the secret.

Parents and educators need to understand the importance of this. The trick is not to discourage them or mock them – 'Why are you wasting time on football, pop music, fashion?' – but to find a way of using that excitement. Get them to write an essay about their favourite footballer, singer or whoever. Putting things together, researching and writing become something that they can learn to do and enjoy.

The other thing is not to go out and buy them a load of books on football or fossils, or get them music CDs. Ask them, 'Would you like to have some more information about that football club?' or 'Why don't you have a look online and see if you can find a really good book about fossils?' It gets them interested, involved, and they take ownership of what they need to do.

To illustrate this point in a different way, I used to help a small private hospital in Bwindi in western Uganda, an area where childhood malaria was a huge problem. Dozens of children in the area were dying from the disease every week. So we raised some money and bought them mosquito nets – a simple solution, but also the best. But the mothers would not use them, it was very odd. An expert who understood the problem, a brilliant man, then told us that we were doing it all wrong. On his advice, we then bought another batch of nets (exactly the same type) but this time told them, 'These are much more expensive and better nets, but unfortunately we cannot give them to you. You are going to have to pay for them. If you can pay a small amount each month, whatever you can manage, it will really help.' The mothers all agreed that they needed to buy them, and this time they actually *used* them. Miraculously, the child mortality rate went down to two children dying of malaria per year. The important point here is that in buying the net themselves and making their own decision to acquire them, they would value them and want to use them. It was no longer something imposed upon them from the 'authority world'.

The same applies to children. If you tell them they have to practise on the piano and you sit with them and watch them, they will immediately say, 'I don't want to do it.' The art is in getting them to want to practise and to make their own decision to do so. Allow kids to be king or queen of their own province, and they will value it and put the work in.

What is most important for parents in those early stages is that they must gain a sense of what it is that interests and inspires their children. Allow them to explore these things, develop their curiosity and let them find something that they can be passionate about, however trivial the subject may seem. Remember, it's about lighting a fire.

Work hard . . .

We live in a fantasising society where everything looks easy and children are told lies from a very early age. The world's largest producer of children's films, as part of its theme tune, unashamedly tells children, 'Wish upon a star and your dream will come true.' This is not only grossly negligent but a complete lie! Try it . . . wish upon a star and see if your dreams actually come true . . . They will not! The *only* way your dreams come true is if you fight to achieve them, and that fight involves what Winston Churchill called 'blood, sweat, toil and tears', and that's the brutal truth.

But the wonderful thing about that truth is that you don't need to be born rich to know how to work hard, you don't need to have been born into an upper-class or middle-class society. You don't need any particular advantage other than a passion for what you are doing.

I have yet to discover anyone who has achieved fulfilment without putting in extraordinarily hard work. This is something that most people may not want to hear, but interestingly, almost everyone I have known that has found fulfilment in life (and I include myself) was invariably shocked to discover that hard work is actually what they *want* to do and is an extraordinary pleasure and the most fulfilling of all things. Noel Coward, a man who achieved an astonishing number of things in all kinds of directions in his lifetime, had a simple motto: 'Work is more fun than fun'. To him it was, and to me it is.

Now for most people it isn't. Work is what they stop doing in order to have fun: 'It's nearly half past five, I can go and have fun now.' For those with fulfilling lives, successful lives, their work can involve the most monumental labour; it's extraordinary, sometimes it can be fifteen, sixteen or seventeen hours a day, but it doesn't seem like it because you don't want to do anything else. Time just flies by.

So if there is such a thing as a 'formula for success', it's probably this: to be curious, find something that you feel passionate about and then work *really* hard at it.

On goals . . .

Not only am I not goal-orientated, I'm actually dead against them, unless your goal is actually to find fulfilment in life. As soon as you start setting goals to get this promotion or that car, or live in this house, in that suburb, you will never be satisfied.

I had what might be described as a bit of a meltdown in the mid-90s, and even to this day, people still occasionally say to me, 'I remember the time when you went off the rails.' And I think, do you honestly believe that being 'on rails' is a good idea? Do you think as a human being with legs and arms and an immortal soul you were put on this planet to be placed on rails? Seriously? A rail is just an inverted rut, and we all know about being in a rut. With goals, you are just making rails for yourself.

There is this metaphorical golden palace of fame and celebrity success set on top of a hill that some people imagine reaching. If you've visited the golden palace, you then immediately want to leave, head away from it and go back downhill . . . and you see people struggling uphill towards it and you say, 'Why waste your time? That's not where you want to be.' But some people still have to find out for themselves.

While goals only set you on rails towards a notional place, that's not to say that there isn't a need to yearn and stretch. That is what we mean when we talk about curiosity and an energy to find out and to learn. There is a wonderful line by the poet Browning where he says, 'Ah, but a man's reach should exceed his grasp, Or what's a heaven for?' The end point or the goal is not the important thing. It's the journey, the looking, the finding, the moving . . . *that's* exciting.

Dealing with hurdles and self-doubt . . .

The worst thing you could do when you face a hurdle or a period of self-doubt or negativity is to keep it to yourself and hidden. One of the great secrets in life, and it's an extremely difficult one to get right, is what I call the gift of proportion. Now, you can look at something physical and determine that it's not bigger than this and it's not smaller than that. The difficulty, though, arises when it comes to hurdles or problems where it can be much harder to get that sense of proportion. You can pretend it's smaller than it is, but that would be an act of denial; on the other hand, you mustn't pretend that it's so big that you can never get over it.

That's where a conversation with someone else, someone that you can trust, is so important. Curiously, it is often easier for people to have a clear perspective on another person's problems than when looking at their own. Talk to a friend or, when you are very young, talk to your parents, a relative or a teacher.

Failure is important and it's natural. You just have to look at a baby trying to walk – the reason it can walk is because he or she has fallen over so many times. All the things we can do later on, all the multitasking, all the amazing processes, these are a result of the failures we experience earlier in life. We are continuously learning from failure.

Be cheerful . . .

The longer you live, the more you realise that it's fruitless to overlay a scheme on humans any more than it is on any other organic being.

Everything we do is human-shaped, and we are a social animal and we rely on signals from others and we need to give signals back. So the great big words like 'Positivity' and 'Positive Thinking' and variations of these are, I think, less important than the slightly more human variations of the same. Whether at work or even socially, everyone will agree that one particular unspoken quality that humans possess, which is also one of the most heroic and yet isn't among the great pantheon of capital letter words, like 'Mercy' and 'Justice' and so on, is 'cheerfulness'.

Cheerfulness is not the same as positivity. It doesn't mean that you think 'everything is going to work out'. Being cheerful in the face of adversity is an act of bravery. It also communicates and it's not egotistical. It's not, 'I have to be positive to make that happen,' it's much more subtle and much more beneficial too. Cheerfulness is like a warm, spreading, joyful thing – as, of course, is kindness.

The ancient Greeks used to believe that if you could propagate cheerfulness, this would cause a cascade of beneficial effects. Their notion of *eudaimonia* was almost a kind of philosophy of 'good spiritedness'. Were something bad to happen to you, if you had a cheerful response to the problem rather than an angry one, the outcome was likely to be more positive.

I have bipolar disorder and my mood swings mean that I can't always be cheerful, but it is something I aspire to be far more than I would aspire to 'positivity' or any of those sorts of things. Cheerfulness is infectious, and I love cheerful people and most people do too. I have lived a long time on this planet now and I've realised that when I go to a party or a drinks function, the people who make my face light up are the ones that are always so cheerful – they bustle, they've really got smiley things to say and it's genuine, not just a fake kind of smile.

Literature and the power of reading . . .

If you go into a bookshop, all the help you will ever need is in the literature section, the poetry section, the science, biography and history sections. You will learn more about who you are and what you can achieve by reading Shakespeare's sonnets than anything else. It takes commitment, of course, and requires concentration, and you need to be curious, but we've been told for all of our lives how important these poems and plays are – people just refuse to believe it though, because it takes work.

And yet there are those who have been so incredibly enriched by art, literature and knowledge of science, who are curious about the world. They have been so enriched that they're able to do anything they want in the world . . . and others say, 'Oh, what is your secret?' Well, the secret is the same secret that you have always been told – *there is magic in those libraries*. They can give you all the power you could ever achieve. But most of those self-help books on secrets, habits or techniques of wealthy people, will give you nothing, zilch, except disappointment.

However, by going to see plays, reading books by great writers and biographies of extraordinary men and women, by understanding history and art and the interchange of ideas and people across history, you will gain an insight into everything you will ever need to know that can unlock every door that you ever want to go through. It's no exaggeration to say that someone who has been curious enough to do all of that can go on to do anything with their lives, because they will have an insight into people, and people's motives, and also how their own brain is capable of learning.

In London, there is the well-known 'taxi-driver' effect. The London taxi driver has to undergo this extraordinary thing called 'The Knowledge', which requires learning the most incredible amount of detail about London's streets and locations. Most taxi drivers are not naturally academic, many will have left school early, but they have to learn and be tested on a huge amount of knowledge, far more information, in fact, than a law student needs to learn to pass a law degree. And then they discover the power of learning. They discover that their brain is actually capable of extraordinary things. FMRI (functional magnetic resonance imaging) studies have shown that their brains have been lit up and neural pathways have been created that weren't there before, simply by this absorption of knowledge that allows them to be capable of things in other directions. Many will go on to study languages or other academic subjects, or simply become avid readers of literature.

Dame Katherine Grainger DBE

As Britain's most decorated female Olympic athlete, Katherine Grainger won a total of five medals for rowing over five consecutive Olympic Games from 2000 to 2016. She won gold in 2012 with her double sculls partner Anna Watkins, after first breaking the Olympic record during qualifying. She also achieved eight World Championship medals (including six gold) and has won the Rowing World Cup in either the double sculls or quadruple sculls on seven occasions. She graduated with LLB (Hons) from the University of Edinburgh, an MPhil in medical law and medical ethics from the University of Glasgow and a PhD in criminal law from King's College London. She is currently chair of UK Sport and chancellor of the University of Glasgow. Among her numerous awards, Katherine has been honoured with an MBE, a CBE, and in 2017 received her damehood for services to sport and charity.

'I still tend to come back to viewing success fundamentally as being happy, because when you find purpose and passion, when you can find contentment and fulfilment in something you love doing, that's where I believe you can find real success in life.'

'I sincerely believe now that until you find what it is that you may want to pursue in life, you have to cast your net as wide as possible. Ideally, there would be no limits on an individual's thoughts or imagination, dreams or desires.'

'The road to success is never direct and rarely smooth. In my experience, the individuals who usually make it are the ones who are resilient, who take the knocks and who come back fighting.'

'I also think one of the biggest gifts that any child can possess, is ambition in life, in the widest possible sense, about what they can achieve, where they can go and the influence they might have. The world needs fabulous people right now, who are going to go out and achieve great things and add real value to the world. I'd like to believe that it's within the power of most parents to help their children to understand that and to fire their imaginations.'

About success . . .

As my life has changed and I have done many different things over the years, my views about success have evolved too. At first, I struggled to define what success would mean for me, but I felt instinctively it would be something to do with being happy – but what might bring that happiness, I couldn't be sure.

It was at university, when I started to become more ambitious within sport, that my view of success would change into something much more definitive for me. By accident, I discovered the sport of rowing, and within that world I found it easy to create targets and goals for myself. My first big ambition was simply to become the best university rower I could possibly be. But as I developed as an athlete, so my ambitions developed and with the encouragement of a brilliant coach I began to think that if I could make it into the British team, then *that* would mean real success. Once I had gained my place in the team, my ambitions were to change again. The next stage was international success in the sport and this would now be defined by winning medals. Once that started to happen, my vision of success became to achieve that ultimate goal in my sport: winning an Olympic gold medal.

So if success in sport can be defined as 'winning', then medals certainly become an incredibly definitive part of that. For me, winning the Olympic gold was the pinnacle of ambition and achievement, and what made it all the sweeter was standing on top of the podium in front of an incredible home crowd in 2012, and next to Anna Watkins, my impressive rowing partner. It wasn't just the medal that defined success; it was the entire journey that led to that defining moment. There were the challenges overcome, the frustrations encountered, the wonderful people that supported and guided, the incredible team that had built around us, and how much we simply enjoyed the whole sporting environment. That journey included all the most brilliant and best things about sport, in my opinion, and was such a positive and enjoyable time for us. Success, therefore, was not just about winning the gold medal – it was about the entire experience and context, and the memories that stay with you forever.

Today, while I'm still working within the world of sport, I'm no longer competing as an athlete. What success means for me now, feels a bit harder to pin down, since it's not as clear or definitive as it was before. Success in my career is now about adding value and leadership. It's about making sure I'm supporting a team that feels valued and is positively contributing to something really important. Unlike competing in sport, it can't be defined by a time on a stopwatch or a measured distance; it's more of a 'feeling', and almost an emotional aspect of success. I think that's why I still tend to come back to viewing success fundamentally as being happy, because when you find purpose and passion, when you can find contentment and fulfilment in something you love doing, that's where I believe you can find real success in life.

Finding my way . . .

It was only when I got to the end of my international sporting career that I started to really reflect on things, because when you're competing you tend to look forward not back. When I look back now, I see there were definite points in my life where the path in front of me had a variety of directions to choose from, and life could certainly have been very different had I chosen a different direction. It is of course impossible to know now whether I would ever have loved the world I didn't choose as much as the one that I did. But I'm lucky to sit here now, content with the choices I made.

Something that I appreciate now – and certainly far more than I would have done at the time – was the huge influence that the people closest to me had on me while I was growing up, and the power of the right person making the right suggestion at the right time. By far the most impactful was my family. My parents and my big sister were always brilliantly supportive and encouraging. There was never one big memorable moment of being sat down and told all about the world in a 'Hey look! Anything is possible!' sort of way. It was always more subtle than that. There was just a constant flow of really positive messages from my mum and dad about seizing the day, thinking about what my real passions were, and encouraging me to try things and get involved. I therefore had the reassurance when growing up, I suppose, of realising that I didn't have to be narrow in my thinking and that there wasn't just one path open to me. I never felt my family were trying to push me in any particular direction either; they simply allowed me to become my own person and to consider my own choices. The sense of freedom I had, together with the continuous positive influence from them, was an incredible gift. I remember being very excited about what life could hold for me and what I might take on. While I saw that 'the world was my oyster', it was also down to me to make decisions about the way forward.

Other people also played key roles as I grew up. At my secondary school in Glasgow, I had an art teacher who also gave karate lessons during the lunch break. I decided to follow my sister and join the karate class, and that teacher ended up being a huge positive influence on me. He was really passionate and very dedicated to his sport, and that was infectious. He also genuinely believed in me – more so than I probably did myself at the time. He always made the lessons fun too; serious training could also be enjoyable. One of the things I love about martial arts is the powerful spiritual side to it: understanding yourself as a person, learning about control and discipline of the mind as much as the body.

Karate was a great formative experience for me, and after a while, I started progressing through the belts. I was the first school student that my teacher took from white belt through to black belt, which I attained just before I left school. At that stage, he was already a very high-ranking black belt himself, and I remember how proud he was of what I had achieved under his pupillage. The day after I passed my black belt grading, I went to see him and gave him a card to say thank you for all that he had done for me. Then, to my amazement, he gave me the very first black belt that he had been awarded when he was a student. That meant a huge amount to me then, and I still have the belt at home now. It's one of those possessions that I would rush to rescue if my house was on fire! That belt has always symbolised something very important to me; when you're young and growing up, with all the insecurities you can feel, when you maybe still don't quite know where you actually fit in the world, having someone who really believes in you and in your ability, who trusts you and who takes real pride in what you can achieve – that is something very special. It can make an important difference to you, especially at that age.

My parents were happy when I decided to study law at university, and they always encouraged activities beyond the classroom too. Just as they had supported my karate when I was at school, they encouraged me to also consider life outside of law lectures. It was during the first week of my law degree that someone, by chance, suggested that I might like to try rowing. I was interested in joining a few different clubs and societies, but I hadn't seriously considered rowing before. I signed up and very quickly felt at home in the club, meeting wonderful, charismatic, fun friends who made training competitive but pleasurable in equal measure. So I started rowing, and it didn't take long before I was really enjoying it – I loved the environment, the physical challenge and the sociable support. Although I improved at the sport, I didn't really have ambitions beyond competing for the university. However, as time went on, a couple of significant people started to gently nudge me to take things a bit further.

First of all, a coach mentioned to somebody else that 'maybe one day I could row for Scotland', and, once that carrot had been dangled in front of me, it became my major focus. I achieved that goal and then a different visionary coach suggested I should go to the next set of British Rowing trials. At first, I couldn't believe it. What he was actually suggesting was that I go for something I hadn't even dreamed of pursuing. Initially, I thought it was a ridiculous idea. It was simply not where my ambitions lay at that time, and I didn't think I was anywhere near good enough to try to compete at that level. It would mean going out and competing against the best people in the country, which seemed just extraordinary to me. When I responded that I didn't think I was ready for such a big step, I was reminded that I was not necessarily looking to beat any Olympic champions just yet. I simply had to show my potential; there were amazing coaches and other wonderful support staff who could then help me fulfil that potential. I just had to take the first step, and I'd find out either way. My coach wisely just let it sit with me for a while.

While the nudges were happening at university, I also had incredible reassurance from my parents at the same time. This is the part that possibly impresses me most now – my parents knew very little at all about rowing or high-performance sport, and had never experienced the situation I was in. They might have seen this as a risky option; it was certainly an unknown one. They could easily have steered me back towards the career I had initially mapped out when I started at university. They were, instead, amazingly supportive, and while it was still a huge decision for me to take, it felt like quite a safe decision, probably because of the secure and positive environment I had grown up in at home, where options were seen as there for the taking. We definitely had a *carpe diem* philosophy within the family about life, to seize the day and make the most of 'now'. My parents held the view that I shouldn't be afraid to take a risk. I should simply try it, see what happens, and if for any reason it didn't work out well for me, then they would always be there for me. In the end, I felt confident enough to go for the trials, along with another girl from university. I really didn't have anything to lose by at least having a go, and so I did – and, by the end of my final year at university, I was rowing for Great Britain.

Another very interesting thing for me when I now look back, is how my rowing career unfolded. When I was at university, my ambition was simply to be the best university rower I could possibly be. I didn't even think about international sport; and I certainly didn't think about the Olympic Games. I just thought about the world I knew and being the best within that. However, as I then developed as an athlete, doors started to open, my world grew that much more, and soon I wanted to be the best I could be within *that* world. Eventually, the world developed again, the challenges got bigger and I had to grow even more to meet *those* challenges. Ultimately, I found myself competing in the Olympics and the World Championships – the greatest sporting stages of all!

Cast a wide net and say 'Yes!' to as much as you can . . .

When I was at secondary school, even after a few years, I still didn't have a clear picture of what I really wanted to do. I remember sitting down with my mum and dad from time to time and having those 'What do you want to be when you grow up?' sort of conversations, but I just didn't know. I couldn't even define what I thought *might* interest me. All I'd say was, 'I just don't want to have a boring life.' When they asked me what that meant I could not define that either! It was difficult because I didn't want to be put into a box, or set on just one path. Nothing I looked at seemed a natural fit for me, and sometimes it's a lot easier to say what you don't want to do, rather than what you do want to do.

I sincerely believe now that until you find what it is that you may want to pursue in life, you have to cast your net as wide as possible. Ideally, there would be no limits on an individual's thoughts or imagination, dreams or desires. It can be daunting not to know your path in life, but I found it helped to talk to people, to read a lot, to learn about as much as I could, and definitely stay open-minded. It can seem a challenge, but you don't need to sit back and wait to be inspired by something; it feels better to go out and look for possibilities, but without narrowing things down too much and too early either. I really did not know what I wanted to do to begin with, but I'd eventually find out over time.

Throughout life, we are all presented with options, activities and opportunities that we can pursue. Before I went to university, someone once said to me, 'The best piece of advice I can give to you is to say "yes" to as much as you can.' It's often far too easy to make assumptions or judgements about something before even trying it, and then to simply reject it out of hand as a possibility. If you think you won't like something or you might not be interested in it, it's still often worth a try. It's just a way of opening doors to more possibilities rather than just dismissing them before you even know. And those doors may lead you to new places or new people who can enrich your life.

That individual piece of advice was to prove very important to me. It was ultimately one of the key reasons why I joined the university rowing club. At first sight, I did not know if rowing was something I would particularly enjoy. I wasn't particularly drawn to it. At the time, it could have been much easier to simply say that I was too busy to the person who introduced me to the idea and to tell myself I'd try something else that I was more comfortable with.

Sometimes it can seem a bit risky to try something new. You don't know if you'll like it or whether you'll be any good at it. Perhaps you don't know anyone there who is doing it. But actually, those are often the moments and the opportunities when you discover the very things that you will end up loving to do in life, or at least you will learn something about yourself from the challenge. The point is, if you don't have a go, you might never find out, and then you will never know.

My own view is that life is short, and it moves at a very fast pace. Life is all the better for finding new challenges and interests, to have enthusiasm and a passion for things. It's a wonderful thing to be inspired, to be excited and moved by things. That is why exploring and engaging all of the different opportunities that are in front of you is so important. When you open up your mind and start exploring, different paths naturally open up for you and present you with choices. It's a big world full of so many different and exciting choices.

The value of education . . .

I came to understand the value of education from quite an early age. My parents were both teachers, and my big sister is still a teacher today.

I enjoyed most of my time at school, and inevitably as I got older things started to feel more serious. I remember thinking that the decisions I made at school, the subjects I would choose or drop, would change the rest of my life – and that felt huge. I think, as you get older, you eventually realise that while they may have seemed like the biggest decisions of your life at the time, they will never actually be 'wrong' decisions. You can always go back and reopen those doors later if you truly want to, because they are rarely actually permanently shut.

Anyone can relearn subjects and re-educate themselves, or even change direction in later years.

At any age, and when facing decisions, it's good if you can be completely honest with yourself about what it is that you really want to do and why you want to do it. It's worth questioning whether you're considering an option because it's what other people are saying you should be doing. Is it truly what you want to do? You might not be sure, but often you will have an instinct, a strong feeling one way or other, and it's worth paying attention to these feelings and instincts. Even if you are not 100 per cent sure, you can make decisions based on the best of your knowledge and understanding at the time about what you want to do, and why. You should not be afraid of getting it wrong, because we all change throughout life. Once again, it is quite OK to change direction later on; at the time we are all simply making the best guess at what it is we think we may want to do.

I remember leaving home for Edinburgh University, and it certainly felt like a big change in my life. I loved my time there, and while I really enjoyed the formal aspect of study, that informal side of learning, as a young adult, was really important for me too. University gives you access to a wide range of experiences, and you meet people from varying walks of life and backgrounds, and from different countries, all of whom bring with them different thoughts and beliefs. I think it's great that many of the ideas and assumptions you might have had growing up – or may have got used to – become challenged. For me, further education broadens everything out and really helps shape you as a person. I certainly felt more independent, and while it may also seem like you have a lot more responsibility, when you compare it with later in life, it's a wonderful time of freedom. Real responsibilities will naturally be acquired soon afterwards, but in the meantime, you can enjoy a relatively carefree time as a student. It's a brilliant time for growing, learning how to think for yourself and how to address problems and issues.

Some of the best informal learning that I gained during my time at university was through sport. In some ways, it was to teach and challenge me the most, and it definitely helped to form my character. In the end, I was to develop two really strong passions: one was for sport and one was for the law, and I was able to choose both. What was very interesting was that the attributes I acquired through being a good athlete made me a better student; while the attributes of being a good student also helped me to become a better athlete. It was very hard work doing both, but for me, they were entirely complementary. When I was exhausted from being in a boat or being in the gym, I would love going to the library or doing something to stretch me mentally. Then, when I got weary of that, I'd love going back outside to train or to work physically with the team. They were both different passions, which for me really helped, and I think if you want to take on two (or more!) big challenges at the same time, you have to truly care about both.

Turning your passion into success . . .

Some young people just seem to find early on in life what they like and what genuinely interests them. It can be often be completely different to what others may be drawn to, and sometimes it might even be something that they wouldn't necessarily want to admit to. I sincerely believe that if you are lucky enough to have a passion for something, then you should follow it and see where it takes you. Nonetheless, 'find your passion' can be a difficult message, because many young people simply won't have one or know where to start finding one. It was not until I was at university that I really discovered what I was truly passionate about. When I was growing up, however, I kind of knew the things I was drawn to, what sparked my imagination and curiosity, and I think that is a great starting point for anybody. It's good to think about what you enjoy, what interests you, what excites you and what matters to you.

Once you have found your passion for something that you want to do, then it can take a lot of work to turn that passion into success. It's a truism to say that people who have become very successful in life will have worked extremely hard in order to achieve that. Even the most talented and most naturally gifted people I have ever met will mostly credit their success to having worked very, very hard to get there. It's not just the hours of effort they put in, it's also that motivation of constantly wanting to learn, constantly wanting to improve, always being curious about how to develop, never feeling they've done enough, never settling. Having that drive will always be a really helpful attribute for anyone that aspires to become successful.

Be prepared to fail and to have doubts . . .

We often see wonderful people doing exceptional things in many different fields. Of course, the danger is that we then talk about their extraordinary success stories and assume that they'll have enjoyed a magical journey without experiencing any issues along the way. I would be willing to bet that every one of them will, in their own minds, have got things wrong at times, experienced massive failures and had huge disappointments. Sometimes it might be through their own doing, sometimes it might be out of their hands, but the road to success is never direct and rarely smooth. In my experience, the individuals who usually make it are the ones who are resilient, who take the knocks and who come back fighting.

When you pursue something that you are passionate about, however wonderful and rewarding it may be, the deal you make is that it can also break your heart along the way. That is certainly the case in sport, and I've had some real heart-breaking moments in my career. Of course, they are never great experiences, never enjoyable, but you survive, you learn from them and you ultimately become better because of them.

I think this is always a fascinating area of discussion because, for a long time culturally, we have mostly sought to avoid failure. The problem is, however, that people can become risk-averse and stop making those brave decisions that will actually enable them to move forward. If people are too focused on the possibility of failure, then often they become unable to make decisions and to try things. Of course, failure is not something I'd actively encourage, but it can often end up being the best way to learn. I believe the right balance is still wanting to succeed, but without being *afraid* of failing at the same time.

Through experience, I have learned it's worth taking things on, despite the perceived risks. When I competed during my last Olympic Games in Rio de Janeiro in 2016 to win my final medal, that was probably the biggest risk of all for me. There was a huge chance at that stage in my career that I could end up crashing out completely, ending my competitive career in disappointment and being seen as a failure. While I was fully aware of the risks, and naturally did everything I possibly could to avoid failure, I also remember thinking at the time that even if I failed in the eyes of others, this would still be another integral part of my journey. In the end, I didn't want the risk of failure to stop me from making a positive decision to compete and find answers for myself. For me, backing down would have felt more of a failure. So we may have to accept that even though failures inevitably have a role to play in our lives, they shouldn't stop us from doing what we have to.

Even when we make brave decisions and positively pursue something extremely challenging, we can still have moments of self-doubt. Everyone has them at some point. These doubts are not easy or comfortable, and we all deal with them in different ways. Sometimes they can be difficult to handle just by ourselves, and so we may need an outside voice to help. It could be someone in your family or a friend, a coach, a teacher or mentor; people that you can be honest with and tell that you're really struggling with this. Another person can help you with your perspective on things, because it's often precisely *this* that may have shifted.

Sometimes, having doubts about something is a good way to highlight to yourself, almost subconsciously, that there's a problem somewhere that needs to be addressed. It could be with you, or it could be the situation you are in, but it helps you to confront it rather than just carrying on regardless. You often subsequently become the better for it. Perhaps the challenge you are facing is something that questions your values and beliefs, and that challenge will help you to see what it is you feel strongly about.

You often hear successful people say that while their journey to the top was always very hard, it's a lot easier in many ways than staying at the top. When starting off, you have the momentum and feel that you are progressing with every step. You can also make big strides each time towards your goal, and it can be very exciting. However, once you get to the top, the steps become smaller. It becomes much harder to keep improving your personal best. It's often a struggle, and that's the time when self-doubt can begin to creep in. You might start to wonder, 'Have I reached my peak?', 'Was it just a one-off?', 'Can I do it again?', 'Can I still do it better?'

When I competed in Rio, while I was positive about participating and knew the risks, I still experienced some serious moments of self-doubt. There were definitely points during my preparation for those Games when I just could not see a way forward, because when you take on such a huge challenge, you have to utterly believe in it and utterly believe in yourself. You have to completely sign up to it, live it and love it. Yet I still recall wondering why I was doing it and if it was perhaps a mistake.

There have been times when a very honest conversation with myself works best. I simply ask some fundamental questions about why I started on this particular journey, what I had originally hoped to achieve, whether I still felt I could do it and why it was important to me. Sometimes just reminding yourself of why you have undertaken a particular challenge helps to reignite everything and put things back into perspective.

I also often look towards external things for help and inspiration. I love listening to great speeches and reading about people who have done truly amazing things with their lives. All of the challenges that you may have to face at some point in your life, others will have faced them too, and much more besides. Many will have found great answers. It's like going for advice to people that you might never meet but who can still help you, simply through their writings.

I also love great quotes. I have many framed on the walls in my office and at home. Quotes are so easy to access from books and online – thousands of brilliant minds from all different walks of life throughout history have faced enormous challenges in their lives with bravery and often humour. Some will have come up against insurmountable problems, had the deepest doubts, yet will have still battled on and found a way through. For me, quotes have always been an amazing source of strength and inspiration. They remind you that you are not alone.

The great thing about quotes is that they're at your fingertips whenever you need them. I might be anywhere in the world, and all I have to do is Google 'self-doubt' or 'inspiration' on my phone to find an endless stream of one-liners. The more I read, the more inspired I feel – and then it's 'game-on'!

Get out there and improve your chances . . .

When I speak about my sporting career, I often say how lucky I was. But sometimes people try to correct me and say 'It's never just luck! You make your own luck!' For me, I see it as a mixture of both, really. Luck can certainly be meeting the right person at the right time in life. In my case, I also happened to get involved with rowing at a time when sport was respected, seen as relevant and was being supported in this country. That was certainly very good timing for me. However, being in the right place at the right time will often follow a lot of hard work or planning. It will mostly involve you putting yourself 'out there', being brave and talking to other people, and getting yourself known.

A lot of this goes back again to saying 'yes' to everything you can, taking a chance on something when you don't even know if you will succeed at it, and then not being afraid to fail. The more you become involved in a particular activity, the more people you meet, the more you will increase the probability of something positive happening. Luck can flow from these things. It might be that you make yourself go to an event, where a chance conversation with someone leads to a fortuitous introduction, which then leads to a significant meeting with an individual that ultimately makes a huge difference for you. It all stems back to you deciding to go to that event in the first place. I find it fascinating when I think about anyone that has been really significant in my life – and I track back to how

I first met them – that they were almost inevitably chance encounters or chance introductions.

When I first went to university, I didn't know many people, but I made myself join clubs and make introductions, and I met some of my best friends that way. They just happened to study at the same university that I decided to go to – it's partly down to chance, timings and decisions, where individual lives simply come together. I certainly would not have connected with the person who ultimately introduced me to rowing, unless I had consciously put myself into a situation, by getting myself out there, where I could meet them in the first place.

Teamwork was always important for me . . .

Personally, I love working with people. For me, allowing others to bring the best out of you, and for you to bring the best out of others, has been a really meaningful part of success. I also appreciate that not everyone will feel the same, and that not every success will necessarily be defined in the context of other people, but my experience has always been participating within a team environment. What I particularly love about my sport is that rowing has a crucially important team element to it, and success has been all the sweeter because I didn't do it all alone. I competed with other people and because of other people, and that helped it to be even more significant for me. It also made success more enjoyable. I truly believe that the spirit of collaboration – that openness and mutual trust – has always been vital to what I have gone on to do in my career.

So how do you build a great team? And how do you make great teams continue to work well together? The challenge is, of course, that every team is different and individuals within a team can represent a range of diverse characters. Although one might seek to have incredible harmony within a team, with everyone agreeing to a common inspirational vision, it helps to have a variety of characters, all with distinct strengths. But it can be a challenge when you have different people with different interests, thoughts and opinions, as this might increase the risk of disagreements or conflict. There is no perfect formula to manage that. It helps to keep everyone as open-minded as possible and listening to each other. Everyone should accept that, however clear your opinion about something may be to you, others may not agree and will see things in a different way, based on their own experiences. And in situations involving high pressure or danger, people will usually have more extreme reactions.

So although it's great to have your own opinion or a strong point of view, you should aim to be good at understanding the opinion of others, especially when arriving at decisions for the team. In an ideal world, everyone would always achieve coherent collective decisions, but it's rarely as simple as that. Fundamentally, it comes down to trust and mutual respect from all the participants within a team.

How mentors can help you to find the answers . . .

When I look back, there were certainly people that I knew who advised me and influenced me throughout my early career and life, that I could naturally turn to for help when needed. But I didn't necessarily define them as 'mentors'.

Having a formal or informal mentor can prove invaluable for any person of any age, because we can all benefit from somebody else's opinion or advice. In part this goes back to the benefit of always being curious and continually learning, never feeling we always have the answers.

In my experience, really good mentors aren't the ones that just give us the answers. In fact, they will normally pose more questions than provide answers. They can make us think about things in a different way or perhaps help us to look at a problem through a different lens. They can be very good at 'reflecting back' to us things about ourselves that we haven't really thought of or asked ourselves about before.

I think we could all be a little more introspective, creating the time to stop and think about what drives us or motivates us, or what our purpose is, what our loves, hates or passions might be. Sometimes we simply don't find time to think about where, or even what, our values truly are. This is something a good mentor can often be brilliant at getting out of us, either directly or indirectly, just by asking the right questions and by making sure we find the answers for ourselves.

For me, whether I was at school or a student, during my sports career or even now, there has always been someone there that I have been able to talk to. Sometimes we need to have what are almost vulnerable conversations with the right person, since it's often then that we feel comfortable enough to admit to any inadequacies or doubts that we might have, perhaps when we've lost our way on something. It's great having someone there who can listen to us and help us find our focus again.

Having a mentor is always a very personal connection. Sometimes they can be highly experienced in your particular field, trained in their role, understanding it completely and doing it exceptionally well. They can be a great first contact. Occasionally, they may be individuals that you just feel naturally able to turn to, that you feel safe with and that you trust. While they may not be a mentor in the formal sense – and they may not see themselves as a mentor, either – that's exactly the role that they can perform for you.

I think it's important for any young person to be aware that there will invariably be people around you, who are also available to you, that you can feel comfortable with and who would be happy to give you their time. Just look out for them, and when you do find someone that takes a genuine interest in you and whom you feel you could talk to, then simply ask for their help.

As you get older and life becomes busier, even if you're very happy with everything you're doing, it can be good to have someone in the background that can check on you and with whom you can have the conversations you wouldn't normally have with others. Their role is simply to talk about you and where you are in life, how happy you are and what your plans are. It is important to regularly schedule time in for this, because if we do not, it simply won't happen; another year goes by and we still haven't done the things we planned to do. A good mentor will hold us accountable to ourselves: 'Didn't you want to do these things by now?' 'I thought you wanted to have more time for yourself?' 'You said you wanted to develop this area in your life?' They can actually help us prioritise what is really important for us.

To parents . . .

It's not hard to see that all good parents want the very best for their children. They want them to be happy in whatever form that takes and will do everything they can to try to help them achieve that. It's probably very hard for parents to know just how much to push, how much to gently encourage and how much to let be. My parents went through a bit of that with me when I was at school, because ironically, considering what I went on to do, I wasn't particularly motivated to try out or join different clubs. My big sister was far more sporty than me at school, and my parents had to actively encourage me to go and participate. I think they got the balance just about right. They definitely had to prod me in certain directions until I felt good about something, but after that, I was off and running.

In my experience, it helped growing up in an environment where I felt I had some ownership of what I was doing and the choices I was making. My parents certainly helped to create that for me and gave me enough freedom, while of course, still setting boundaries for me.

Perhaps one of the greatest gifts from my parents – both of them were teachers – was to instil in me a feeling of just how important my education and learning would be. As a value, that has always stayed with me. I still believe we can all continue to learn and develop, whatever our age.

My parents also gave me the confidence that if I found something I really liked, and worked extremely hard at it, then I might get the opportunity to do great things with it. However, they also helped me to understand that while the work-ethic side was important, so too was the enjoyment side of things; it was about having fun, making wonderful friendships and to never forget that life was to be relished. Work was important, learning was invaluable, and fun was crucial too.

I also think one of the biggest gifts that any child can possess is ambition in life, in the widest possible sense, about what they can achieve, where they can go and the influence they might have. The world needs fabulous people right now, who are going to go out and achieve great things and add real value to the world. I would like to believe that it's within the power of most parents to help their children to understand that and to fire their imaginations.

I'm aware that parents can also play a part in how their children's attitude evolves. Character is developed throughout our life, and it ultimately defines who we are and how the world sees us. It is a very personal and individual thing, and it's fascinating how two siblings with similar genes and the same upbringing can develop into two completely different characters.

When I was a child growing up at school, it was difficult to appreciate just how important attitude and character would be. Even without fully understanding it, character is something we all ultimately find for ourselves. Perhaps it starts with how we begin to differentiate right from wrong. But of course, it's difficult because there are a lot of grey areas, yet one of the greatest of human attributes is how, as we develop as a young person, we gradually acquire our moral compass. This then invariably plays a major part in the attitude we develop. For me, that was part of the reason I chose to study law; I felt from a relatively young age a real sense of justice and injustice, and a need for fairness, and I really wanted to make a difference in the world.

However, while the development of a young person's character and attitude is mostly a personal journey for them, parents can have a positive influence too. Looking back, I think that when my parents had the most effect on me, they managed to do it in a subtle way, not by lecturing me on how things should be, but by simply helping me to appreciate and become more aware of the consequences of my behaviour and actions, whether good or bad. They also instilled in me how important courtesy, respect and politeness were, and I thank them to this day for that.

Of course, as both adults and children we can easily upset someone else, either deliberately or unwittingly, and sometimes without appreciating the consequences of what we have done. It can then be useful to consider the 'why' or the 'how'. It might be a good time to ask, 'Why do you think that upset them?', 'Why do you think that was the wrong thing to do?' and 'How do you think they feel about you right now?' And if, on the other hand, someone does something to upset you or your child, it can be useful to ask, 'So, why are you upset?', 'What are you feeling right now?' and 'How do you think the other person should have behaved?'

And finally, when I think about the many great parents that I know, as much as they will have disciplines and rules, they always strive to make home feel like a safe place to be for their children. Then, if anything goes wrong – and everyone gets things wrong or make mistakes sometimes – children can go home, and have a totally honest and open conversation with their parents about what has happened. I had that with my parents, and I love them for that. I still feel the same way about home now.

Balance and prioritisation . . .

When I was at university, we had a really good coach, and he taught us something that would have a big impact on me then and help me throughout my life. He said that we all needed to identify three main areas in life that imposed the biggest draws on our time, for which we then needed to find a balance. For me at that time, they were my studies, my rowing and the combined world of my friends, family and social life. Sometimes, one of those areas would naturally prioritise itself, for example, when I had exams to do or an important essay to hand in, or perhaps when I was competing in trials for rowing. What my coach was particularly good at conveying to us was that while there always needed to be a balance, there would rarely be a perfectly equal balance. Each area would compete with the others for your time. They would all be very important to you, and you'd have to make sure that you were always spending *enough* time on each one. You needed almost constantly to monitor what was getting priority, and to see when there was sometimes a requirement to correct that balance.

One of the interesting things is that if you become too focused on one particular area and spend too much time on it, by shifting the balance towards doing other things, that can actually help you to be even better at doing the very thing you might otherwise be obsessed by. It's all part of the balance, which in the end helps you to be better at all three of the areas you choose to prioritise. I've found that if I feel out of sorts, but I can't quite understand what's wrong, then usually something is a bit out of balance with how I'm spending my time.

For me, I've realised that if I'm not doing some sort of exercise, then I feel unsettled. I've found that being active in any type of sport or physical activity – not necessarily organised sport – is simply good on so many levels. It is clearly physically good for you, but mentally it can also be hugely beneficial too; getting your heart rate going actually means you become better at focusing, better at concentration, better at dealing with problems and challenges. Sport has also taught me values and life lessons in a better way than I have learned from any other source. Sport can also help you learn about personal responsibility, time management and working in collaboration with other people. These are all hugely important things to learn when you are young, as they are valuable skills to have throughout life.

And, in an increasingly demanding and fast-paced world, even going for regular walks can be a huge help. Walking can clear our heads, and give us a different perspective and space to think about things, also helping us to manage stresses and pressures. Sometimes the simplest of things we can do in life can be the most important and beneficial.

Setting your goals . . .

One of the most important things that I did when I was an athlete was to set goals. With my coach I would set them, revisit them constantly to see how I was doing, and regularly adjust them to ensure that they were at the right level. With big goals, you generally won't be able to achieve them easily. If you can, then you simply need to raise the bar. Ideally, your goals test you and stretch you.

For me, there were always two types of goal. The first is the truly ambitious goal, the one that's so big, you're almost too scared to admit it to anyone else. It's the goal that may remain very personal to you, especially early on. It may take many years to achieve, of course, but it's the one that really motivates you.

The second type are the smaller goals – the ones that are more immediate, manageable and doable. They should still be challenging, but they're also the ones that you could achieve today or this week, and when you do so, you can tick them off while knowing that each one is moving you step by step in the direction of your big goal.

Sometimes, when you are pushing hard to achieve one of the smaller goals you've set, it can be extremely hard work and challenging, and you might also be fed up with your day-to-day tasks. You may ask yourself, 'Why on earth am I doing this?' But those are the moments when you then think, 'It's because of *that*!' Then you remember your big goal, and it's exciting and it inspires you. On other occasions, the big goal may seem like you're climbing Mount Everest. It seems just too big to achieve and you think the summit is too far away right now. You feel that reaching the top might be too much, but you can manage to think of moving a bit further up the slope. That then becomes one of your smaller goals: relatively doable compared with the big goal, but one that will still move you forward towards it.

When you set yourself goals, be prepared, and be open-minded enough to change them too. Because, once you set your big goal, while it should be like a rock and a clear vision for you, sometimes the path to that goal may have to change, so you still have to be flexible.

You might find a different way to get there, or things beyond your control can happen; as an athlete you might get injured or you don't get selected. You may then need to adjust your smaller goals to still get you to your big goal. The destination will remain the same, but the way to get there – the journey – might alter.

And sometimes, even your big goal can change. You might get to the top of the mountain, and then you see another peak in the distance emerging through the mist that you hadn't seen before and you think you'd like to tackle that one. Or, you may have a goal, and then something entirely different emerges that becomes big enough to supersede it. That's what happened to me at university. I was passionate about pursuing law as a career, which was the big goal for me. Then the opportunity to compete seriously at rowing emerged, and it was to take over. Eventually, winning at the Olympic Games was to become my new 'big goal'. So, while your big goal should be your rock and you should be absolutely resolute about achieving that, it's still wise to be open-minded about the possibility that something more compelling might come around. It's possible that it will distract you and give you a different focus, but you might actually gain more from it, because the fact remains that a lot of people will go on to achieve great things in their lives, things that they would never have dreamed of achieving when they first started out on their journey. That's part of what makes life so exciting, challenging and fun.

Tanni, Baroness Grey-Thompson, DBE

As one of the most successful British athletes of all time, Tanni Grey-Thompson won a career total of eleven gold medals, four silvers and a bronze across five Paralympic Games, together with five gold medals in the World Championships. During her athletics career, she was a dominant force in wheelchair racing for the 100, 200, 400 and 800-metre disciplines. Tanni was the first woman to break the 60 second barrier over 400 metres, at the Barcelona Paralympics in 1992, and has set no fewer than thirty individual world records. She also won the London Wheelchair Marathon six times. Since her retirement from athletics, she has been a tireless campaigner for disability rights and is now an active member of the House of Lords. During her career, she has accumulated numerous accolades, titles and awards, and is now a much sought-after public speaker, TV presenter and sports commentator.

'I was certainly good at making myself train hard, but I was also good at pushing myself to train for the things I *didn't* like doing. Because in reality, the things you don't like doing are usually the things that you're *not* so good at and you need to improve.'

'If I had the power to change one thing, it would be to see all young disabled people assume naturally, and by default, that they have the right to pursue anything that any non-disabled person can do.'

'Success is often about how you deal with failure. When something goes seriously wrong, you can either give up or you can dig deep, recover your self-belief and focus once more upon your goal. It's all about your attitude and being positive, even when everything sometimes seems stacked against you.'

'Parents must spend time with their kids and talk to them. Have proper conversations. Don't just sit them in front of the screen because it's convenient. Have dinner together and talk. Communicating with your children and getting them involved is one of the most valuable things you can do.'

About success . . .

While my life can be split into quite distinct segments, I think of success as having many different layers. When I was an athlete, it was all about winning gold medals or breaking world records (which didn't always coincide). But during the last four years of my athletics career, success for me was also beating my personal best in the 100 metres, by just one-hundredth of a second. I might not necessarily have won those races, but whenever I achieved a new personal best time, it was absolutely huge!

I have always found it fascinating how other people's perception of my success can be so different to mine: 'You're a successful athlete because you've won so many medals . . .' But, when I look back, if I had to pick what I think were the top ten races of my career, only half of them would actually be gold medal-winning races. The others would be races where, by my own personal standards, I had simply done incredibly well, but without necessarily winning a medal.

I also don't think about my life just in terms of sport anymore. In a way, I've gone well beyond that part of my life now. I'm also a quite forward-looking person. So, when someone says to me, 'Hey, you're that athlete!' I find it both funny in a way and strange, because actually, my life has since moved on. 'Yes I am, but that was over a decade ago!' Today, I'm immersed in politics and campaigning for disability rights as a career. Success for me now might be winning a vote in the House of Lords on an issue I have been working hard on. And sometimes, it may be deciding *not* to take something to a vote and just settling for what I may have gained from the ministers, on a matter that could ultimately make a significant difference for disabled people.

So, being successful has never been about just one thing for me.

Finding what you want to do . . .

The key to finding what you want to do with your life is to try lots of different things. I tried loads of sports before I found wheelchair racing. If you don't explore different things, you might never know whether any of them could have been just right for you. One of the things I get frustrated about is when I see young people – they get to fifteen or sixteen, and their lives are already so narrow or closed-off, just because they don't know what's on offer out there. They simply don't know about the vast range of things that they *could* do with their lives. How would they ever know that they could have made a brilliant sound engineer or a great journalist or whatever, unless they have been exposed to the possibilities of those sorts of things? Young people should therefore read more and dedicate more time to finding out about different careers and different jobs. But they also need to be motivated to explore; some of this is down to parents, some is down to schools and some is naturally down to the young people themselves.

Success as an athlete is always hard-earned . . .

There is very little chance of any athlete becoming an 'overnight success'. It always takes a huge amount of commitment and hard work to get there. But I think today, a much greater understanding exists than ever before about what an athlete really has to go through in order to get to that point. In the past, there was often this common perception that it was all glamour and non-stop parties for top athletes . . . I think it took until around the 1990s for this myth to eventually be dispelled. TV programmes began to expose the reality of what it actually takes to become a successful athlete, showing how hard they have to prepare, and just how painful and tedious the training can be.

Yes, it could be amazing at times! For me, competing in a demonstration race in front of 110,000 people at the 2000 Olympic Games in Sydney was really cool, but most of the time it was simply *not* glamorous at all. When people see the amazing snapshots of you competing at prestigious events or maybe you're seen dressed up for some function or party, they automatically think that this is your life. But the hard reality is nothing remotely like that – in between you are training extremely hard, twelve to fifteen times a week, in all weathers and all times of the year. It's train, eat, sleep, and not much else. So, throughout my athletics career I have always tried to remain grounded, while mentally separating the reality of my life from the perception that other people might have of it.

Work hard but train smart . . .

I didn't win my first race for a couple of years. But actually, that was a good thing because it helped me to realise just how hard I would have to work to get to where I wanted to be.

In fact, nobody thought I had any talent at all until I won my first 100 metres in the Junior Nationals. It was only then that people started saying, 'Oh! You're really talented!' When looking back, I think it's quite funny how just one race changed everyone's opinion about me. While I knew I was getting better and quicker with every single race, most people would only look at my position across the finish line. I might have been fourth, or third or even second in a race, but because I still wasn't winning then, nobody would look at the times I was doing and see that actually, they were improving.

I was certainly good at making myself train hard, but I was also good at pushing myself to train for the things I *didn't* like doing. Because in reality, the things you don't like doing are usually the things that you're *not* so good at and you need to improve. But we all prefer to do things that we enjoy doing . . . So I believe that one should spend less time doing the things you like doing and spend more time on the things you don't like doing! For example, my race starts were never that good, so every day I would practise and work hard at improving them. Although I never really got that much better at doing them, I soon learned how to handle my starts and how not to panic.

I have always had an inner *drive*. My mother had it and my grandmother had it too, so it was in our family. It's that absolute desire to do well, while recognising the hard work that also goes alongside. For me, this is incredibly important because as an athlete, you need to have talent, but you also have to possess a very strong desire. I always wanted to do more and to do better.

I get quite frustrated sometimes when I see really, really talented young people who say they want to achieve great things, but they're not prepared to work hard or train for them. If you are highly talented, but you don't want to do it, then that's fine, because nobody should be forced to do something that they're not truly passionate about. But when I hear young athletes say to me, 'I really want to make the GB team!' and yet they're only prepared to train three or four times a week – well, the reality is, that will simply *never* get you there. I will often say to young people, 'If you want to make a career in sport [or whatever it is that you decide you want to do with your life], you've got to genuinely like it, because you're going to have to spend a lot of time doing it if you want to become good at it!' In other words, find something that you love doing first, and you can *then* worry about what you have to do to become the best at it.

Anyone can train very hard in sport, but that doesn't mean you're going to always hit your targets. You have to learn to train *smart* as well, and this was something I really picked up from my parents. Because it's not just about working hard all the time; when you're young, you can train hard, you recover quickly, and so you don't necessarily have to train smart. As you get older, however, perhaps by your mid to late twenties, you *have* to train smart and you *have* to be mindful of all the other things you can do to help you grow. But, if you train smart when you are younger too, this can also reduce the risk of injuries that athletes are often prone to later on. It's a bit like a jigsaw, where you've got to get every piece right, in order to come out well at the other end.

Something my dad always encouraged me to do was read lots of books about sport and to learn more. I would also talk to other athletes all the time about the technical aspects of racing, such as what gloves they wore or perhaps different types of chair. I used to regularly explore many diverse things that could help me to improve my racing, but I'd always do so in a methodical way; try something out, measure it carefully and evaluate it. If it didn't work, I'd try something else new (not on the day of a race, of course), by building it into my training routine, planning in failure points and having time to assess it properly.

Another aspect of training smart is to *plan* effectively. I like lists and I like spreadsheets, and I was always good at planning. Once you have planned something, it just becomes easier to do it than to not do it. Athletes should either find a good coach who can do the planning for them or they should learn to plan themselves.

At the end of the day, you have to be totally honest with yourself about what you are doing and what you really *want* to do. If you are only prepared to train three times a week as an athlete – or indeed in any sport – that probably means that you simply don't want it enough. But even if you are training frequently, it's not about looking back either and trying to justify to yourself, over a macro-cycle, how well you think you might have done overall. Having that honesty is actually more about, 'Did I do my *very best* and work the *hardest* I possibly could in that *last* training session?'

When I was training as a wheelchair athlete, we used to do something extra that was never an agreed part of our programme. We would start by warming up on the road, followed by the usual long, hard training session. On our way back, we would use the last couple of miles to 'cool down', but every single time we got to the very last turn before reaching home, we would all have a big sprint for the house! It was something we never missed, and we always wanted to do – just a fun thing at the end of a hard session, always difficult and certainly not necessary. But it was also doing that something extra, over and above the training, that would end up pushing us that little bit further each time.

In some of the sprint sessions I'd train in, there were guys who would deliberately push me all over the track. They would try to block me, they'd cut me up or even shove me out by four lanes so that I was forced to go around them. You couldn't do that in a proper race, of course, but in training they'd try to make it extremely hard for me. None of it was serious, and we also had some good laughs, but it was also about finding different ways to make ourselves stronger.

My training group was really close, and that was very important too. We were also always honest with each other. If we did not get something right in a training session, we'd then work hard to get it right in the next one. You couldn't just ignore it and blindly carry on, thinking it would be fine the next time around. If we didn't question what went wrong, and specifically what we had to improve in the next training session, then six months down the track we could find ourselves nowhere near where we needed to be.

I loved that feeling when we got to the end of a training session! It was difficult to train so hard every day and always be able to enjoy it, but if a session had gone really well, it was all 'pennies in the bank' for me – that's the way I'd look at it. So, as a group, we would always try to make each training session interesting and fun. It was also important to make sure that everyone enjoyed participating. If one person was winning every week, it could be quite demotivating for the rest of the group. So we'd always make sure that the training group was more 'even' and that everyone had a chance to have their good moments. Because, actually, you are stronger when you're in a good training group rather than just training on your own.

Some people just assume that because you are competing as an individual, you won't necessarily be a team player. But the reality is that there was very little that I could have done in my career as an athlete all by myself. The vast majority of my time was spent training with different teams and working with the help of other people. The only time I was ever truly by myself was when I competed in a race.

Most of my training groups would include a whole range of different people. Some would be GB athletes, some not, and others were just friends. There was one person I used to train with sometimes who was not that quick as a sprinter. We would start at the same time, but he would do a 200-metre sprint and I'd have to cover 400 metres over the same time. I was always determined to beat him! Sometimes it was really close, but when you are going absolutely flat out over 400 metres and you're chasing someone 200 metres in front of you, that's exceedingly tough. By the time I finished, I had nothing left . . . in fact, the only thing left on the track was half my lungs! But it was a great way for me to push myself to the limits. Training like this was always tough, but it was also about finding different ways to get the best out of the people who were there.

Being careful about nutrition is, of course, critical. But I also used to see some athletes train incredibly hard, and then go down to the pub and have lots of drinks. Yes, the training might be tough, and it's nice to relax and unwind afterwards, but why waste all that hard effort? When I was competing, I would probably have one or two glasses of wine a year – I didn't want to waste all that pain and bruising, and all those blisters, over a couple of drinks! I'm not saying that you have to be totally rigid and should never waver, of course . . . I would be lying if I said that I never ate chips! I recall one occasion when I had just finished competing in a half-marathon, and there was always a burger van near the end by the finish line. You couldn't fail to notice that lovely aroma of burger and fried onions, especially after a race in which I'd probably just burned off around 700 calories. But I remember at the time, I just couldn't resist saying to myself, 'I'm going to have a burger!' And that's OK once in a while – you can waver and indulge yourself a little bit sometimes.

Nonetheless, if you want to be a serious athlete, you really have to be strict with yourself, and you have to make some hard choices. For me, I couldn't be both an athlete and a party animal, so I picked being an athlete.

Failing is always important . . .

You should not be afraid to fail. But the problem is, while that's quite easy to say, failure can also be very hard to deal with. Because, when you start becoming successful as a young athlete, failing is not always seen as something good, nor is it seen as positive. It's how you deal with failure and how you come back from it that counts, however, and it certainly helps to have good people around you to support you when you do fail.

There are two types of failure for an athlete: failure in racing and failure in training. Both are an opportunity to learn about everything that you do. When you are relying on equipment, you have to try various things during training. You have to test and measure it, try different methods for doing something, and then push it to the limit – to the point of failure. When it comes to your personal performance, how you are feeling in training is one part of it, but it's also measuring things like your heart rate and your speed. There are many devices and bits of equipment available to measure these things. So failure in training is important – and failing a lot – because it's the best way to find your limits, what you can improve on and how you can perform better.

One very helpful thing that I did throughout my whole career was to keep a training diary. I kept my diary up to date for *every* training session I did. This enabled me to look back when I was having a good spell and to understand why, and I could always go back and evaluate where things were going wrong when I was having a bad spell. My diary would always provide a context for what I had done. So if ever I got to a point where I hadn't achieved something I wanted, I could usually find clues to what had gone wrong by tracking back analytically through my training history.

Failure in racing is also important, because you learn in a different way to failure in training. You tend to be much more self-critical when you fail than when you win. But I believe you have to learn to balance this, so that you are less self-critical when you fail and more self-critical when you win, and I think it's important to do that equally. When I've coached athletes in the past, at the end of every race I would tend to ask, 'OK, what did you do well? What could you have done better?'

Being disabled should never limit aspiration . . .

A congenital disorder is a medical condition that's present at birth, and in my case, I was born with spina bifida. While I was able to walk a little at first (I was never really able to walk properly), the limited mobility I had soon deteriorated as my spine began to collapse. By the time I was six years old, I was paralysed. Although it's hard to recollect that time now, I'm aware that it was a real struggle for me then, and certainly *the* most difficult period for me as a child.

And so it was from the age of six that I became a wheelchair user. While up until that point it had been really difficult, once I was given my wheelchair I actually felt a great sense of freedom. It was completely liberating for me, because I could now play with my mates, go to school on my own and do all kinds of things in many different ways.

My parents were brilliant. They never told me that having a wheelchair was a limitation. There were those, of course, who would try to convince my parents that my being a wheelchair user was a big problem, but Mum and Dad would never tell me that. As I got older, other people would also say to me 'how sad it was' that I should be in a wheelchair, but I'd just go, 'OK, fine. Think that if you want . . .'. For me, I've never felt that there's anything that I've not been able to do, simply because I'm in a wheelchair. Granted, I haven't done a bungee jump yet, but that's only because I'm afraid of heights! I certainly could do so if I really wanted to, and there are, in fact, *loads* of things you *can* do, even though you have a wheelchair.

But of course, some disabled people do find it more difficult – I have friends in wheelchairs who really struggle. They find it hard to come to terms with their disability and feel that they have had something taken away from them. It's a complex area, because it depends not just on the mindset of the individual and the environment they're in, but mostly, perhaps, on the people around them. The problem is, if you have a child that is born with a congenital impairment, the first thing parents are told is, 'I'm very sorry to have to tell you this, but . . .' And I think it's very sad that the whole language around disability is still so negative today, because ultimately, it can set the tone of *non-aspiration* for any young disabled person.

Media coverage of the Paralympic Games in recent times has certainly been really good for changing attitudes and stimulating an interest in disabled people in many positive ways. The Games are now seen as a mainstream sporting competition for disabled athletes and not just as a sideshow for the Olympics. But at the same time, it is frustrating when you hear – as you often do – that a young disabled person has been told, 'Don't worry, you can still become a Paralympian!' When one thinks about it, this is actually both naïve and absurd. It is just the same as telling a non-disabled child, 'You're *not* disabled, so you can therefore become an Olympic athlete . . .' Because the demands on a disabled athlete are just the same as those on any non-disabled athlete – you still require talent, you still need a huge amount of training and hard work, and you also need a bit of good luck. So, when a young disabled person hears something like that, all we are really doing is shutting down their aspirations and telling them that because of their disability, their options are now limited, so their only hope is perhaps to become a Paralympian . . .

When I was young, by good fortune, we lived in a part of Cardiff that was relatively accessible and wheelchair-friendly. I was attending a mainstream school when I first started to use a chair, and my parents campaigned hard to ensure that I could go on to attend a mainstream high school as well (which included threatening to sue the secretary of state for Wales over my rights to do so at the time!). They wanted to make sure that I could have as normal a life and education as possible. When I look back now, what my parents fought so hard for and managed to achieve for me was *hugely* important. I will always be enormously grateful to them for that.

There is another common misconception about disabled people: the assumption is that because someone is disabled, they must also be ill, and this is where a lot of people become confused. Of course, some disabled people will also be ill, but most are not. In my case, I have never really been ill – I have only been disabled.

We need to encourage disabled people to be forward-looking. They need to be able to feel positive about their future, that they can lead a normal life, and can enjoy being part of the same community and society as any able-bodied person. But at the moment, it's still fairly hard. Once again, the language around disability remains quite negative.

I recall recently hearing a non-disabled person talking about a group of wheelchair users and referring to them as 'wheelies'. I felt compelled to point out to that person just how rude and deeply offensive a description like that can be. The world has since moved on with equality and protected characteristics, and we now know what we should and should not say when describing others. But the same values, unfortunately, do not seem to always apply when describing disability. Referring to someone solely by their personal appearance in this way should also be considered inappropriate, because such language and such a tone can only serve to depress once again, the aspirations of a young disabled person – especially if they become conditioned to being only described by the wheelchair they're sitting in.

Today, I spend a lot of my time using the platform that being a member of the House of Lords has given me to campaign for disability rights, and to help change attitudes and beliefs. One of the most widely held perceptions that needs to be overhauled is that just because someone is disabled, we should not automatically assume that they *can't do* anything. We should actually be demanding *more* from disabled people, not less.

A huge amount still has to change as well with regard to transport and access, as well as to the attitudes that can make this possible. And, it really shouldn't be so difficult today for the parents of a disabled child to get them the right education and social care. Everything still becomes such a fight and it really shouldn't be that way.

Attitude and positivity . . .

There are times in one's life when things do not go according to plan. Sometimes, it seems totally unfair. And it's completely OK to say, 'That's not fair!' But I believe that it's much better to say, 'That's not fair but that's life, and *this* is what I'm going to do about it!'

When I was no longer able to walk, even at such a young age I kind of knew that there was nothing I could do about it. I just wanted to get on with all of the things I *could* do. I did not want to dwell on the things I couldn't do.

I was fortunate when I was young because my parents were so positive. They always refused to accept that I was unable to go to a mainstream high school, which is why they worked hard to get me in. If they had not have done that, if they hadn't been such a positive force around me, I'm not sure if my life would have turned out the same.

When one has low expectations for disabled people, or any young person for that matter, the chances are that they'll grow up believing that they'll never be able to 'achieve'. And, it's primarily because the people around them believe that in the first place. If I had the power to change one thing, it would be to see *all* young disabled people assume naturally, and by default, that they have the right to pursue *anything* that *any* non-disabled person can do. Sadly, many of our young disabled today just assume instead that there's this whole mass of things that they will never be able to do.

We have a saying in my family, which is to 'aim high!' Set yourself a goal that stretches you, dream about achieving it and just go for it! Unless you try, you will never achieve. And that's exactly what I did. It is then about creating the right attitude around what you have to do, working hard and being persistent, building your self-belief and simply being positive about your future. When talking with others about my time as an athlete, I still often get asked, 'So, what did you have to sacrifice?' (the inference being that there also has to be a downside). But I will always say, 'Nothing!' Because, essentially, being an athlete was what I actually *wanted* to do.

Your attitude is such an important part of how you deal with problems throughout life. I know that I can definitely achieve a lot more when I am feeling positive, because it can be difficult dealing with life's emotional ups and downs. When things go wrong, you need to get back to focusing on your goal, just keep going and always look forward. This has certainly worked for me during some of the biggest challenges I have had to face in my life.

It was during the time I was competing in the Athens Paralympic Games that I had a particularly difficult few days at the start of the competition. My first race was in the 800 metres. The semi-finals went quite well, but while I was on the track for the final race, I just 'knew' that I was not going to be my best. In the past, I have had moments when I had absolutely no doubts that I was going to win a race or break a world record, but this was completely the opposite – I had a real sense that I was going to fail. I started off pretty well in the race, but then things started to go wrong. I ended up finishing in my worst position in any Paralympic race, and it was also one of the worst 800 metre performances of my career.

I was completely distraught at the end of the race. When I saw my husband, he was also upset. I then had to provide a trackside interview for the BBC, which was not easy. I felt that I had let my team down and my country down, and not least my family and friends, most of whom had naturally come to the race to watch me perform well. I finally got to the stands where they were seated, and everyone was visibly upset. Many were completely lost for words. I then looked for my young daughter Carys, who curiously seemed blissfully unaware of what had just happened. I asked her if she saw Mummy's race, and she simply said, 'No, I was eating a hot dog.' It certainly changed the mood at that moment and brought a smile to everyone's face, but it also helped me in a way to put everything into perspective. This was just a single race in my career, a big one to lose, of course, but not the end of the world. The biggest challenge for me now was that I had three more big events to compete in, for which I needed to somehow mentally prepare myself.

The next two days of training before my next event, the 100 metres, were incredibly hard. It was crucial that I rebuilt my confidence, and I knew that I had to remain positive. I reminded myself over and over that I had actually performed really well all season and there was no reason why I shouldn't be doing well at these Games. But I remember on the day of the 100 metre final, I was as nervous as I have ever been at any time in my life before a race. Jason, one of my team coaches who was looking after me on the day, was hugely encouraging, and I remember my husband Ian, who was trackside, wishing me good luck with a smile. Both of them really helped.

But one of the most extraordinary things occurred when one of my principal competitors in the race, an Italian athlete named Francesca

Porcellato, came over to talk to me. I knew her well. We had competed against each other over many years, and during the last year before the Paralympics she had consistently come second to me in every 100 metre race. She would also be going for gold in this, the most important race of the year. I told her in all honesty that I wasn't feeling good after my 800 metres fail (she had won a medal in that race). Francesca then did something really incredible, which I will never forget. She could easily have tried to play mind games with me to spoil my concentration before the race, but instead, she smiled and said, 'You are the best in the world. No one has come near you this season in the 100 metres. It's your race to win . . .' What she did was not only exceptional but one of the kindest things I have ever experienced in my sporting career. I knew I had a mountain to climb after the last race, but her words and encouragement really helped me.

I went on to win gold. It was one of the happiest moments of my racing career, and when I left the track I felt really good. I also felt ready this time for the interviews and to see my family and friends, and I was now far more confident about the next two important races that were ahead of me in the Games.

Success is often about how you deal with failure. When something goes seriously wrong, you can either give up or you can dig deep, recover your self-belief and focus once more upon your goal. It is all about your attitude and being positive, even when everything sometimes seems stacked against you.

Listening to the right people who can help you . . .

When I first started wheelchair racing, I wasn't very good. I had to follow the right steps and in the right order so that I could improve. I was, of course, incredibly lucky to have such a huge amount of support from my parents, who helped me to plan for what those steps looked like and how to get organised.

I knew I had to get on the school team first. After that, it would potentially be the junior team, then the junior Welsh team and then the junior GB team. Beyond these were the four-year cycles to aim for: the European Championships, the World Championships, the Commonwealth Games and, of course, the Paralympics. So my parents helped me to map out this whole life in front of me, with all the events and dates included.

My mum and dad were also incredibly grounding, as well as being supportive. They encouraged me to do well, but they were also the first to teach me not to be scared to fail. In the early days, when I was failing a lot (I actually lost a lot of races throughout my athletics career), my parents helped me to draw from the good and the bad that I did, and how to learn different things from both winning and losing. My father was also very keen that I had other things in my life, and not just sport. He told me that I could go off and become a full-time athlete once I'd got my degree at university. He would encourage me to read and acquire knowledge, of course, but also showed me how to do other things and how to contribute in different ways, and not be entirely focused on being an athlete.

I remember once, I had been away training in Australia for about three months. When I got back home, I went for dinner with my parents and I started telling them all about the training I'd done, where I was doing it and what it was like. After a while, my father said, 'OK, so you trained a lot. I've got that, let's move on. Did you do anything else?' It was really his way of bringing me back down to earth again. When you train hard, it's easy to get too internally focused in a way, because it all becomes very personal, and requires a certain level of selfishness and determination. But still, my family did allow me to be selfish; they let me miss lots of parties, birthdays, Christmases and other events because of my training. But they also encouraged me to retain a balance.

Having that support and that amount of honesty around you can be really levelling. I know of some athletes who didn't have that, but I think it really helps when you do, and it doesn't necessarily need to be from your family. It's all about having people close to you who understand what you want, who can calm you down when you do well and who can pick up the pieces with you when you don't. My family certainly understood what my drive was and what I wanted to do. And whether I won or lost, my dad would always tell me what he thought of my race. My husband Ian, who was also a Paralympic wheelchair athlete, would also tell it to me straight. Such honesty from those closest to me was really cool and always helpful.

What you *don't* need as an athlete is people telling you that you're 'brilliant' all the time, because that's not the real world. That doesn't actually make you any better! It just makes you self-centred and even complacent. Yes, of course, as a successful athlete, when people recognise you, and they come up to you and say, 'You're Tanni. Hi,' that's really nice, and people are often lovely. But my dad would always say, 'Don't believe your own publicity.' I think that was good, important advice and grounding once again. I soon learned to recognise a need to 'separate' myself in a way, and to keep my own view of 'me' distinct from the public's view of me. In the end, that certainly worked well, and it almost became like having two different lives, really.

And I think it's really important to have what I call 'critical friends' in your life. These are the people who are both aware of what you are doing and who are also sensitive to the right way and the right time to tell you about something you need to know. Because there are certain times when you can tell someone that they need to sort themselves out, and there are times when that's simply not right. It's back to honesty again, because your critical friends are those that you can rely on for *real* advice. You also know that they really care. It may be a family member or a close friend or a mentor, but their views are held separate from all of the opinions and advice that may be offered by others. I soon learned it was always much better to listen to my critical friends than to listen to 'other' people.

I've had journalists say to me, for example, 'That was the worst race I've ever seen you do!' I would say, 'Okay. Thanks!' I could detach myself from that and not take it personally, because that's their job. And sometimes, when perhaps I've made a mistake and done badly in a race, people have come up to me and said, 'What did you do that for? I'd never have done that!' The problem is that everyone has got an opinion, especially in sport. Some might have an opinion that's well-meaning and right, while others may have an opinion that's well-meaning but wrong. Sometimes people can also be malicious, so you have to always take a step back and understand the motivation behind what you're being told, because everyone's motivation will be different. That is much easier to do when you get older, of course – it's not so easy when you're still young.

So it's important to detach yourself from the opinions of other people. You need to rely more on what *you* know yourself about what *you* have done to get to where you are now (which is why keeping a training diary is so important), and to listen only to your critical friends. When I competed in Barcelona at the 1992 Paralympic Games, I won four gold medals and one silver. Four years later, at the 1996 Paralympics in Atlanta, I won one gold medal and three silvers, and I vividly recall a particular team manager telling me that I was now 'all washed up and should immediately retire'. I was really shocked! I remember saying back to him, 'But I'm not ready to retire!' and he said, 'Yeah, but you *should*, and *now*!'

While I have seen other athletes in similar circumstances have a knee-jerk reaction and say, 'Right that's it! I'm retiring!' I wanted to wait until I got home first so that I could discuss it with my family, with my critical friends, and take time to assess everything very carefully. Thankfully, I decided in the end to carry on for another four years . . . At the 2000 Paralympics in Sydney, I went on to win four more gold medals.

Mentors and influencers . . .

There were a number of people that I think of as mentors, who helped and supported me throughout my athletics career. My parents were my early mentors, of course, and were definitely a huge influence during the early stages of my becoming an athlete. Chris Hallam was an extraordinary sportsman and coach, who achieved an enormous amount in his time to promote wheelchair racing, well before the

Paralympics even came into existence. He inspired me to get involved in the sport and was a great mentor to me.

My husband Ian was one of my biggest influences and mentor, mainly because I always wanted to beat him! He was an accomplished wheelchair racer himself and competed in two Paralympic Games. I knew whenever I was training, that if I could get even close to his best times, I had a chance of becoming the best woman in the world in the sport. So this became a key target for me to achieve, every day that I went out and trained.

Having mentored several young athletes myself, I know that the relationship between mentor and mentee is a special one, but can be finely balanced. For a relationship to work, a mentor has to feel that they are genuinely adding value, in order to remain invested and interested. A mentor also has to care about the individual they are mentoring, which means they have got to really know them well. But it's not always quite so straightforward – sometimes a mentee may be reluctant to talk, or even speak out about a specific issue, and a mentor has to be able to read some of those nuances. The best relationships are where there's an open dialogue and trust. It also takes time to build a relationship, which is not a quick or easy thing to do. I always wanted to see any mentee of mine perform in lots of different environments, because only then can you truly see how they react to different situations. Their own feelings about how they are performing on the track while their heart rate is racing at 195 beats per minute will usually be different to what I see when I'm watching them from the side.

In sport, I think a young person can look for a mentor quite early on, certainly while in their teens. Finding a mentor is a challenge, though, and has to be done in the right way. It starts with finding someone you can talk to easily, that you can have an open dialogue with, and who is genuinely interested in you and what you are doing. It's also being not afraid to ask; when I was a teenager, I was really, really shy, but sport soon pulled me 'out of myself', because I very much wanted to learn and to become better. It made me talk to people, and ask them for their help and support. But there is a certain way to approach people, and there are important skills that need to be learned. They include understanding how to communicate, and knowing how to write an email or a letter properly.

Goals . . .

It is, of course, good to have a main goal (or a few goals), but it's also important to have smaller goals, or stepping stones, in between that can enable you to reach your end goals. You don't go straight from winning a junior championship race to winning a gold medal in one leap! There are lots of important steps in between, and it's essential to know what these look like.

Setting goals is really about knowing where you are going, and it starts with a plan. Once you have an end goal, you can work back to your starting point (where you are now) and then plan for all the steps you need to reach, while anticipating potential obstacles you might encounter along the way.

But you also have to be flexible. As you improve or you change, you have to adapt your goals and targets accordingly – it's a continual process of re-evaluation. When I was training, there was always a number of different targets that I would be aiming for within a year. My short-term goals might be to reach those targets, but if I hit one earlier than expected, I would immediately revise that target and raise the bar.

Your education . . .

Education is hugely important, and was massively so for me! Whether it's through your formal education or apprenticeships, reading the newspapers, volunteering or any other form of learning activity, education gives you choices. It creates opportunities too.

But it's also learning about the world we live in, the environment that surrounds us and the valuable platform that having this knowledge gives us. I recall many years ago the legendary basketball player Michael Jordan saying that his best advice would be 'to read the newspapers every day'. He was going to functions, he was going to dinners, meeting high-powered business executives and politicians all the time – they might want to discuss basketball with him for a while, but a point would come when the talk would move on to other things, and he didn't want to find himself being excluded from those conversations.

Being educated also helps us to know *how* to take advantage of opportunities when they are presented to us.

Making the most of opportunity . . .

Educating yourself, dedicating time to preparation and working really hard (training, in the case of an athlete) puts you in the best position to make the most out of opportunities when they arise. It's a way of 'making your own luck'. The widely acclaimed golfer Gary Player is often credited with having said, 'The harder I practise, the luckier I get.'

And we've all heard the expression, 'being in the right place at the right time'. That certainly happens, but it's doing everything you can to *put* yourself in that situation in the first place that really counts. It's knowing how to prepare for those opportunities and recognising them when they're in front of you. One thing I have always aimed to do is to make the most out of every single opportunity that has ever been presented to me, and there are very few that I've not tried to take advantage of. I have always been more concerned about failing to realise when there has been an opportunity, and then missing out on something extremely important as a consequence.

You can be the fastest person on the start line, but that doesn't necessarily mean you're going to win the race (I've certainly been there . . .). But I've also *not* been the fastest person on the start line and have still gone on to win the race. So yes, one can sometimes be lucky or unlucky, but that's why you have to do everything possible to improve your chances. Once again, it's all down to a combination of learning, preparation, hard work and then making the most of an opportunity.

Part of preparation is also being organised. I have seen incredibly talented athletes who have failed to secure their place on the national team, who then missed out on an entire four-year cycle, simply by not being organised. I recall one athlete who hadn't realised when the closing date for selection was and thought it was two days later; they made the required time but had to be told by the A-team manager, 'Unfortunately, you haven't actually qualified because the closing date was yesterday!' I recall them saying to me, 'I didn't think that was the *real* closing date!' I personally thought that was both incredible and unforgivable. As an athlete, I always learned everything I possibly could about the selection processes, all the dates, and what needed to be achieved by when.

To parents . . .

I firmly believe that parents should allow their children to go out and explore. Just let them go, let them try different things and find out what they like to do for themselves. Be there as a parachute, but don't try to wrap your kids in cotton wool. Most children are quite resilient; they just need to be given a chance to see what they like and what they don't like. But one of the difficulties in saying that, of course, is that it very quickly comes down to resources – some families may not be able to allow their children to try *everything* they would like to do. So parents may also need to be creative in providing different experiences and finding different options for their children to sample. The point is that they should not just leave it all up to their kids to find out.

Throughout my life, my parents have certainly encouraged me to try out new things and to always aim to be the best I can possibly be. When I chose to become an athlete, my family were amazing.

They understood that completely and supported me throughout, and it was very good to have that from them. At first, my mum thought it was quite funny that I should choose to be a wheelchair athlete, but then it was like, 'Well, OK, if that's what you really want to do . . .'

Having travelled extensively, and after working at lots of different things, my experience of life is naturally quite broad. I can now sit down with Carys, my teenage daughter, and ask her, 'So, have you thought about this?' But even then, I cannot realistically know everything that she might like or not like. There might also be things that she's contemplating doing but cannot yet quite articulate to me or my husband. And I've said to her, 'Don't just let the world pass you by. Create something from it for yourself.' With the internet today, young people can discover all sorts of different things in a way that simply was not possible before.

I also think it's good to get kids involved in domestic activities from an early age. When Carys was quite young, I used to get her to cook and bake – yes, we had to sample some rather 'interesting' cakes, but she also made some really good ones too! It was all about encouraging her to take a bit more responsibility for herself, and it's what my parents also did with me. Because it's a great way to get kids to learn about trying and failing (at the smaller things), and it builds their resilience too.

Some children are naturally more resilient than others. But again, I think it's important for parents to let their kids try things and then fail, to learn from those things by themselves (while being there as the support to pick them back up).

Learning about making choices is important too. We used to present Carys with lots of choices from quite an early age. With clothes it might be just, 'It's this outfit or it's that one – you choose,' but she also knew that once she had chosen, *that* was what she was going to wear. So, from these small steps, she would begin to learn about the consequences of good choices and bad choices. And, in a way, children need to make some bad choices, so that they can then learn from the experience. In years to come, when they are presented with really serious choices, they will have a context to help them to choose wisely.

Being a good parent is always challenging, especially when you lead a busy life. Trying to get the balance right between work life and home life can often be very difficult. But I remember someone once telling me, 'You don't need to be the best mum in the world; you just need to be the best mum for Carys.' I have always thought that was really sound advice.

And finally, parents must spend time with their kids and talk to them. Have proper conversations. Don't just sit them in front of the screen because it's convenient. Have dinner together and talk. Communicating with your children and getting them involved is one of the most valuable things you can do.

Anya Hindmarch CBE

World-renowned accessories designer Anya Hindmarch founded her business in London in 1987, and has since built a global brand with over 30 stores worldwide, including flagships in London, New York and Tokyo. With creativity, craftsmanship and personalisation at the heart of everything she does, her bags and accessories are highly prized today. A passionate advocate of British design and arts, Anya is also a UK trade ambassador, a non-executive director of the British Fashion Council and a trustee of both the Royal Academy of Arts and the Design Museum. In 2017 Anya was awarded a CBE in recognition of her contribution to the British fashion industry. She has also received several prestigious annual designer awards, including three British Fashion Awards, three *Glamour* Awards and an Elle Style Award.

'I think there are three things that a young person needs to understand the importance of, when preparing for a successful life: confidence, doing things to the best of their ability and hard work.'

'The harder you work, the sooner you'll get where you want to go and the more you'll get done. Also, the harder you work, the more you push and the braver you are, the more you'll begin to *make your own luck* – and more doors will open for you.'

'Having a positive attitude is absolutely essential if you want to become successful in life. But you *can* learn how to develop the right attitude, and it also *really* helps to surround and associate yourself with people who have a positive attitude as well.'

'We have to continually remind ourselves again and again to trust in our kids because they *are* smart and *are* able to work things out for themselves. We should tell them they are *good* and that they must trust their own judgement – having a sense of 'self' and the confidence to 'listen' to it is really important when they are young.'

About success . . .

When thinking about success and what it means to me, it tends to revolve around my work and my business, which is something I love doing and is such a major part of my life. But it's much more than just growing your business or making profits; for me, it's about the whole team that's involved and also the journey – both are unbelievably important – and the legacy we're creating as well. When I think about my business as an entity, for me it's the people, the positive force and positive culture that exists within it.

The world of fashion is fast-moving, with a high element of risk, which makes it very exciting but at the same time, *you're only as good as your last collection*. So I never dwell on success, and frankly, I don't have time to.

For me, the journey I have taken is endlessly scary, and I'm perpetually focused on what I have to do next. I never sit down and think, 'Great, we've achieved that.' I'm more likely to think about what I *haven't* done, and I'm always anxious about the next thing, albeit in a positive way. Fashion is exciting, but also a tortuous place to be sometimes. I do believe, however, that the moment you stop and think, 'I'm a success,' that's when things will start to go wrong. So I'm only ever thinking about the next mountain to scale, really.

Starting your journey . . .

I was sixteen when I was given an old Gucci handbag by my mother. I still remember how that made me feel at the time, and it was to spark my early interest in the world of fashion – and bags in particular.

After a year studying in Florence, I was impressed by Italian design and decided to import into the UK a number of drawstring leather duffel bags that had become fashionable in Italy, which I then sold successfully through a readers' offer in *Harpers & Queen* magazine.

That was really the *naissance* of my business, but having always been fascinated by how things are made, I then started to both design and manufacture my own range of high-quality bags in London. I sold them initially through luxury retail stores in London before seeing them reach outlets in New York, Tokyo, Paris and elsewhere.

Fashion has always fascinated me. When you think about it, no one really needs another piece of clothing. Most of us have enough clothes to keep us warm, dry and for all seasons, but we still go out and buy more clothes than we actually need. But of course, fashion is fundamentally about how we want the world to see us. When I leave home, how I dress, how I hold myself, how I wear my hair and how I project myself – it says an awful lot about me. It's an amazing set of tools in a way.

Speaking as a woman (but it's the same for a man), I know that if I dress a certain way, I then feel confident about what I'm wearing. I'm just being *me* and I'm able to feel good. There might also be times when I want to wear something a bit more *directional*, and other times I might go to a board meeting and need to dress in a certain way because I want to be taken seriously.

There's a whole range of unwritten 'rules' in fashion that people can follow, with different tribes they can join and ways to either respect or mess up traditions, both of which can say loads about the person. So, it's a totally fascinating 'other language', and I find the psychological value of fashion really interesting, and especially how it can really empower people.

It was certainly a very fertile time in the UK when I first started my business. It was 'Thatcher's Britain' then (love it or loathe it), but it was also a time for entrepreneurial creativity and momentum. It was almost like a 'lab' for start-ups – a lot of businesses that are very successful today were first created around that time. I was also fortunate because I came from an entrepreneurial family, which was really helpful when I got started.

My first big turning point happened when I opened our first store. It was on the first floor because I couldn't afford a ground-floor store at that stage, but it provided a great opportunity to engage with the customer directly, as opposed to selling through other stores, where they'd meet the end-user. This was pivotal for me, because being able to talk with your customer really focuses the mind on what you need to do.

As our reputation grew, opportunities to export overseas unfolded and we soon established our first international store in Hong Kong. I was still quite young and barely knew what a 'franchise agreement' was at the time, but my eyes were opened up to a huge export market. I discovered that England was just a small island, really, and we'd got this whole wide world to sell to. From the learning curve of establishing that first franchise, this enabled us to open stores in Japan, Singapore and Malaysia, and on it went.

When you grow your business, there are definite steps you take and levels you have to reach – it's a bit like going from nursery to junior school to secondary school . . . There are deals you may do and contracts you might sign, some good, some bad. I think it's a combination of all of those things – not necessarily one single thing – that enables you to move forward. It's just constantly tightening screws, and it's definitely a real journey.

The people who support you . . .

People are fundamental to growing any business. It's about finding your team – the people you want to surround yourself with and spend your days with (it's a bit like putting together a really good dinner party). You learn how to manage and keep them, to be honest with them, value and get the best out of them, and also to give them the best of what you are doing collectively as well.

We all need a support system to help us, especially when building a business. It can be very lonely without someone you can turn to when needed. I'm unbelievably lucky to have the support of my family. My father, in particular, has always been there for me. Whenever I have a problem, I can literally ring him at three o'clock in the morning and he'll happily talk it through with me, worry about it for me, sleep on it and then call me back in the morning. He has always been like a mentor to me, but at the same time, my harshest critic. It's important to have someone like that in your life who is really honest with you and who will tell you, 'No, that wasn't good.'

My husband has also been hugely supportive and works with me in the business. When you are running an organisation, you need to be bright and positive, but there are times when you do want to crawl into a hole too, because we're all human. Having somebody close that you can do that with is very important – someone who you can show your face to, lock the door and then just talk to.

When you are much younger, it can also be very helpful to have an older person you can turn to for advice. It could be an uncle or a godparent or a close family friend, but someone who likes you and with whom you have an affinity. There are usually lots of people around who would be happy to help. It can also be very rewarding for someone to feel that they have been able to help a younger person. One of the most wonderful things is to receive a letter from somebody saying, 'you have made a big difference in my life.'

So don't be afraid to ask someone for help. Just say something like, 'It would be lovely if we could meet up for an hour or so once a month, to brainstorm things with you and ask for your advice.' Someone that likes you and who is in a position to help will probably say yes. But, it's still 'a big ask', so never take that person for granted. Be sensitive about the time they're willing to give you, and prepare a list of things to discuss so that you can be organised. You also have to give them back loads – dote on them, bring them cakes, remember their birthday. It's just common sense, really.

You can also start with people who naturally 'offer themselves' to you – teachers are amazing people and should not be underestimated. I'm sure that 90 per cent of teachers go into teaching because they genuinely *want* to help children. Kids will often view them as just 'teachers', but it's really quite a tough job, not necessarily the best-paid one, and they do it because they want to make a difference. If you like a teacher and they like you, then just ask them if you can seek their advice from time to time. Teachers have feelings too, and it's a special thing to be wanted and appreciated.

It's fundamentally important for all young people to learn early that there's as much pleasure in giving as there is in receiving. But it must not be giving in expectation of something in return. It's just giving for its own sake.

There's a lovely concept called the 'favour bank' that my son's godfather wrote to him about, on the day before his confirmation. He was a banker, and he described in an amusingly self-deprecating way that while 'all bankers are terrible', the favour bank is actually the truest bank you can have. It's a bank into which you regularly pay *favours* – it might be when you're especially kind to somebody, or you do something that really helps them out, or spare them some time when they have a problem . . . You pay these favours in and you never expect anything in return. But actually, one day when you need some help yourself, the bank always pays out. And life is truly like that – if you give generously without any expectation, when you need something yourself, people will always be there, happy to help you.

So for me, it's been about all of those people who have been kind and generous enough to want to help me and to mentor me during my journey. It's an unbelievably generous thing for them to give, something I will always truly value; and actually, it's something that I feel a real responsibility to be able to give back over time.

Prepare for the journey . . .

I think there are three things that a young person needs to understand the importance of, when preparing for a successful life: confidence, doing things to the best of their ability and hard work.

Confidence is the thing that empowers you to take each decisive step along your journey. If you look at any successful person at the top of the tree, and then work backwards and plot how they became successful, it's because they did this, which led to that, which then led to this and so on . . . It's essentially a 'decision tree', which you can track all the way back down to the beginning. Some will have been good decisions along the way and some bad. The good ones will have taken them up, the bad ones may have taken them in the wrong direction or down again – it's a bit like snakes and ladders.

Once you have made a decision to do something, if you do it to the very best of your ability, you will be noticed, and new doors will naturally open up for you that can lead you through to greater things. But if you decide not to open a door that's presented, or you end up doing something badly (so that the door which could have opened, will not do so now), you may never know about that amazing route that would have been out there for you to take.

When my son was asked recently to do a speech for a friend's eighteenth birthday, I remember telling him, 'Just have a go and do it really well, because if you do, you'll probably be asked to do something else again, and that could lead to something extraordinary that you don't even know about yet.'

It's about striving, pushing and taking every opportunity to shine. So, at school, just put your hand up in class and say; 'I'll do it!' Wow the pants off whoever you are trying to do it with and be amazed by what happens. Just make the best effort you possibly can because with every step you take, you will also know now that 'I can do that!' and your confidence will grow.

Hard work is also really crucial. The harder you work, the sooner you'll get where you want to go and the more you'll get done. Also, the harder you work, the more you push and the braver you are, the more you'll begin to *make your own luck* – and more doors will open for you.

And one of the nicest things about doing something that you really love is that it actually doesn't feel like hard work!

Finding what you want to do . . .

You have to try *lots* of things. It starts with being cheeky, opportunistic and literally volunteering yourself to do things. For example, once you have an inkling about what you would like to do for work or as a career, try approaching firms in the field that you are interested in – write a letter to the owner or the boss and simply say something like, 'I have read everything about your company and love what you do. I'm thinking about my future career and I would give all of my pocket money to be able to spend a morning at your office, even just sitting in reception, to watch and learn more about you.'

Any good employer would think, 'This kid is really keen' and will probably want to help you – and who knows what this might lead to. So you have to be willing, you've got to be charismatic, and also that little bit cheeky.

I once received a letter from a girl who was working in one of my stores in which she said, 'If I pay you £1,000, can I come with you to Paris Fashion Week?' She didn't have a £1,000 to spare, of course, and I wouldn't have taken it from her anyway, but I remember thinking, 'I like you, you're a bit cocky – and that's interesting.' And lo and behold, I took her into our office, she soon became my PA, then became head of PR and subsequently set up my office in New York. She eventually moved on to work for the wife of the British prime minister in Downing Street and, ultimately, set up her own business . . .

On another occasion, a young guy approached us for a job. I remember saying to him, 'We have nothing available at the moment, but our receptionist is off next week. Why don't you come in for a couple of days? I'll pay you a little bit and you can just learn . . .'. So he came in and was just great – he brought in a large box of chocolates for everyone at Christmas and he even said, 'Can I repaint that door for you? It looks like it could do with some paint around the corner.' He just *wowed* me, and I'll do anything for that person now.

So you've got to be a bit cocky in life, but in a charming way. Charm is so important, and it comes, really, from being more interested in the people you are talking to than trying to make them interested in you. Charm is also being bright-eyed and bushy-tailed, and this naturally makes you more charismatic.

When people impress me, I'm willing to do a lot for them. Kids need to learn this early too, and it starts at school. When you impress your teacher because you put your hand up and volunteer to be in charge of 'recycling' or something, they will think, 'You know what? You're smart, that's initiative . . .', and they will look out for you. One day, when you ask them for help with something, they'll be happy to do so because they like helping people like you . . . and so it goes on in life.

I am also much more impressed with kids that take their own initiative to open a door for themselves. I'm less impressed when it's their parents who are trying to open doors for them. While we're all asked to help our godchildren or the children of friends, I always keep a 'quota' for kids who independently approach me, who are brave and who show initiative. And I believe it's incumbent on all employers to always give kids like that a chance.

Education . . .

I think education *can* be fantastically important, and I have fought very hard to provide the best education I can for my kids. I went to a very good school, but paradoxically it didn't work so well for me because I think I learned differently to most. I was diagnosed with dyslexia early on, which was interesting because while I know I have a good brain, I recollect that I didn't *feel* bright at school and it didn't seem like I was thriving. There was also very little learning support in those days, which might have been more helpful. It is ironic now how I just love to learn, but when I look back at my schooling, I feel that I didn't really learn enough at that time.

But I did go to a convent school, was taught by nuns and had a more spiritual education. It certainly made me think about how I behaved, what my responsibilities were and how to treat other people, which was all very helpful. So for me, there are a million versions of different school environments, and in one school I think you can be educated in a hundred different ways, some positive, some negative . . . There are some people who will thrive at school, while others will not. I know a lot of what I call 'very stupid clever people', and I also know many very clever but not necessarily academically successful people – so I think your education should not really define you.

I do believe the best education is actually *self-education*, when you're naturally motivated to learn. I will always value emotional intelligence (EQ) *far more* than IQ. EQ will actually usually get you further, I think, than IQ, although it depends on what you are doing. The dream is obviously to have both a healthy EQ and IQ, in equal measure.

Self-doubt and failure . . .

When I speak to young people about being an entrepreneur, it's usually very reassuring for them to learn that *everyone* who starts their own business and who ends up enjoying real success, will have had the same sense of self-doubt – and will have had to manage the same hurdles and negativity along the way – as anyone else.

It can be really tough at times, and there are occasions when you just want to hide yourself away. You don't know the answers, and you're just trying to figure your way through. But, do you know what? That's just *completely normal*, and we all just have to learn to live with that.

As a designer and an entrepreneur, one of the biggest challenges for me is having to put out a collection, with my name above it, exposing it publicly while saying, 'This is what I like, everyone. Judge me on it, give me a score.' And that can be very hard sometimes. You have to know that along with the peaks you will also have the dips, and these *will* happen at regular intervals. You have to be able to take them when they come, and that's all part of the life of an entrepreneur. Some people find it too hard, which is fine, because there are lots of other career opportunities out there where you can find success with less risk.

We all sometimes lack a little confidence about doing something big, and it can be a struggle. Whenever that happens, the best thing you can do is to think back to when you have previously done something similar – it might be recalling the speech that went down well, or the presentation you delivered excellently at school, or where you volunteered to do that project and it turned out fantastically . . . Take yourself back to that place, and remember how brilliant you were and how good it felt. Tell yourself, 'I did this well once before, and I know I can do it again.' And that is why it's so important, especially when you are young, to do lots of things and get as many successes as you can under your belt, so that you can draw upon them in the future, when required.

And should something occasionally not go well for you, then you have got to be able to say, 'There are always going to be one or two,' and then think back to the occasions when things *have* gone well. Because success is usually made up of a patchwork of failures. If you're sailing a boat, you might be going from A to B, but you have to tack a bit to the left and then tack to the right, and each time you are actually going in the wrong direction – so it's a hundred failures, but you will eventually get to your correct destination. Winston Churchill once famously said, 'Success is going from failure to failure without loss of enthusiasm . . .' If something doesn't work, don't give up. Go back, and try, try and try again . . .

When big mistakes happen, which they inevitably do from time to time, everyone must be really honest about them. You have to be frank with yourself and with your team about what happened and the reasons why. You must be able to say, 'OK, what are we going to do now to put this right?' while communicating about everything in a very clear way.

You should never duck an issue or try to blame someone else. I'm OK when mistakes happen in my organisation and someone tells me, 'I've really messed up, but I know what I've done wrong and I'll make sure it doesn't happen again.' For me, that's fine. They have admitted their mistake, they know what to do about it and, by learning the hard way, they are much less likely to make the same mistake again. It is when someone tries to spin what's happened or attempts to cover it up that I become concerned or angry. They are far more likely to do the same thing again by not being honest about things – and by *not* learning from their mistakes.

Attitude . . .

I think that attitude is *everything* and is absolutely essential for your journey. I can never stress this enough when talking to young people.

It's just amazing what you can do with the right attitude. When leading, you can take your people over the trenches if you have to: 'Come on, guys, we can do this!' It's simply teamwork and good leadership. Your family is a squad, your company is another squad, and you've got to be right in there, banging the drum, making it the best team in the world, making it have a sense of identity.

Finding a positive attitude as a young person is partially down to mindset (whether you naturally see that glass as half full or half empty . . .), but there are also plenty of ways to train your brain, because anyone can actually develop the right attitude. It starts, though, with embracing the fact that your brain is really capable of so much more, and then you have to *want* to change and *want* to learn how to.

I used to have a pathological fear of public speaking, to the point where you could offer me a million dollars and I still couldn't do it! One day, I decided that this was just not good enough, and so I looked for a solution. I discovered neuro-linguistic programming, and this enabled me to completely conquer my fear. I can now stand up in front of a thousand people and speak with relative confidence.

Having a positive attitude is a much healthier way to approach any issue within an organisation, and I try hard to make it the only way that is acceptable in my business.

When a company has a sales meeting, for example, a manager could say, 'I'm fed up with all of you! We're way off-target and none of you have done what I told you to do!' But, they might say alternatively, 'Look, guys, we've had a tough time recently and we're well behind on our sales target, so this is how we're going to get there. And, if we can achieve *that*, it will be cake all round!'

I like to see all meetings run in a positive way. If a member of my staff says something negative or critical during a meeting, I'll either nicely squash and override it, or I may take them aside afterwards and say, 'Look, I thought you were rather negative in the meeting, and that can simply kill everyone's mood. Let's find a more positive way next time to express things.'

So having a positive attitude is absolutely essential if you want to become successful in life. But you *can* learn how to develop the right attitude, and it also *really* helps to surround and associate yourself with people who have a positive attitude as well.

Goals, visualisation and discipline . . .

I think goals are important, and I also believe in creative visualisation. If you can visualise where you want to be, it is more likely to happen for you. Sportsmen and women often do this, where they *imagine* that they are competing and winning – 'You're running the last lap of the race, you hear the roar of the crowd, you get to the tape and finally, "Boom", you are there!' It's all about *sensing* the experience. It opens up the 'neurological pathways' in some way and reinforces belief.

When I'm preparing to give a big speech (which can still be quite scary!), I will often imagine myself being there at the podium looking out over the hall, then speaking my first line and getting a positive response from the audience. It really helps. Visualisation helps you to break down those barriers. Where you can visualise the endgame, you can then chunk it down into the steps you need to take to get there – and these become your goals.

I find in business, when you are so busy, with everyone demanding so much of your time, you end up mostly running on instinct and following your nose. Management meetings and board meetings therefore become your business goal-setting moments, as a formality and as a discipline.

Discipline is for me very important. It's really all about being 'on time and on budget'. I normally work every Sunday to prepare for the week ahead, to clear the decks and not least my bulging email inbox (which builds up inexorably during the week). I like to start Monday with a completely clear head and with my lists fully prepared. List-making for me is my form of personal goal-setting, and definitely the best way to organise my brain.

For young people, discipline can be a challenge, but there's little point in saying that you are going to do something and then end up not doing it. Whether it's that email you said you would do or that 'Thank you' note you were going to write, you need to be disciplined about getting things done.

And once again, *hard work* is perhaps *the* most important discipline of all. It is something that is absolutely essential to master if you really want to become successful at anything.

Health, well-being and balance . . .

When you have an incredibly busy life, as I do, you have got to learn how to manage the demands of a hectic business alongside managing your family, and everything else. How you cope with this mentally while trying to find the right balance is something that I've given a lot of thought to recently. Mental health is a very topical subject right now, of course, because it affects all of us, and that includes me, my kids, all of my people at work: How happy are you? How good are you feeling about life right now?

I believe that exercise is very important, because it definitely helps your brain. I have found a pattern now (after having tried everything else), which is to go for a four-mile walk, with a girlfriend, three times a week – just walking and talking. For me, it's a really nice way to nourish your body and mind.

I also believe that one of the keys to mental well-being is having someone close to you, that you trust completely, who knows you well too, with whom you can completely offload and discuss any concerns or issues. I can feel so much better after sitting down and talking with *that* person, even for just ten minutes – it's like mind therapy for me.

Some people might look at me and think that I am completely immersed in my work, but I'd say that because I love it so much, half of it is actually fun. My family are also involved with my business, so it all nicely merges together. But there *are* times when the business demands that you give it everything – and you have to make sure that everyone around you understands: 'It's going to be a really tough week, so please bear with me. And if we make it through to Saturday, I'll get the pizzas in!'

Sometimes, you might think, 'I'm feeling really tired, but I've actually done pretty well this month, so I'm going to take a weekend off.' And you must then commit to that – you *must* remember to look after yourself. If you don't take time out to relax, then you cannot operate at your best. Whenever I'm doing endless long-haul travelling, I always make sure I take some personal time out in between, just for me. It's like my little stepping stone in the middle of a busy river, which is a boring sacrifice sometimes, but I just need that to keep going.

I am a great believer in holidays, and we take a lot of trips with the kids to far-flung places. I quite like it when we're on an itinerary and I find it quite relaxing in a strange way, having a guide telling us something about 'that temple' – it really helps to empty the mind and brings you nicely into the present. When I'm just lying by a pool, my mind can easily drift back to work . . .

So be as kind to yourself as you would be to other people. I am actually quite a kind person, but often I'm not as kind to myself, which is probably a typical female thing! So keep pushing and working hard, but be prepared to cut yourself some slack sometimes. Be aware of what your business, your children and your family need, but listen to what your mind and body are telling you too.

To parents . . .

It would certainly be the dream of any average child to have two supportive parents who are 'together' spiritually, with healthy communication and a positive attitude. This is fundamental to good energy flow within a family and most of us accept that it is important.

But that's not to say that someone cannot become successful when they come from an adverse background or from a dysfunctional family either – very often, kids who do experience this end up possessing a drive that's second to none. There are many famously successful individuals who will point to a very difficult start in life, such as losing one of their parents at an early age, for example. On the other hand, family can sometimes be so 'comfortable' that kids just don't find that desire to really push out.

Where there are two parents, it doesn't matter really if they're married, not married, divorced, same-sex or whatever – they must be a positive force for their children's lives and cannot be a distraction. Children are wonderfully selfish and just want to be cared for, and if things are complicated between their parents, it can be hugely disruptive for their children. Kids should almost be in this lovely tunnel of warmth and stability, just pushing on without any distractions, but if they have to hold on to the sides because something bad is going on, it can be horribly upsetting for them. The healthier the family environment, the healthier a child's mental state will become – and their confidence too.

Parents must be positive towards each other when around their children. What some parents forget, and which is fundamentally important, is that when they are talking with their children about their partner, the child is 'half of them'. When they criticise their partner, they are also criticising their child, and that can really knock the child's confidence in themselves.

Helping our children to build their confidence is one of the most important roles for any parent. We have to continually remind ourselves again and again to trust in our kids because they *are* smart and *are* able to work things out for themselves. We should tell them they are *good* and that they must trust their own judgement – having a sense of 'self' and the confidence to 'listen' to it is really important when they are young. When you affirm to your child that they are good, they will *become* good. But if a parent keeps telling their child, 'You are so naughty and do everything wrong!', they will almost certainly end up becoming what their parents tell them they are.

But if one were to say something like, 'OK, I respect your decision, you're not stupid, go to that party but please be careful because I love you and would hate anything bad to happen — you are a bright boy (or a bright girl) and you'll be sensible, and I trust you,' then this becomes empowering. It's a terrifying thing for any parent to say to their children, of course, but actually, they are enabling their children to *become* trustworthy. It's back to the mantra that your children 'will become what you project', which is why this is so important.

Similarly, if someone tells their child they are 'useless' and that they 'will never be able to do that', they might just grow up completely lacking confidence in their abilities to do things. We all have an inner voice that's *set* at a very early age, and parents can have a huge influence over whether this becomes a negative or a positive inner voice. It is a big responsibility for parents, because if their child forms a negative inner voice, it will become *very* difficult, if not impossible, to change later on.

And when, as they will, your children *do* mess up, it's far better in my view to talk through what went wrong rather than just being angry and critical — 'Look, you are normally great at this, but this time you've made a big mistake. Let's think about what you've done, really learn from it and then move on.' But that's also not to say that everything should be kept all lovely, comfortable and soft, because that's not real life either. My father has always been quite tough on me, but in a very constructive way, not a negative way, and I have genuinely learned a lot from that.

As a mum, we can struggle a bit sometimes, trying to do everything perfectly, when the truth is that it cannot always be perfect. But it's important to remember that we all have a real responsibility to be happy *for* our children. It's much better to be upbeat and have a laugh with your kids over dinner than to be stressing about getting the food ready, on top of everything else you have to do, and then being angry and frustrated with them because you're tired and can't play. Your kids will always remember the mood far more than the detail.

Declan Kelly

Born and educated in Ireland, Declan Kelly is one of his country's most respected and decorated businessmen. From very humble beginnings, he embarked on a career in media, becoming an award-winning journalist before moving into communications. He founded his first public relations business in 1999, disposing of it three years later prior to moving to the US. As economic envoy to Northern Ireland (appointed by Hillary Clinton when she was secretary of state), Declan was highly praised for the contribution he made to the economy of Northern Ireland. He is best known as co-founder of Teneo, the hugely successful international consulting company headquartered in New York, where he remains CEO and chairman.

'Good luck finds those who make the effort, have the right attitude and who are persistent.'

'Through the sheer volume of your effort, the law of averages will work in your favour. If you cast a line in the water, you might catch a fish. If you cast fifty lines in the water, you are *going* to catch a fish.'

'Having a good positive mental attitude is something that saves time, saves energy and it gets you to a place faster than you would otherwise get if you're just meandering through life without that attitude. It's your positive attitude that will get you past obstacles, that will help you deal with your failures and mistakes, and that will ultimately help you to reach your goals and succeed.'

'There is always an inherent conflict between being a parent and being a friend to your kids. As a parent, you have to apply discipline and lay down the law, but if you can be friends with your children at the same time, they will be your friends for life.'

On success . . .

I believe that one's personal view on success is shaped by where you have come from and your early experiences in life. Success for me is not defined by money, nor by individual achievements or perhaps those landmark moments in your life that you can stand up and tell your kids or colleagues about. It is not about the medals you have won or awards that you have been given either – those things are nice and make you feel good for a day, they can go on your résumé and they might even 'validate' you in some way, but they still do not mean success for me.

I think of success as the fact that I've advanced from where I came, into the person and to a place that I *never* dreamed was possible, and the incredible journey in between. Every day of my life, I wake up and remember where it all started. It's that extraordinary feeling, thinking about where I am today and looking back to the younger me.

So for me, it's a sense of satisfaction in having personally driven the huge changes in my life to bring me to where I am now – that means success for me.

Humble beginnings . . .

When I grew up in Ireland, my family was very poor. Both of my parents left school at twelve years of age and each had to work at three jobs every day, just so that our family could survive. From the age of five, I was helping my father to sell potatoes by the side of the road. We would go from one village to the next, trying to sell produce that we had grown in the fields.

It was very tough for us as a family living from day to day. It was not until I was seven that we actually had running water. On one occasion, our house was burned to the ground and I ended up living with my grandmother for a year while my father built a new house with his bare hands.

My whole raison d'être at that time of my life was survival. And that certainly forms you as a person, because after you've gone through all of that, nothing else you have to face in life can really ever be as scary. So from an early age, I *knew* that I had to escape and get myself to a completely different place in life. I needed to advance myself, and it was *having* to survive that ultimately drove me to want to succeed and, metaphorically, never to go back.

My parents were wonderful and totally dedicated to our family. Their whole mission in life was to help me and my brother to get educated and go on to university. When you grow up poor, as I did, seeing your parents working so hard all of the time – and when they sit you down every night to tell you that they're doing this for *us* – it really inspires you.

I was tremendously impacted by my parents. My mother had the most remarkable, amazing influence on my life, and still has to this day. She has this indefatigable spirit and just wanted to dedicate her entire life to her children. While my brother and I went on to pursue our careers, she has continued to do some extraordinary things, including raising lots of money for charities.

For me, I had no option but to work very hard at school. I would come home, help my father with the cows and then lock myself away in a room with a table full of books, and study solidly for five hours. My parents would leave me alone, except to feed me, and once I was done, I would go off to bed. I did that almost every day for six or seven years.

I will never forget the night when I learned that I had secured my place at university. It was also critically important that I attained the required level of exam results to avoid needing financial support from my parents. I was working that night with my mother in a meat factory. Our job was to clean up the offices and workspaces at the factory. I dialled the telephone number of an automated service to hear my results. When we learned that I'd obtained a university place together with full financial aid, I remember just sitting there with my mother in the middle of the floor, just holding each other for twenty minutes and crying, because we both knew the real significance of that moment.

It has always fascinated me how those little moments in time are so poignant. It's almost like a 'roll of a dice', where the outcome can actually determine the direction of the rest of your life. If that moment hadn't gone the way it did for me then, I would be doing something completely different now.

Work ethic, goals and humility . . .

I think that hard work is everything. It's not something you acquire by accident, it doesn't come easily either, but there's no substitute for working hard.

It's a bit like exercise. If you want to win a race or run a marathon, but you don't put the work in and exercise hard, you won't get the results. So it doesn't matter how smart you are, it simply will never happen for you unless you are prepared to put the hard work in. There are very few geniuses in the world, so the average person *has* to work hard.

You also have to know what's important from what's not, and avoid wasting a huge amount of time on stuff that doesn't matter. I was able to prioritise things from a young age, and created a simple formula for writing down every day what I was going to do the next day. Today, I use the same lists; they have the meetings I need to take, calls I need to make, emails I need to send, documents I need to read and approve. Until that day is 'completed', I will not make another list. Every day since I was eleven years old, I have been working by this organising discipline.

If you can learn to do this at a young age, it will follow through into almost every aspect of your life. It will help you to know how to conduct yourself, how you organise meetings, how you interact with people, friends and family, how you spend your time and how important it is to take leisure time. When I was young, I could not afford to waste time because I simply had too much on the line. I believe that people who are less organised tend to do less well.

Setting goals is vital. I set goals every day of my life. Some are for the end of the day, some for the end of the week and some for the end of the year. Your biggest goals must stretch you. If you do not set extremely challenging goals that seem almost insurmountable, you can't really hope to achieve the things in life that you thought were impossible. I never ran seriously before, but around eight years ago, I got out of bed one morning and decided that I wanted to run. I worked hard, and as I improved, I started to set goals for the distances and times I wanted to achieve. I have since competed in five marathons, while pushing my body hard to places where I never thought it could go. And it's the same thing with your personality, your heart, your emotions and your brain. Why does it matter if I run a marathon at 3.41 as opposed to 3.45? It doesn't really matter for anyone else, I suppose, but it does for me!

I have always believed that it's important *not* to take yourself too seriously. I grew up in a house that was naturally very serious, because of what we had to deal with day to day. But it was also a house full of laughter, music and dancing. We were never afraid of making a fool of ourselves, just because it's fun. Having that humility and in a way, having the sort of *personality* that's comfortable with showing your vulnerabilities, are very important, I think.

I started a band in our company some time ago, which I still belong to. If you can stand up and play a musical instrument in front of six hundred people who work for you, and let them laugh at you, they will not be afraid to do it themselves when they get the opportunity.

I also admire any leader who's willing to stand up and admit in front of their people, 'I have made a big mistake,' 'I did a bad job,' 'It's my fault,' and to make fun of themselves over it.

Reading . . .

Reading is very important, in my view. I tell people who work for me that they should be reading something all the time. It can be fiction or non-fiction, but it must be outside their comfort zone, not something that naturally 'floats their boat'.

I am amazed, however, when people say to me (including teachers talking to me as a parent) that everything can now be organised on a tablet. You don't even need to write anymore – you can read it and type it all on a keyboard.

Having been a journalist for many years, I believe that there is no substitute for actually thumbing through the pages of a book and properly reading it. While one can also listen to audio books today, I think that there is still real value in actually reading the words from the page and allowing your brain to connect with the structure of a sentence in its visual form as opposed to its audible form. Listening to an audiobook can be helpful when you are driving for several hours, but have you actually *read* the book? How much really goes in? There's a certain value that comes from the *effort* required to read through the pages of a book. It also naturally brings you silence and presence.

Choosing what to do in life . . .

I know that most people will say, 'Cast your net far and wide' and 'Try as many things as you can to find what you want to do.' I personally have a different view.

If a young person gets to seventeen or eighteen years of age and they still don't have any idea what they want to do as a career, I think they're potentially in trouble. By their mid-teens, they should have already been 'given' directional signs, either organically or inorganically, that tell them what they are good at now and what they're likely to be good at for the rest of their lives. If they are still casting a wide net at that stage and looking at lots of options, something has gone wrong, in my view.

I think it's sad, whenever I talk to a parent whose son or daughter is studying a particular subject at university, and they say to me, 'I don't really know why they're doing it, but they seem to enjoy it.' It is, of course, very difficult for parents to know what to tell their children, because everything is changing so fast. Many university courses available today didn't exist, even as a concept, five years ago. So, if a parent left university twenty-five years ago, what advice can they realistically give their children about what they should do today? Most parents end up relying on their kid's school to help them decide what they want to do.

The problem is, at thirteen or fourteen, children will not necessarily know what they want to be doing at that stage either. But somewhere in between, I believe that they should start 'corralling choices', based on what their perceived strengths are at that time. At fifteen, I knew that the sciences were of no interest to me, and that I'd probably be appalling at chemistry, biology and physics. This naturally led me to make choices in favour of subjects I thought I *would* be good at. In the end, sociology was a subject I really enjoyed when I was at school and one I excelled at. While I did not pursue sociology as an occupation, it was enormously helpful during my career as a journalist.

Mentors . . .

I not only believe in the value of mentorship, I think that having a good mentor is critically important in developing one's career. I had two special mentors in my life, without whom I would not be where I am today.

But, I think there is a big difference between the sort of mentoring you need when you are young and the type of mentor you need much later in life. So the real question is, at what point in your life do you need a proper mentor? A young person up to their late teens doesn't really need a mentor at that stage; that's what parents, close family friends or even career-guidance councillors are for.

My mother fulfilled that role for me when I was young. She was actually more than my mother – she was my friend as well, and we have always had this amazing relationship. I was blessed to have someone who, despite never having had a formal education, possessed tremendous common sense.

Mentorship programmes can be very helpful to guide young people from their early twenties into real career opportunities. When I was appointed special envoy to Northern Ireland, I founded the Northern Ireland Mentorship Program in partnership with the American Ireland Fund. I have seen for myself at first-hand how valuable such programmes can be for these youngsters, providing an initial one-year placement with large corporations in the US, as a precursor to helping them find full employment and a career.

I personally feel that you do not require a mentor, in the formal sense, until you reach your late twenties and early thirties. At that time, you are making decisions that are really definitional in terms of where your career is going.

When I first arrived in the States, I was fortunate to meet a man named John Sharkey. He was running a huge part of MCI WorldCom at the time. I called him up one day from a phone box – he had no idea who I was, but he took my call and invited me over to his office. He soon took me under his wing, and over time he introduced me to hundreds of people throughout New York, to help me with my career. He was like a second father to me. He had no reason to do this except out of goodness, and he saw something in me that he thought he could help flourish.

My second mentor was the late, great Don Keough. He was the president of Coca-Cola for many years, and one of the most celebrated businessmen in the US. Like John Sharkey, he also took a deep personal interest in me. Without these two mentors to help me, I would not have been able to achieve what I have done in my business career.

Both of these great men, however, helped me after I had already established myself in my career. When someone can take you and introduce you to people that could be really good for your business, or they observe you in a meeting or public speaking, and they tell you, 'Don't do it that way, do it this way,' and you take their advice on board, that's proper mentoring. But once again, this level of mentoring is far more appropriate for someone much later in the development of their career.

To parents . . .

Children naturally observe the behaviour of their parents, and this certainly helps to form them. My parents demonstrated the importance and value of hard work to us. Interestingly, when I work with someone now, I always try to explore the organic nature of their personality, where they came from, how they grew up and what their 'frame' was like when they were young – because these things really find their way through to how they become as a young adult and eventually, a mature adult. By the time a child is eight years old, I think one can already observe what kind of person they are going to be.

Education really matters. It is critically important. Education was my path to a better life, and I feel bad for people who don't understand what it's for or who don't enjoy it. The fact is, if we do not educate our children, the world can't get better.

I genuinely believe that most children take their attitude towards learning, once again, from what they observe in their parents, and this can take one of two forms. They may look at their parents, as I did, and see that they are working incredibly hard with little spare time and perhaps didn't have the education to be able to help them fully with their learning. Kids in these circumstances really owe it to their parents to do everything *they* can to learn and succeed, through using their own initiative. Or they may be in the fortunate position where their parents are both educated and able to spend the time with them. In this case, it is the *parents* who have an obligation to help their children fully understand the value of learning, such that they can achieve as much as their parents have done – or even do better.

There is always an inherent conflict between being a parent and being a friend to your kids. As a parent, you have to apply discipline and lay down the law, but if you can be friends with your children at the same time, they will be your friends for life. This also provides the opportunity for your children to learn *with* you as opposed to learning *from* you (just handing down knowledge). It is important for parents to appreciate this distinction. If your kids can learn with you, it becomes a very different way of thinking. I always try to impart to my children 'how I would do something', rather than just explaining to them what they need to do. This also means being more involved with your children and participating with them in activities so that everything is more collaborative. It then becomes natural for them to *learn* collaboratively with you too.

Parents should also continue to learn and evolve – I always make a point to take myself out of my comfort zone every day to learn something new so that I can continue to be relevant to my children, because frankly, they are learning things faster than my ability to keep up with them. Only by doing this are you enabling your kids to keep pace with what's really going on in the world. The problem is that this is hard, and it takes time, which is why many parents don't bother, but it's important to do.

Young people today are older at a younger age than before. They are exposed to a lot more of what I'd call regular adult information than previously, and their innocence is lost much earlier. Technology provides a whole set of experiences that children also never used to have, which I find fascinating. Rightly or wrongly, they're being exposed to decision-making at a young age, and this will necessarily form a big part of their lives in the future. And for parents that haven't grown up with the digital social media revolution, it's hard for them to know whether or not their kids are equipped with the right tools.

Luck follows persistence . . .

Good luck finds those who make the effort, have the right attitude and who are persistent.

In our company today, every time we see a business development opportunity, there will be those that tell us, 'It's never going to work.' Perhaps the phone doesn't get answered or the client says, 'We're OK, we don't need any help right now.' But we never give up. We might make twenty attempts trying *something* to get through, and eventually we crack the code and get heard. People then say, 'How did you manage to do that?' And the answer is always the same – persistence. We didn't want to take no for an answer and we didn't give up. It's the same thing we did yesterday and the same thing we're going to do tomorrow.

When I first went into communications in Ireland, I was a junior guy looking for my first big client. I read something in a newspaper about a company, so I called up the office of the person who was running a particular project and asked if I could speak to him. His assistant told me that he wasn't there, and she eventually revealed that he was on his way to the airport to fly to a certain place. I told her that I'd call him the following day, but instead, I drove to the airport, bought a ticket, saw him on the plane and swapped with somebody so that I could sit beside him for the forty-five-minute flight. He had no option but to talk to me, and when we got off the plane, he agreed to have dinner with me that evening. That night, I got the business. At that time, it was the largest account I'd won in my entire life.

I'm still not sure what drove me to do this. Was it desperation? Was it because of how I'd grown up? A fear of failure? Did I have to succeed and to win at all costs? Since then, I have always believed in taking every meeting, taking every phone call and pursuing every rabbit down every hole. I will always find a way . . . Once again, if you've got the right attitude, work hard at it and are persistent, luck will find you.

Through the sheer volume of your effort, the law of averages will work in your favour. If you cast a line in the water, you might catch a fish. If you cast fifty lines in the water, you are *going* to catch a fish. So yes, being in the right place at the right time is important, but if you pursue every opportunity, don't take no for an answer, possess incredible self-belief and work incredibly hard, you reduce the percentage chance of failure very significantly.

Self-doubt and failure . . .

I have been told my entire life, 'You can't do that.' Frankly, that has always spurred me to go and achieve whatever it is that I am told I can't do. So now, I don't even listen to people who tell me that.

I grew up with two parents telling me constantly, 'You can do *anything.*' While, of course, I can't really do absolutely anything, I certainly believe that if I put my mind to something, I can make it happen as well as the next person can.

Self-doubt is a good thing, but the problem is that it can be a very dangerous thing and may lead to bad decisions and very serious mistakes. To narrow down the scope for self-doubt, you have to build yourself a toolkit that enables you to survive in almost any circumstance. You do this by learning, and knowing what your strengths are. It goes back to narrowing your options as a young person – identify the things that you are really good at and focus on them. You will quickly find that you can become very good at those things if you work very hard at them. And if you do that, the likelihood of self-doubt won't really arise, because you're already geared up for and focused on those areas that matter and where you are strong.

Life is full of barriers, obstructions and problems. When you meet an immovable object, you have to find a way to get past, and if you can't get around it, you have to go under it or climb over it. I don't indulge the concept of defeatism. If you have no alternative but to succeed, you *will* find a way to succeed.

People fail all the time. I fail at things every day and make mistakes. But I don't allow my failures to define me – I learn from them and move on. You need to reflect on your failures and mistakes, but I do not advise anyone to get so wrapped up in 'what happened' and 'why it happened' that they're rendered immobile. Reflection and analysis are important, because anyone who's not self-reflective is lost. The greatest leaders in the world have all been people who have sat back and reflected on what they did wrong.

When you have set your mind on something to achieve, you have to be decisive. There is no room for dithering. You have to make decisions and stick to them. When a 1,500-metre runner is competing in the finals of the Olympic Games, as they get to the last bend of the race they have to decide when to make the kick. There's no point in thinking, 'I'm not really sure if I should do it now or not' – they have twenty-four seconds in which to make that decision, and then go for it.

And that for me is a metaphor for life: you make your decision, you go with it – and hopefully, it's right. But if you fail, then OK, you learn from it and the next time you do it differently.

Your attitude is also crucial. I think it's very important to have a smile on your face. I know people who work in deep therapy, who practise smiling and laughing in the mirror with their patients so that they actually feel more positive when they walk out of there – it's actually a very healthy thing to do.

Having a good positive mental attitude is something that saves time, saves energy and it gets you to a place faster than you would otherwise get if you're just meandering through life without that attitude. It's your positive attitude that will get you past obstacles, that will help you deal with your failures and mistakes, and that will ultimately help you to reach your goals and succeed.

Work-life balance . . .

When I was growing up, for me it was the work-work balance! I'm now a great believer in the work-life balance. I take my time off very seriously. When I'm off, I'm off! I also encourage and insist that all the people who work for me must take their time off too. I spend a huge amount of time at weekends with my kids, doing things that are important for them. I also read avidly, play music and exercise a lot – they say that a healthy mind in a healthy body is key, and I think that's been proven beyond doubt.

Companies like Google and Facebook are doing the right thing now to elasticate the work-life balance to a place where outputs are much greater. Our office is all open-plan, so people can collaborate more. Our staff can take time off and we don't look anymore to see whether they've come to work or they haven't, whether they're working from home or from somewhere else. We trust our people to do the right thing. And this is an evolution in corporate thinking that has helped to make people much more productive.

So, I think it's important for kids at a young age to know that there is a work-life balance, and it's important to have that, but the *work* is just as important as the *life*. When you are between seventeen and twenty-five, I think it's 'work first' and 'life second'. Once you have established yourself and you get a job you like, a career and a life, then it's time to rebalance. I know many people in New York who work eighty hours a week and they love it (or that's what they tell me). I also know lots of people who want to die in the office when they're ninety years old – I'm just not one of them! To me, it doesn't make any sense. When you eventually go down into the ground, as the guy once famously said, 'I don't think they'll be putting on my tombstone: "I wish I had another hour in the office."'

Martha, Baroness Lane-Fox CBE

At twenty-five, Martha Lane-Fox co-founded lastminute.com, a high-profile and pioneering internet-based company that offered late holiday deals online. Her professional life was abruptly halted in 2004 by a serious car accident that left her with life-changing injuries. After two years in hospital, Martha started to rebuild her career, co-founding the karaoke business Lucky Voice and also joining the board of Marks & Spencer. She was appointed Digital Champion for the UK in 2009, and has since become a widely respected proponent for the responsible use of technology. In 2013 Martha joined the House of Lords, becoming its youngest female member, and was also appointed chancellor of the Open University. In the same year, she was awarded a CBE. As an avid campaigner for human rights and women's rights, Martha has founded or acted as patron for numerous charities and foundations, both at home and abroad.

'Your attitude towards other people is key. Being generous, kind and polite to others, showing compassion and empathy for the other side, will not only help you to feel better as a human being, it will also come back around for you too.'

'I think optimism is an interesting thing, because as an entrepreneur you want to be optimistic about your ability to get things done, while at the same time not wishing to be unrealistic. I believe that optimism and realism are very important when they work together in tandem.'

'Hard work is an absolutely *vital* ingredient for achieving success. I have very strong views about this, because so often we tend to give the impression to others that things will just 'happen' in life or that they're easy. But you always have to work *really* hard!'

'Right from the get-go, just read to your children all the time. There's no question in my mind that this has already made a massive impact on my kids' language and their curiosity. So just keep reading to them and ask them questions.'

About success . . .

I do feel very strongly that every individual has to determine their *own* values for success and what it really means to them personally. One of the things that I perceive often leaves people feeling insecure, anxious or unsettled is when they try to define success according to how they believe *other* people may be thinking.

This is especially important now for young people during this new age of mass information and the vagaries of social media; it's that ability to know so much more about what everyone else is doing, while also putting yourself 'out there' in a kind of connected way. And that is why I believe it is so vital that you have confidence and resilience in the things that really matter to *you*. But you must also have confidence that these are the things that *should* matter to you, and that you never lose sight of them.

To me, for example, it really helps if the activities we pursue can generally contribute to humanity rather than detract from humanity, or contribute to the planet as opposed to harming the planet. These particular things will always be essential values for me and fundamental to my own view of success.

Defining success on your terms, however, usually involves having a predefined ambition. While for some, that might be simply raising a happy family, for others it may be to build a billion-dollar business or even to become prime minister. Once you have defined your goal, whatever that may be, it then becomes much easier to work out what steps are required to move yourself in that direction and what sort of education you may need.

I have never had a master plan. A lot of what has unfolded in my life has been the result of serendipity, both good and bad, but what I have always tried to maintain at the core of it all are a few key principles. First, to always try to be kind and generous-spirited, and whether that means I'm having to fire someone from a company or when I'm doing something as inspirational as being chancellor of the Open University, the same values will always apply. Second, to try to keep a sort of strong public-service ethos in what I do, because I think it's important that when you have had some good luck in life (as I was fortunate enough to have early in mine), you should also think about how to help the next wave of people to find their luck too. And third, you should think continuously about what you can do to help improve society.

I know that on one level I have been successful. I see the material evidence of that around me and know that I have been able to create resources that few people will probably be able to achieve in their own lifetimes. When I had my car accident in 2004, having those resources behind me certainly helped save my life. So, once again, I think I have been immensely lucky. But when I think about 'success', I still feel like I'm a *work-in-progress*. I still have a kind of restlessness in me and a drive to want to contribute more.

When I think about the things I have been involved in throughout my life and career, they have mostly revolved around technology. But there are many who think, and I would argue too, that technology as a sector has not exactly covered itself in glory in recent times. I certainly don't feel that I can honestly say – especially as someone who's had a high profile in the UK technology scene for a while – 'Great job! Well done, tech! You've certainly helped humanity!' So that's why I think there's still a lot of work to do, and why I say that for me, it's a continual work-in-progress.

While I am not particularly active in legislation in the House of Lords, I am very active on my committee. And while politics is not exactly covering itself in glory either at this time, nor is it really addressing our problems using the tools of the modern age, I also feel that there's a lot for me to do there too. But I suppose one of the things that I have enjoyed pursuing and want to continue driving is my belief that while we've all put a lot of thought into building technology businesses, we've been thinking a lot less about how we can most effectively *use* technology for the benefit of society. That was a journey that started off for me in 2009 when I was appointed Digital Champion for the UK, which then led me to set up the Government Digital Service. In my view, this was an enormous opportunity – which we still have – to drive positive change and to deliver in its broadest sense, really valuable and essential services to everyone. I still find this challenge extremely motivating.

So although I have enjoyed some personal success in my life, I still feel that on a professional level there's still a lot I have to do, while working on the things I really care about. For me, success really comes in many forms, not just one.

Choosing what I want to do . . .

I don't believe young people should get too obsessed or worry too much about having to find the right career for themselves at an early age. When one considers recent data, which show how young people today are likely to have double the 'jumps' in their career compared with just twenty years ago, that's a pretty significant shift! So the age-old notion that you might 'go into accounting' or 'go into retail', and then remain there for the whole of your career, this is actually a complete nonsense these days.

When I was much younger, I was very interested in acting. But, for a long while, I was also fascinated by the criminal justice system and wanted to become a prison governor. I then studied ancient and modern history at university. After I graduated, I became interested in the media and thought that I might like to pursue a career in journalism or work in a media business, and so I looked at jobs in those areas. In the end, following a purely chance meeting through a particular network, I started working for a media and telecoms consultancy, where I then met my future business partner, Brent Hoberman, with whom I would eventually create *lastminute.com*. For me, this all demonstrates quite poignantly that while plans are great, while goals are great, it is essential not to be too rigid – these curve balls will invariably come at you throughout your life!

So don't feel too stressed or vexed, and don't think, 'Gosh! I still have to discover *something* I need to do, and then make it my career!' Just stay calm but remain active. Approach everything with a testing mindset, have lots of different experiences and be open-minded. When you eventually find something that you believe you might like to pursue, you can then think about what you will need to do to become successful at it. 'What do I need to learn?' . . . 'Who can I talk to about it?' . . . 'I'll probably need to meet some people in that area to broaden my network.' But while it may be helpful to set a few goals and start working towards them, always remain open to other possibilities. These are still steps along the way and part of your journey of exploration.

But when you think you have found something that really interests you, that's the time to be tenacious. If you can find someone working in the same area, someone whom you respect and admire, don't be shy to approach them and ask for their advice. If, for example, you decide that you would like to become a doctor, and there's a cool doctor in your local hospital or general practice, simply ask them if you can go and spend some time with them. In my experience, most people really like being asked by young people to help them or to advise them. And unless you ask, you will never know! You might even find a future mentor, or a way into certain networks and places that might otherwise seem unattainable. These days, it's so easy to find someone on LinkedIn, on the internet and through social media. Just get in touch with them and see what happens!

Preparing for the future . . .

The world is changing rapidly. It's a tougher place for young people today, and they're going to face many challenges that our generation never saw when we were growing up. I am a middle-class woman who was fortunate to have a great education and better resources compared with most people when I started my career. But even people like me, who are born today, will have to deal with a completely different set of circumstances and challenges in the future.

One of the most critical issues facing young people today is the future for our planet. It is surely hard for anyone to argue that the world is not facing a cataclysmically bad scenario around climate change at this moment. We have got ourselves into a real mess, and yet the attitude of many governments – and far too many people – reflects an almost blind optimism that everything will somehow sort itself out. And while I do believe in our amazing human ingenuity and the extraordinary capacity we have for innovation, the world continues to be either in denial or completely underestimating the scale of the challenge ahead of us. I still feel that climate change is not yet fully at the heart of every business, political or technology conversation – as it should be. I honestly believe that when we look back in ten years' time, we will all think that we were on the wrong side of history.

I feel very keenly for our young people – and for all of us! – and what they will have to face and deal with in the future. I am also a firm believer that a special kind of intellectual dexterity, resilience and curiosity will be fundamental and that specific skills will be needed in the area of technology. So being able to engage fully with technology – and not being frightened of it – will always be very useful. While I am slightly ambivalent about learning to code (I think that machines are going to be doing all of that pretty soon, indeed it's already started), I still think it's a brilliant route into learning about and having confidence with technology. It's also just like learning a new language, which is always a useful thing to do anyway.

So I really believe that equipping oneself with technical skills – and by that, I mean not shying away from the digital world but learning how to be curious about it, how to make and create it – will always stand you in good stead. We often talk about young people as being kind of 'digital natives', or that they have a better understanding of everything digital than we do, but I don't think that's true. It's just that the game has changed. I think they simply have a different relationship with technology today because they are twenty-five years younger than me. But that doesn't mean that they can build it and own it and drive it for their own different ends – there is naturally a big difference between being a consumer and being a creator. So if a young person can understand technology better, and they can fall on the side of *making* or *creating*, that will certainly help them significantly in the future. They will always have a head start if they can engage with the technological world around them confidently and in more depth.

But whatever the future may hold for us – and for our young people with regard to technology – I do feel deeply that it's going to be a very long time before computers become 'human'. In the meantime, we should all double-down on *being* human ourselves. For me, that goes back to being values-driven, to family, to kindness and being generous, but also to empathy, the personal connections you create, the interactions you have with people, the mental dexterity that you can bring to solving problems and understanding what it is to be a human being while living in the world today. It's not *just* about solving problems through code – it's about intellectual curiosity, building resilience and being wide-ranging. I would always say to young people, 'Have confidence! Because being human is a quite remarkable thing.' So how do you build that 'human' muscle? Well, you build it through reading and learning, you build it through understanding culture, you build it through travel, through creating and expanding your networks. All of these things are so incredibly valuable.

What I like to read . . .

While I read a lot, I often get asked, 'What's your favourite business book for success?' But being truthful, I have only ever skimmed through maybe a handful of business books, and invariably put them down pretty quickly! What I do read endlessly, however, is poetry and classic literature. I love *War and Peace*, for example, but I take refuge in books of all kinds, and can honestly say that whenever I have been inspired by something I've read, which has then led to an idea or perhaps making connections between things, it's far more likely to have come from something that I've been reading before going to sleep than any book that I feel I *have* to read in order to understand some sort of 'management style' or whatever.

I was very heavily influenced by Mary Wollstonecraft when I was young (like many other young women will have been), and still feel like she's one of the great unsung heroes of the planet, let alone the UK . . . and let alone women! The fact that she really did change the dynamics of education in this country at an incredibly complicated time in history, was married to a highly complex man and then gave birth to Mary Shelley, this all presents a truly fascinating life story. I would far rather read biographies of such people from the past, and try to think forwards, than some entrepreneur's 'my-rise-to-success' business story.

How others can inspire you . . .

I've been very fortunate to have had a number of very significant people at times in my life who have helped me to think about various jumps throughout my career (and I don't mean necessarily sitting down with me to talk things through). My first boss at Spectrum was a brilliant man called Kip Meek, who gave me far too much responsibility for my age at the time! The company was a start-up he was growing. I was the eleventh employee when I joined, and when I left it had a 150 people. Kip was in media and telecoms in the early nineties, a sector that was exploding. He would send me off all over the place by myself, and also gave me a lot of responsibility internally within the company. Giving that to a twenty-one-year-old, who had very little experience, was certainly a very brave move! He's always been hugely important to me, and even now, when I have those moments of introspection in my career, I will go and have lunch with him, not for him to mentor me, but purely because I really value his opinion.

I have even discovered people from outside my network who may seem poles apart from me and often have a completely different view of the world. They have nonetheless become friends whose opinions and advice I value, and I find that really interesting and energising. But as time moves on, I now find myself looking towards younger people, rather than older, as being the most helpful for me. I've often been intrigued why it's so widely held that mentors always have to be older than you.

So, for me, there are formal mentoring relationships that I may have, and then there are simply people that I enjoy spending time with. I know some brilliant young women, for example, some who work in tech and some who do not. They probably don't even know that I'm getting something from them, but just the way they think or the way they use technology or the way they're building their own careers can be really interesting to observe and learn from. But inspiration and help can come from many different sources – I love going to the theatre, and before I had children it was very much my default 'happy place'. I would go every week with a friend, and afterwards, thinking about the experience or learning something from the play or simply watching human relationships unfold, has been as valuable in many ways for me as any formal mentoring relationship.

Being a parent . . .

My parents have always been, as for many people, an incredibly important part of my life. While I still think today of my life as a work-in-progress, I also measure myself in terms of, 'Am I doing OK according to how my parents would score it?' . . . 'Would Pa think that I'm reading enough books?' . . . 'Would he be proud of my intellectual curiosity?' My father is an academic and a polymath, and has always been incredibly rigorous intellectually. He has real integrity and certainly instilled a strong value system in me. My mum is an extraordinarily resilient person and gives out to everyone in her network. She has always taught me the importance of being graceful, generous and kind. Both my parents have given me the confidence while growing up to be who I am, and even to feel completely at ease as the only woman in a room full of men – and that's been hugely valuable to me.

I remember a close friend of mine, who has four kids of her own, once saying to me, 'As a parent, you think you can tell your kids *how to be*, but in the end, it's *how you are* that's most important.' It's all about being 'your best self' for your children when they are around you, so they can learn and pick up from that. Being polite to your partner in front of them, for example, showing interest in their work and being engaged in yours, and always being respectful to others. These things will have far more impact when your children see you *doing* them compared with just saying, 'You have to do that!' It's *being* and *doing* how you want them to *be* and *do*. I really, really believe in that now.

It's never too early to talk to your children. Mine understand about my work and understand when I have to go off to do something that's important to me, because we talk about those things. And right from the get-go, just read to your children all the time. There's no question in my mind that this has already made a massive impact on my kids' language and their curiosity. So just keep reading to them and ask them questions.

When you're out with your children, engage with them and ask them questions about what's going on around them, and what they can see or hear – 'What's going on in that tree over there?' . . . 'What has that truck got on it, can you see?' If, as a parent, you continually express interest and curiosity about these things, then they will start becoming interesting for them too. They begin to think for themselves and to ask questions. They become curious.

For me, one of the benefits of having had children later in life is that I can just feel a bit calmer about everything, both at home and professionally. I am not having to wrestle now with that 'peak time' of my career, which many younger parents have to face. And while it can be easy to start panicking about having to do so much for your children from so early on, I do think it's essential to remember that having children is a long game and it's a long journey. Kids will, of course, need different things at different times, but there's no need to try to do everything all at once.

Whilst my mum never gave me a book on parenting, she did give me lots of anthropological books to read about how different cultures bring up their children. I still find it fascinating today that perhaps the most fundamental wisdom that has come from all of those books is that parents should simply 'back the hell off!' Be much calmer about everything and just 'let them be' more.

I feel that the language you use with children and the culture you build around them is really crucial. It's about helping them to build confidence, but without arrogance. It's also helping them to solve problems, but not to think that they are 'the best in the whole wide world!' for doing so. For me, it's better to say, 'Well done, you did it!' than to say, 'Wow, that's absolutely brilliant, just look at you!'

Helping your children to feel confident and loved is obviously essential, but for me, confidence and optimism come from children feeling that they are in a safe place, where things can screw up sometimes, and yet it doesn't really matter too much. Instead of saying something like, 'That was such a silly thing to do!', for me, it's perhaps better to say, 'OK, so that's gone wrong. What do you think you should have done? What are you going to do from now on?'

You still have to be strict, of course, and you have got to show them who is in charge – that is always non-negotiable! I can be furious sometimes with my kids, but still hug them and cuddle them. So as a parent, you can draw your boundaries, but without making them feel that love is ever in question. That's fundamental.

It's extraordinary, though, how often you see parents forget that they always need to put themselves *second* in order of importance to their children. One often sees this when relationships go wrong or parents break up. When my own parents divorced, my mum was amazing at not making me feel as though it was all about her or it was all about my dad. She was listening, hearing and feeling, and she certainly made me feel seen and heard.

It's really all about *not* putting yourself or your own emotions at the heart of matters. That's not to say that you should spoil your children all of the time; I just think it means not being emotionally greedy *of* your children. My parents did that brilliantly with me.

I spend around one week a month travelling, and like every working parent, male or female, I will often agonise over whether that's OK or not. Now, whenever I have to leave, I will refrain from saying something like, 'Oh, I'm going to really miss you. Come here and give me a big hug.' That's not helpful for my kids and it's not particularly helpful for me either . . . Instead, I may say, 'I'm off now. I can't wait to speak with you tomorrow on FaceTime.' When I get back from a trip, it might be, 'I'm so excited to see all the fun things you did while I was away! What would you like to do now?'

Making the most of good fortune whilst handling bad luck . . .

Fortune or good luck are important elements in anyone's life, and I think this is often very much understated by people who have been successful. I was born in London and raised in a middle-class home. My parents were able to feed us and send us to good schools, which, right from the start, was an enormous piece of good fortune for me. I really appreciate the importance of that, because I am also aware that for many people there are sadly still situations that are almost impossible for them to fight their way out of. If you are born into poverty, for example (which sadly we see far too much of everywhere), it can simply be much, much harder for you to break free from that and to move ahead. And there still seems to be this prevailing liberal conceit that just because everyone has access to education, they can somehow make their lives better. I really don't think that's always true.

Whatever your circumstances may be, however, I also believe that you can, in a way, make your own luck. Because there are certainly things within your control, such as your behaviour and your attitude, that can make a big difference to how things unfold for you. When Brent and I started building lastminute.com, we were tenacious, we pushed really hard and we badgered people all the time. We were relentless! Hopefully, we weren't ever cruel or unkind, but we were certainly determined. We constantly tried to make clever leaps and find creative ways to make things happen for us. In this way, we were continually increasing our chances of moving ahead successfully.

We were also lucky because during the late 1990s, the zeitgeist was clearly going in our direction too. And then, we also had some completely random good luck as well; on one occasion, we mailed our business plan to a particular company, but sent it to the wrong address! The people who were in that building decided to open our package and just happened to be venture capitalists . . . They liked what they saw and ended up investing in our business – it was to be a really lucky break for us. So when I reflect now on how luck may have helped us in our particular journey, it was a combination of good fortune initially (both coming from privileged backgrounds), making our own luck through hard work and having a positive outlook, and with some elements of random good luck thrown in as well.

But then, you can sometimes have extraordinarily bad luck too. When I had my car accident in Morocco in 2004, I was very severely injured. I broke twenty-eight bones around my body, including a shattered pelvis, and I had a stroke as well. I was to spend two years in hospital. When I eventually left my hospital bed, I had to learn to do everything all over again as though I were a baby. It was like a fundamental 'reset', where every aspect of my physical life was affected, from walking to eating, and that was really hard. But my way of dealing with it then was by not dwelling on it. My attitude was 'It is what it is,' and you either choose to go forwards or you don't. In a way, I managed to face up to it all through denial – even today, some people think I have completely recovered, but that's more to do with my attitude about it. The reality is that every day I still have to manage my life to make it *seem* like there's not very much wrong with me. From a practical perspective, it's a constant mental risk assessment for me, to calculate what I can or cannot do each day. But while the accident happened arguably at the peak of my career and, of course, was a real setback professionally, I always refused to let it conquer me or overwhelm me. Many of the significant things that I have done in my career – and have been recognised for – have happened since the accident. I could easily have given up, but I still had a lot I wanted to achieve and do with my life, and that helped to shape my attitude and motivation to get through these especially difficult circumstances.

Self-doubt is part of being human . . .

Self-doubt can be very hard. Everyone feels it and everybody faces it from time to time. One of the good things, hopefully, that has come out of all of the light that has recently been shone on mental health issues is perhaps a much greater appreciation that this is really just a part of the 'human condition'. However, while one can debate exactly how helpful all the discussion around mental health has been for everyone, I do think that there is *real* power in people being able to open up and say, 'I was vulnerable too' and 'I feel vulnerable now.'

I can certainly reflect on a number of occasions when I have experienced significant moments of self-doubt in my professional life. When I was at lastminute.com and the share price famously collapsed, I was seen by many as the 'villain of the stock market'. I received three thousand handwritten letters at my office telling me everything from 'You're a bitch,' to much, much worse. I don't often retreat to my bed and have a bit of a mental breakdown, but for forty-eight hours I did, because it was completely overwhelming at the time. I had to then get up again and face the company. I had to try to show everyone that it did not matter, that it was all 'just noise', and that we had to brush it off and continue in our efforts to build a great and successful company. It was certainly an incredibly tough time to manage.

And then, of course, while my car accident was to leave me physically challenged ever since, I do continuously feel self-doubt on a very personal level – 'Am I going to be able to cope?,' 'Am I going to be able to get through to the end of today?' But it wasn't just my legs that were broken at the time, my confidence was on one level shattered too – what was I going to do next? I had been on this amazing trajectory in my professional life, and now I would have to build this weird kind of 'portfolio life' at the age of thirty-five that I always assumed I wouldn't have until I was sixty-five.

It has taken some time to feel more settled, in being a generalist now, and no longer being able to say, 'Yeah, I do this! This is my thing!' in a focused and dedicated way. And while there are still things that I would like to spend more time pursuing, in the end, I'm trying to derive strength from the fact that I'm now doing this whole bunch of good stuff, and that's OK. But, without exaggeration, I still feel self-doubt about it every single day. I still feel this endless restlessness around 'Am I really doing the right things?'. . . 'Am I actually making a contribution here?'. . . 'Is this really the best version of myself?'

I mention all of these things because, if someone like me – who might outwardly appear to others as this successful and confident person – can feel self-doubt on a daily basis, then young people, please take heart! Self-doubt is something that it's really OK to admit to having. We *all* have to live with it, and we all have to learn to be at peace with it. Once again, it's just part of being human, and I honestly can't think of a single person that I know who will not have felt it deeply at some time in their lives.

Failure is inevitable . . .

The world of technology, where I come from, started off in a way with a kind of philosophy that it was great to break things and make a mess of things, because this would ultimately drive change in a positive way through 'disruption' (my least favourite word ever!). Arguably, however, technology has not always done a good job of being responsible around the things that it's breaking, and this naturally raises many important questions. But, of course, technology does have this 'culture of failure' at its centre, because it's fundamentally a science where you are always testing, failing and learning from those things and then moving on. I think

I learned a lot from that because, being an entrepreneur, you fail every day, all the time – it's almost like the *default*. So you have to get used to failing and you have to find your way past obstructions, over hurdles, around corners and so on.

Throughout my career, like most entrepreneurs, I have had my fair share of spectacular failures, both personally and professionally. I failed at many things at lastminute.com, from failures around the IPO to when we bought companies and then failed to integrate them properly, to bad marketing decisions, to many bad hiring decisions . . . and I have had many more failures since then too! The point is that experiencing failure is normal, especially when you are pushing hard and breaking new ground.

For me, while failure is inevitable, the key thing is not to dwell on things incessantly or to beat yourself up over things that go wrong. You need to move on – but with 'helpful reflection', in my view. I have seen some people fail, who then spend a lot of time tormenting themselves over it, navel-gazing while in a kind of negative cycle, and they end up losing their confidence.

When failure happens, you need to channel it in a way and *build it into* making progress. You need to analyse what your role may have been in that failure, and even get other people to challenge you around it too. You then need to ask, 'How can we make sure that it doesn't happen again?' But at such times, you have to be realistic and honest with yourself too. I certainly hope that I'm always someone who doesn't mind being challenged and that I'm self-aware enough to be able to take criticism. I think that is really important to try to preserve.

With my team at Doteveryone, whenever we do something major, we will usually have a 'wash-up' session afterwards in which we look at everything that has happened, both good and bad, and then look for what we may need to change and do better next time. I think that's a pretty good way to approach lots of things, especially when they may not have gone so well or as planned.

Looking back . . .

As someone who has studied history, I am quite used to looking back, but in the much broader sense of course. Some people, however, like to reflect on things they've done or that have happened and to analyse them meticulously. That's not really the way I like to operate. While, of course, it can sometimes be helpful for me to reflect on the past, I do not think it's ever helpful to dwell too much on the things that you cannot change. I much prefer to look forwards. Once again, if I reflect on my car accident, how helpful is it really to keep thinking, 'I wish I'd worn my seat belt'? It might be helpful as a reminder that I should always wear a seat belt, but it's simply *not* at all helpful to keep going over that stuff.

Attitude, goals and working hard . . .

Having a good attitude is fundamental. Any 'success' that I may have had in my life or achievement in the things I've wanted to do can, I feel, be attributed largely to my being a confident, optimistic and resilient individual, able to cope (mostly!), while also being able to see a path through any difficulties or challenges. These, for anyone, are attributes in which I would always put a lot of stock, and if you possess them, I think they will always be a valuable resource and of incredible service to you.

I think optimism is an interesting thing, because as an entrepreneur you want to be optimistic about your ability to get things done, while at the same time not wishing to be unrealistic. I believe that optimism and realism are very important when they work together in tandem. And you build 'realistic optimism' through learning it and understanding it first of all, and then by sort of *acting* it. Eventually, it becomes a way of being.

Your attitude towards other people is also key. Being generous, kind and polite to others, showing compassion and empathy for the other side, will not only help you to feel better as a human being, it will also come back around for you too, I believe. That can be as true when you are using social media as it is when you are in a meeting with someone, or when you're interacting with others at school . . .

Goals, I think, are really, really important. Goals can be huge, like 'I want to go to university,' or they can be smaller – 'These are the things that I need to do by the end of this month.' For me, they can be work-related goals, where I might be thinking a year ahead to things I want to achieve professionally, and they can be personal goals too. I have a kind of mental priority list going around in my mind pretty much all the time – a bit like the flight-announcement boards at an airport that keep updating. That can be very strengthening because you can 'feel' it when you have achieved something you set out to do, and you can also be grateful for the things you have done. I think that's always helpful. But it goes back to being kind to yourself too, because setting your goals shouldn't be completely rigid or rigorous either. I think it's just really helpful to have a proper sense of the direction in which you're heading, and to be able to mark off those achievements, big or small, along the way.

Hard work is an absolutely *vital* ingredient for achieving success. I have very strong views about this, because so often we tend to give the impression to others that things will just 'happen' in life or that they're easy. But you always have to work *really* hard! On a personal level, I had to work incredibly hard and relentlessly to be able to stand up again after my accident, and then to walk again. But I have also worked extremely hard throughout my professional life. Things *don't* just happen because you are there. You need to *know* your subject inside out, you have to *show up* and be *present* and be a fully active part of things, and that is all about hard work! It becomes about delivering fully what you're meant to deliver, doing your job properly and doing it really well, in whatever area that may be. To me, that's the fundamental bedrock on which success and fulfilment in life are built.

Achieving the right balance in your life . . .

Finding the right balance in your life depends very much on what you choose to do. If you want to become a professional sportsperson, for example, you will certainly need to dedicate a huge amount of time and effort to that. And while you might not find that your whole life will be fulfilled by it, you might find an enormous sense of fulfilment in achieving that particular goal. When you're starting and growing a business, it's really hard to have much of a work-life balance, but the notion that you have to work at it 24/7 has been widely proven to be a nonsense.

I believe that you can be focused and work really hard on one dominant priority in your life, and still find room for other activities that may not be as important but which can still maintain 'a bit of you'. You do that in different ways at different phases of your life too. When I was building lastminute.com, that was a really dominating part of my life, but I also kept time for other things; I helped to start Reprieve, a human-rights charity, quite literally working from a cupboard at the office. It wasn't an everyday activity for me, but it gave me energy to have another dimension to my life – and this was incredibly useful for me at that time. I think it helped to make me better at my day job, but it also helped make Reprieve better too.

Today, while I don't have a full-time job, I enjoy having the time to be around my children in the mornings and for this to be something I can prioritise. I do often work late at night and can often be on email 24/7, but that's fine because I can feel in control of it. So I think it's just about finding the right balance for you, while thinking about the different phases in your life. It also depends on what your goals are. If you want to become incredibly good at something or really 'successful' at whatever you might determine success to be, you have got to be realistic. It will probably require you to make some sacrifices. It's simply not possible to be friends with a hundred people, to read a hundred books a year, go to the theatre every week and spend time with your kids, while also dedicating yourself to running a business. Something will have to give. Precisely how you balance that is down to you!

Joanna Lumley OBE

An award-winning actress, voice-over artist, former model, author and activist, Joanna Lumley's popularity has spread across the globe. She is perhaps best known for her comedic role as Patsy Stone in *Absolutely Fabulous*. She has also played leading and supporting roles in numerous highly successful films, TV series and plays. More recently, her travel documentary series from around the world has been hugely popular. Among her many awards, she has been the recipient of three BAFTAs and in 2017 was honoured with the BAFTA Fellowship, in recognition of a lifetime of achievement. She has also received a string of honorary Doctorates from British universities and is a Fellow of the Royal Geographical Society. Joanna is a keen advocate for human rights and is also patron to several charities.

'Do everything to the best of your ability, enjoy it, and success will come from doing something that you really love.'

'When you smile or put on a happy face, it's amazing what a difference this can make.'

'I have always tried to be kind because I was taught to be courteous, and one of the great kindnesses in the world *is* courtesy.'

'As children grow older, parents shouldn't become ambitious *for* their children. Sometimes parents have a vision of how their son or daughter will turn out, what they want them to be. Don't dream too much for your children, simply be there. See what they want to do.'

What success means to me . . .

I have never really thought of myself in terms of being 'a success'. I certainly feel exceedingly lucky – and lucky to be alive – but I've never thought, 'Oh, I'm a success now, how marvellous!' or anything like that. And it doesn't matter how many prizes and plaudits one gets, I still don't think I'm a success in that way.

The only thing I have ever 'pursued' is to try to be *good* at whatever I'm doing. I have never been particularly ambitious, except perhaps to know the world. I've always loved acting and I still love doing it today, but it's not my life. I have never thought, 'I've got to get that part!' I have never longed or fought for those things, but when I *have* got the part, I've simply tried to do it well. I have never had any ambitions or set myself any goals except to do everything to the best of my ability.

I've had opportunities to do all sorts of things because I was born in a suitcase. I was brought up in the Far East, and being a soldier's daughter, wherever you are, it's home. So you already get to know the world a bit in that way at an early age. Personally, I have never looked for a 'pathway' through life and have never really had a goal at the end of it.

I suppose for me, success means being able to wake up every morning with peace in your heart and excitement in your mind – unbelievably hard to get, especially when you're young, but I firmly believe that success spirals out of something that you really love doing.

Follow something that you love . . .

The turbulence of being a young person is quite often not knowing what you are going to do. I wanted to act, but I didn't really know what the future held. I didn't think much about the future then anyway, but I couldn't think 'how to be' at the time either. I was too 'jumpy' and didn't want to train, I didn't want to swat or slog at something. I definitely did not want to work in an office – those things I knew I didn't want to do, but I couldn't think how to join the circus.

I tried to get into drama school when I was sixteen. I was turned down and it hurt so much! I wasn't even prepared at that age and I don't know why I went up for it, it was ridiculous. When they turned me down, I thought, 'What if I apply for several drama schools and they all turn me down? Does that mean I can never be an actress?' So, rather than hear any more 'no's', I thought I would sort out another way of doing it later on. I fell into modelling for a while and soon, when the time was right for me, I eventually found my way into acting, and was given a chance to pursue what I really wanted to do and would always love doing.

Sadly, we're driven by money in the West, and that's not so good. When I talk sometimes to young people about acting, they don't ask what they need to do to become an actor, they ask, 'How can I get to be famous?' All they want is to be rich and famous. They look at Hollywood stars and want to be like them. The irony is that 98 per cent of all actors are out of work at any given time and, across the board, we are the lowest-paid of all the professions by far! It's really hard. Unfortunately, what they see in the media or on social media makes everything appear easy, but it's not.

A lot of young girls will be influenced by what they see and read about glamour, and say, 'I want to do something in make-up or hairdressing.' Nobody has ever told them that they could become an engineer. If they're guided by what they see on reality TV, why would they ever want to be an engineer?

I have also seen bankers suddenly halting their careers and going off to run a home in Africa or joining a choir. They wake up one day and realise that they don't want to do it anymore, they've never liked it. Everything they've been taught about having a 'grown-up life' and making lots of money is wrong for them.

So, in order to find your own success, it is important that you find something that you *really* love doing.

Politeness, kindness and courtesy . . .

You can never fail if you are polite. Politeness opens all kinds of doors, it's astonishing. I am so conscious of children or young people who are polite.

I'm dazzled by them. I walk about saying 'Hello' to everybody and people say 'Hello' back, but sometimes the ones who don't say 'Hello' back are a bunch of school children walking up the road and you say, 'Hi guys' and they just ignore you and walk past because they believe it's 'not cool' to be polite. Well, I'm here to tell you, Darlings, politeness will get you to the very top! It can even mask a lack of ability. It can mask all kinds of inadequacies . . . Kindness and courtesy will always help take you much further!

I have always tried to be kind because I was taught to be courteous, and one of the great kindnesses in the world *is* courtesy. It's a shame that this seems to be disappearing and is not insisted upon as much these days. Even if it seems automatic, saying 'Please' and 'Thank you', standing up, opening a door or picking something up for somebody – these small courtesies make you a magic person. Being courteous and nice also brings you a kind of energy that makes you feel good about yourself and other people. Sadly, the concept of being kind and courteous is not even taught in schools any longer.

There are all kinds of things that are hard lessons to learn sometimes but that are so important. Being punctual is a courtesy – everyone appreciates someone who turns up on time. When you are meeting someone, show that you can be bothered and make a little effort to dress nicely. If you commit to doing something, stick to it! Sometimes days are going to be horrible, sometimes stuff is unbearably boring, but if you said you are going to do it, stick to it and do it with good grace. Don't just turn up and say, 'Yeah, I'm here.' Show some enthusiasm; 'OK, so what are we going to be doing today?'

Write 'thank you' letters. When someone gives you their time or does something for you, however small, they will always appreciate even a brief 'thank you' note – it's another courtesy. I write 'thank you' letters all the time. You feel good about doing it and people love to receive them. They will also appreciate that you have taken the time and made the effort to write. Today we seem to be going back to hieroglyphics with emojis – you don't even have to say, 'Thank you, I was thrilled to receive it!' You just go 'tap', and without any effort at all, you've sent a grinning face or something. It's not the same . . .

Being brave and facing difficulties . . .

We all have to face those difficult moments where one must be brave and one must be strong. If you're feeling inadequate, don't indulge it. Get hold of it and shape up a little. For an actor feeling terribly nervous on stage, you go on, your heart's banging and you think, 'I can't speak . . .!' and someone says, 'Just get on with it and do your darn lines!' and so you just get on with it. Once you've successfully read your lines, you think, 'Oh, OK, I've done it!' You've managed to push past your inadequacy at that moment. But it's the learning and the doing of it that makes you stronger, and from now on, when you do face another challenging moment in the future and your heart is banging away, *you know that you can do it*! So, just be brave and be strong.

In the famous musical *The King and I*, when Anna is on the ferry on her way to the court of the King of Siam, she's very nervous. She sings:

> *Whenever I feel afraid*
> *I hold my head erect*
> *And whistle a happy tune*
> *So, no one will suspect*
> *I'm afraid . . .*
>
> *Make believe you're brave*
> *And the trick will take you far*
> *You may be as brave*
> *As you make believe you are*

This is why I love acting – you can act anything, and you become it. You are on stage, you're in the wings and you feel flu coming on. But you still go on and you act as though nothing is wrong. By the end of it, Dr Theatre has more often than not actually cured you. We find this all the time – you pretend to be well or you pretend to be fine, and you become so.

When you smile or put on a happy face, it's amazing what a difference this can make. A long-distance runner I know was told that when you're coming into the last bend of a run, start smiling. Strangely enough, when the endorphins kick in or whatever it is, something positive happens.

There's the wonderful poem, 'If' by Rudyard Kipling (see below), that I have printed on an old Irish tea towel and pinned to the back of my study door. I know it by heart. For me, it's a guide to life that literally cannot be bettered. I would pass this on to every young person if I could, and often tell young actors to get hold of it and read it. Although the poem ends '. . . you'll be a man, my son', it's still relevant to everyone.

Virtually everyone will face dark days at some time in their lives. When I was around twenty-four my life was turned upside down. I had a hospital operation, went back to work far too early and suffered a major breakdown. I was in a terrible state. I tried counselling myself at that time as best I could, and even though things were really, really bad, I just wanted to get back to being well again. As part of my self-healing, I remember trying to envisage all sorts of scenarios of being in trouble and imagining what I needed to do to get out of them. In every case, a small voice would tell me, 'Kind people will help you.' And this is something I have believed in ever since. Whenever you are in doubt or in trouble, ask for help – and kind people will always help you.

Asking for advice and finding a mentor . . .

As a young person, you are very often terribly self-conscious. You're concerned about how you look, what other people think. You may be completely caught up in yourself, because that's the nature of being young. But if you can, try not to worry too much about yourself. Try to be interested in other people and make the greatest effort to listen to what they have to say. Don't just have an opinion, listen to other people and ask questions. The world is full of kindly people who can help you and who love being asked. If you don't know something, ask. Don't think, 'They'll believe I'm stupid' or 'They might despise me' for asking a question. People adore being asked questions, especially by the young.

As I have got older, I still ask questions all the time from everybody: 'How do I do this? What should I say? Did you know that . . .? Where did you go? Tell me, tell me, tell me . . .', and people love it, they love telling.

When you are young, you can often find advice, answers to your questions and even a good mentor from within your family. Quite often, mothers are very busy with younger children or they are out working. Dads may be too busy and sometimes it's a grandmother or an uncle or aunt that helps out at home – an older, steadier hand. They can also be good mentors. Grannies have nobody in their heart but you, so they are bound to tell you the truth!

My grannies were not able to be my mentors, unfortunately, because we lived in the Far East. I didn't know them, and I never sat in their laps. We used to write to them, so one was called 'Kenya Granny', since that's where she lived, and the other was 'Bedford Granny'. My parents were wonderful, and I suppose they were my mentors when I was young. Later in life, as I began to do more travelling, Lord Shackleton was a mentor to me, and very helpful he was too on some of the tougher journeys I have done. He encouraged me to become a Fellow of the Royal Geographic Society and put me in touch with people who'd be useful on some of my more hairy trips. As you get older, you appreciate more how helpful a mentor can be.

A school teacher can be a good mentor (if they have time, poor devils). Sometimes they can spot the shining ones, and quite often you might hear someone say, 'Mrs Phillips was just great – she knew when I was the bad boy in class but also knew I loved music, and so she put me in touch with the oboe.'

So mentors are people that you can learn from and turn to for advice. But you have got to 'want to know', and you have got to have questions to ask in the first place.

Make your goal to be your best . . .

I have never been ambitious, and because of this, I have never been disappointed. I have never had any goals, except to *do everything well*. If you want to become an actor, don't set yourself the goal of becoming a Hollywood star. If you want to be a singer, love singing and focus on doing your very best. What if you want to change direction later on? If you thought you want to be a solicitor and you decide later to become an opera singer, don't feel like you've missed the goal and let yourself down.

Life is so thrilling, and that is why I've never had any deep regrets. I look at all the wonderful things that have come out of what I've done. As an actress, I have done so much second-rate work in second-rate films that have never gone anywhere. But from it, I have made some of the best friends you can imagine. We've laughed and cried about some of the stuff we've had to say or do! But, we've done it to the best of our abilities, we've paid the rent, and we've made some great friends. My job is acting and I love doing it. If the big job isn't there, I'll do some small stuff or voice-overs, which I also love doing. So don't kill yourself chasing the big dreams or the big goals. Do everything to the best of your ability, enjoy it, and success will come from doing something that you really love.

To parents . . .

My advice to parents would be to give your children love, love, love. That's about all you've got and all you can ever do, and you must never withdraw it ever, ever, ever. Unconditional love – seems hard, but just do it. That is the first thing.

Giving children advice when they are young is very difficult. It's hard for them to make sense of it. It's also funny how so often you remember perhaps what the English mistress told you at school or what your mother said to you or what your father advised . . . and then it comes back later in life, maybe in your thirties or forties, and it sits with you and you're guided by it and it all makes sense. It makes sense now, but not when you first received it. When you are young, you say, 'Yeah right! Do you really think I'm going to do *that*?'

While it's difficult to give children advice, it's often quite hard for a young child to ask for help too. Sometimes it might be worth a more indirect approach – ask your child for help with something you can do together. So, if Mum or Aunt Lucy asks them for help to prepare the carrots at suppertime, she can use the time to say perhaps, 'Do you hate maths or do you love it, like I did?' Because you are doing something else together, things can be said in a relaxed way that kids don't mind hearing, and they are more likely to ask questions or ask for help too. Stuff can come out and be discussed that they might not want to talk about normally. If my parents were to say, 'Jo, I want to talk to you about something,' I would probably resist and not want to listen, but if during a car journey when nobody's looking at each other, stuff was talked about, I was more likely to listen and things could sink in.

My parents believed in literature and the importance of reading. If you can read books, know how to read a map, how to use a reference book, dictionaries and quotation books, have Shakespeare in the house, you can then learn so much. They helped us to appreciate reading and to build an appetite for it (you can't bang it into children). When I was a child, we read all the time – we read at meals, read at night and I am still passionate about reading today. If children don't like reading at first, encourage them to listen to audiobooks.

Encourage your children to learn. Education is so important for young people. Through education, you can teach people how to look after themselves so they won't fall ill, and you can teach them how to avoid falling into crime.

I believe that we should spread everything in front of children. I cannot bear the way that we have stratified society by music. We have largely taken classical music out of schools, so some children cannot grow up knowing if they love it, because they will never have heard it if it's not played at home. I would bring back singing and music to schools, in plenty. When you sing something together, it unleashes all sorts of things. I have never met anybody who sings in a choir who doesn't come back feeling happy and invigorated.

As children grow older, parents should not become ambitious *for* their children. Sometimes parents have a vision of how their son or daughter will turn out, what they want them to be. Don't dream too much for your children, simply be there. See what they want to do. Take them off and do things with them away from home (but not the normal holiday stuff), where you can do things together. Go on a walking trail with them. Have some great songs that you can sing as you go. Do something where you're *there* with them and see how they manage. It's extraordinary what children can learn from these adventures and it helps parents connect and 'be in touch' with them too.

'If' by Rudyard Kipling – written in 1895

If you can keep your head when all about you
Are losing theirs and blaming it on you,
If you can trust yourself when all men doubt you,
But make allowance for their doubting too;
If you can wait and not be tired by waiting,
Or being lied about, don't deal in lies,
Or being hated, don't give way to hating,
And yet don't look too good, nor talk too wise:

If you can dream – and not make dreams your master;
If you can think – and not make thoughts your aim;
If you can meet with Triumph and Disaster
And treat those two imposters just the same;
If you can bear to hear the truth you've spoken
Twisted by knaves to make a trap for fools,
Or watch the things you gave your life to, broken,
And stoop and build 'em up with worn-out tools:

If you can make one heap of all your winnings
And risk it on one turn of pitch-and-toss,
And lose, and start again at your beginnings
And never breathe a word about your loss;
If you can force your heart and nerve and sinew
To serve your turn long after they are gone,
And so hold on when there is nothing in you
Except the Will which says to them: 'Hold on!'

If you can talk with crowds and keep your virtue,
Or walk with kings – nor lose the common touch,
If neither foes nor loving friends can hurt you,
If all men count with you, but none too much;
If you can fill the unforgiving minute
With sixty seconds' worth of distance run,
Yours is the Earth and everything that's in it,
And – which is more – you'll be a Man, my son!

Dame Carolyn McCall DBE

One of the United Kingdom's most respected business leaders, Carolyn McCall's reputation began while working at *The Guardian* newspaper. She joined as a researcher in 1986 after obtaining her master's degree in politics, and steadily progressed to become CEO of *The Guardian* and *The Observer*, and eventually CEO of the Guardian Media Group. In 2010 she was appointed CEO of easyJet and successfully led the airline's transformation into a customer-focused success story, with record growth in passenger numbers and business travellers. In 2018, she was appointed CEO of the commercial broadcaster ITV. Among her numerous awards, in 2008 she was named as the Veuve Clicquot Businesswoman of the Year and was also awarded an OBE. In 2016 she received her damehood for services to the aviation industry.

'If you are positive, energetic and happy in your work, you will naturally stand out. People will begin to say, "Would you like to work on this project?" or "Do you want to work with this team?"'

'There's this popular myth that once you reach a certain level, you stop learning. I think that's completely bonkers! I'm still learning all the time.'

'If you are afraid of failure or taking risks, this can seriously hold you back. Most people believe that they *can't* make a mistake, and the fear of doing so often stops them from getting on with things.'

'One thing that my parents gave me was a very secure home life – I knew I was loved, and I therefore always felt secure. They never told me that I couldn't do anything. Instead, they would say, 'You can do whatever you want to do.' It was that ability to feel I *could do* anything and that I had the *freedom to do* so that was really important.'

Finding your happiness . . .

While some people will make it their goal to 'become successful', I have never really thought like that. I think having a focus on *happiness* is far more important, and being happy has always been *my* goal. Success is just an outlook, and something that comes as a result perhaps of having a more balanced, fulfilled and happy life. I decided quite early on in my life that I wanted to be happy, but I also did not want to have to make unnecessary compromises along the way.

For me, happiness comes from knowing first of all that my family are happy, safe and secure. Second, that I am able to work at something I really love and enjoy doing, which is worthwhile and where I know that I'm making a positive impact on a business or on the community within which I'm working and a positive difference to the people whom I work with in that company. And third, despite living a hectic life, having real friends and being able to maintain normal friendships through thick and thin.

These three things are the most important for me. So I don't ever think about success like many other people might do. For me, it's all about finding happiness.

Choosing what you want to be . . .

It can be difficult for a young person to know what they want to pursue as a career at a young age. The world is also changing at an incredible pace and who knows what roles will actually exist in five years' time. One has only got to look at the whole field of artificial intelligence, for example. People talk about it incessantly now, and yet little was known about it outside the realms of academia just a few years ago.

I do think education is very important. Apart from the grounding it provides, it can certainly ignite some of the interests you will pursue in later life.

If a young person is lucky enough to have a vocation, I think that's great. You often hear about kids at the age of ten or eleven who want to be a doctor, a nurse, a vet or a pilot. They should certainly follow their vocation, but for those that do not have one, they should actively look for different opportunities – get out there and explore what it is that they might like to do and keep an open mind.

I am a great believer in work placements and paid internships. These allow someone to dip in and out for perhaps a week at a time within different industries, be it accountancy, media, law, banking, retail or something else. They can provide a young person with real insight into a particular sector and to get a feel for what a company's culture is like. They can also help them to eliminate the areas they may not like. I remember once putting someone into work experience at an advertising agency. When she came out, she said, 'I thought that's what I really wanted to do, but I now realise it's absolutely *not* for me.'

It seems that everyone now wants work experience when they're young. I would certainly favour some form of government initiative to provide a more structured approach that involves corporate businesses – a coordinated work-experience programme that provides at least two different companies for each student to explore. Finding work experience is really hard when every school is asking sixteen-year-olds to find it.

Follow what you enjoy . . .

I can honestly say that I have enjoyed every single job that I have ever done. I think this is very important, because if you enjoy what you do, other people will enjoy working with you too – and this can certainly help you move ahead in your career. If you are positive, energetic and happy in your work, you will naturally stand out. People will begin to say, 'Would you like to work on this project?' or 'Do you want to work with this team?'

It started for me when I went to university, where I was able to pursue the subjects that I really enjoyed studying – History, English and Politics. While my university life was good, I also really enjoyed the work, which is not something that a lot of students will say. But I also *wanted* to learn. Even now, I read a lot. There's this popular myth that once you reach a certain level, you stop learning. I think that's completely bonkers! I'm still learning all the time.

My pathway meandered a little during the early part of my career, when I was seeking something that I would really enjoy doing. After my graduation, I trained as a teacher and spent a year working at a London comprehensive school. I then studied for my master's in Politics while working at a civil engineering company, doing risk analysis. I eventually decided that I might like to do something in media, and my first big turning point came when I got a position at *The Guardian*, where I embarked on a new career as a researcher. I had no idea where it was going to take me, and I didn't really care either. I just enjoyed being there. *The Guardian* was a meritocracy, with a very 'open' culture – great people, very creative, very bright and very collaborative. I liked it so much that after just three months in, I knew that I had finally discovered what I really wanted to do and where I wanted to be.

I loved being in research and I could happily have stayed working in a highly academic research function forever, but one day my boss said to me, 'You should do sales.' I remember telling her, 'I don't want to do sales, I'm a researcher!' But she persuaded me. 'You know what? You can do all the research you want, but I think you'll be *very* good in sales.' I asked her, 'If ever I want to move back again to my job in research, can I?' And she said, 'Yes, you can. Your job will stay open for you.'

Coincidentally, I had recently met a hugely successful businessman, and I recalled him saying to me, 'All the best people start in sales.' I now realise that selling actually teaches you a huge amount. When you work in sales, you begin to understand all aspects of a company's operations. In media sales, you learn to work with the creative side, because you're selling the product. You have to understand marketing well too, and the closer you work with marketing and understanding your audience, the research and all the insights that you have, the better you become at what you do. At the same time, you are continually facing customers and therefore account managing and trading all the time, and you have to become a good negotiator. And so I took the plunge and moved into sales. This was to become the big turning point in my career and a huge kick-start moment for me.

It was in sales that my career really began to make good progress, and I soon found myself being promoted to sales management, and, in time, moving up to manage more people and bigger teams. A little while later, an extraordinary new opportunity opened up for me. I had joined *The Guardian* in 1986 and at that time, no one was talking about the internet. By the early nineties, however, I felt right at the centre of it all, managing the launch of *Wired* in the UK. This was a *Guardian* joint venture with *Wired* in the US, and an amazing time for me to learn about digital enterprises. From that experience, I went on to launch, with an editorial partner, *The Guardian* website. My whole digital background and experience has really come from these two digital ventures, and I still use the enormous amount of knowledge that I acquired from that time in my work today.

In the twenty years that I worked at *The Guardian*, I took on a new role virtually every eighteen months. I was able to work very cross-functionally, and, being such an open culture, if you were good at what you did, they would let you move around a lot within the organisation to gain more experience. In the end, it was like a massive graduate training programme to become a CEO, and was extremely valuable for me. From general management, I became managing director and eventually chief executive officer.

One thing that I learned from being CEO of a creatively led media business like *The Guardian* was how to be collaborative, but perhaps at a much more sophisticated level than would be normal. The whole structure of the ownership trust really exists for editorial independence and, ultimately, to protect *The Guardian*'s legacy into perpetuity. One always had to balance sensitively the commercial interests of the business with its editorial side, and you soon realise that you have to work *with* people and really collaborate effectively. There was no point in trying to bulldoze or bludgeon your way through with things, because they just wouldn't happen.

Another thing that I have learned during my career, as a manager and as a leader, is the importance of making the workplace an enjoyable space for your people. It has become something of a mantra to always 'create a place fun enough for people to *want* to come to work'. I believe that you can create roles and an environment where people genuinely enjoy their work. The last thing I would want is for someone to return from holiday and think, 'I really don't want to go back to work today.'

When the Guardian Media Group was looking for a new group CEO, the company undertook a rigorous four-month recruitment process, searching both internally and externally. Even though I thought that everyone knew what I was capable of doing (I had already been on the group's board and had been running a key division for five years), I still had to go through due process, prove myself in an interview and explain the reasons why I felt I could do the job. It was actually very good for me, applying for a big job internally, but also one of the hardest things I have had to do in my career! Once I got the role, I was then exposed much more to other areas, like mergers and acquisitions, corporate finance and private equity, all of which were to be hugely valuable for my career.

I enjoyed each and every role that I was given at the Guardian Media Group over the time I was there. But after a while, there was nothing else that I wanted to do within the organisation. I'm not a 'vertical' person, but I couldn't realistically go horizontal or vertical. The time naturally came to cut the family ties when I was offered an exciting new role as CEO for easyJet.

While it was a big risk for me personally at that time, it was also a great opportunity, but not without its challenges. The company's founder was no longer at the helm but was still a major shareholder, which was to prove quite difficult at times, as has been widely publicised. I recall thinking, before I decided to take on the role, 'If I don't take a risk now, I never will.' I knew that I had built up a good track record and reputation in the media industry, and if I needed to go back, I could probably do so – not to the same job, of course, but hopefully to a key role in the industry. I would certainly not be making myself unemployable by changing sector.

My role at easyJet from the outset was definitely at the very sharp end of operational intensity. The business had a lot of issues when I joined, with considerable operational problems, customer problems and people problems to sort out. But with the experience I had gained from all of the roles I'd previously taken on, I was ready to meet the challenge and felt able to make a big difference for the airline. In the end, I really enjoyed my time working for that company, and I feel a real sense of pride for the contribution I've made to creating a customer-facing airline, with engaged and high-performing people delivering market-leading returns.

Finding a mentor . . .

I think it's important for a young person to have somebody other than their own family to talk to about their working life, about their career, their future and their motivations. The more they can talk to someone knowledgeable about what it's really like to work in certain businesses or sectors, the more informed they will be. As you get older, if you are the kind of person who loves to learn and wants to hear what other people think, then it's a natural step to find a mentor.

One needs to find someone who'll challenge you and who can help you to see the broader picture. Even later in life, a mentor can play a crucial role in helping you to visualise your future. A wonderful mentor of mine told me when I was at the Guardian Media Group, 'You can do anything now.' I remember saying to him, 'I can't do *anything*,' to which he replied, 'Of course you can. You can be a CEO anywhere.' Although I didn't believe him, it certainly opened my mind, so much so that when easyJet called, I know he helped me be brave enough to take that on. He was also good at telling me, 'This is what you need to do less of' and 'This is what you need to do more of.' He also persuaded me that my network was too media-focused, and that I needed to do less media and marketing dinners and do more 'business' dinners, to build up my business network. He was brilliant for me and crucially helped open my mind to greater possibilities, before I made the move to easyJet . . .

Attitude . . .

Whenever I am speaking to children in schools or speaking at events to women and men, I will always express how important it is to have a positive attitude. People like being around positive people. No one likes to be around people who drain them or who moan and complain all the time. If anyone has something to complain about, they should just _do_ something about it. If you don't like your job, you need to try to move on!

One of the best ways to cultivate a positive attitude is to surround yourself with people who have positive energy. You can also get energy from different places and activities. Some people find it in sport. For me, I get a lot of energy from playing tennis with friends. I absolutely love it – it puts me in such a good mood. It could be raining, but I'll still have a good time playing.

I also get a lot of positive energy from going out with some of my girlfriends. Nothing to do with work, it's just literally having a chat; talking about the kids, talking about what's going on in their worlds. It's a simple thing, but it always lifts me and gives me that energy.

How parents can help . . .

I never want to live my life through my children. Unfortunately, I think that does happen quite a lot with parents in some families. I also believe it can be quite dangerous, heaping your own expectations on your children, when these may not be a recipe for their future happiness! They may end up becoming relatively successful in the eyes of their parents, but it might not necessarily make them happy or well-rounded individuals in later life.

Where parents come from a professional background, the expectation might be that their children should follow in their footsteps and become, say, a lawyer, a doctor or an accountant. But if one of their kids really wants to do something creative, just let them do it.

I believe *the* most important thing that parents can and should do is give their children the security and confidence to be able to go and pursue whatever they believe they should do in order to be happy.

Building self-confidence is hugely important for a young person. If they lack self-confidence, it will almost certainly hold them back. I see this a lot in young women and girls. Even when they have self-belief, they can lack the confidence to vocalise it and they usually don't 'behave' it. Typically, they might go for a job interview and get asked the question (I ask this all the time when I'm interviewing), 'What are you really good at?' They're quite likely to reply, 'Well, you know, what I need to develop is this' or 'I need to work harder at that . . .' Whereas most guys will say, 'I'm really good at delivering on my numbers' or 'I'm good at leading from the front.' Men tend to be more assertive about what they are good at, while many girls or women will often be more modest and hesitant.

This is an area where parents of young girls can play an especially big role, through helping them at home to feel happy, confident and secure. It's important to give girls that confidence, to avoid them being swayed by the usual peer pressure – what they think they should look like, how they think they should be. Parents can do this by keeping a line of communication going all of the time. This can be easier said than done with teenage girls, but I know that you have to keep talking to them, no matter how frustrating it is and how mad they drive you! So my aim is to keep communicating, and be 'reinforcing' rather than undermining.

One thing that my parents gave me was a very secure home life – I knew I was loved, and I therefore always felt secure. They never told me that I couldn't do anything. They would never say something like, 'Oh, don't be daft, you can't do that.' Instead, they would say, 'You can do whatever you want to do.' It was that ability to feel I *could do* anything and that I had the *freedom to do so* that was really important.

My children really like sport, and I think that's a very good thing for them. It gets them outdoors and keeps them active, fit and away from being stuck watching a screen for hours, which is increasingly becoming a dominant part of teenagers' lives these days. Another good reason is that it helps kids to become *passionate* about a sport, be it football, rugby, hockey, tennis or netball, and it becomes something that they *want* to do. They enjoy playing with their friends and they learn about being part of a team. Not all children like sport, so it's always about broadening their interest in whatever they might enjoy, be it drama, music, art and so on.

Resilience and self-doubt . . .

In order to deal with challenges, especially some of the bigger ones, you need to have resilience. Becoming resilient takes time to acquire and is, in my view, sourced from two things. First, you have to be fairly 'seasoned' and have to experience a few knocks along the way to develop your resilience. Working in sales, for example, is very good for building resilience, because of how you learn. When you start 'presenting', your peers will tell you how to improve, and you have to listen and absorb. And then, you have to learn how to deal with rejections. It's an integral part of sales that people will say 'no' to you all the time – they don't want to buy from you, for whatever reason. So you get knocked back, and you've got to learn to get up each time and start again. That helps build resilience.

Second, having an 'anchored' life helps to make you more resilient. That's why I firmly believe in having a well-rounded life with balance at home in my family life, and having real friends I can rely on who have known me for many years. Because when things get really tough, having your family and your friends really gives you resilience. These anchors are very important for me and provide a lot of positive energy when I need it.

It was the day after the Brexit vote when I found myself having to summon every ounce of resilience I possessed to manage the implications that leaving the European Union would have for easyJet. No one at the airline believed that the UK would vote to leave, but the potential impact on the business was going to be huge if we did. Although based in Luton and a UK company, easyJet is a European airline – half of my staff were from the EU. I had to address my people straight away – they were all concerned and anxious, both about the company (the share price fell by 40 per cent) and the effect on them as individuals. I didn't know what resilience really meant until I experienced being faced with that. I had to meet with my teams right across Europe, the whole network. I needed to present a face of assuredness and pragmatism, while expressing confidence in the business model, the structure of the business and the people in the business. I had to say, 'We have a plan, we have a contingency. This is what we're going to do – and don't worry, it's going to be hard, but we're going to be fine.'

I also had to see the UK government and civil service to understand the implications, and meet with European governments and regulators in order to implement our contingency plan of setting up an airline in a European country to protect our flying rights. I was also very involved in trying to manage the UK media. It was an exhausting time and, of course, I still had to lead the day-to-day business.

During difficult times we can all experience periods of self-doubt, and that is when you have got to have the right people around you – the right team, the right mentors. These are people that want the best for the company and for you, who can give you positive energy, who you can trust and talk to about your concerns, worries or anxieties. They can help you to look at things in a different way. Having self-doubt is normal and makes us human. In fact, if you don't have self-doubt from time to time, you probably will never be successful.

Dealing with failure – a learning culture . . .

If you are afraid of failure or taking risks, this can seriously hold you back. Most people believe that they *can't* make a mistake, and the fear of doing so often stops them from getting on with things. But actually, people are normally forgiven if they make a mistake over something that was 'well-intentioned' – when you make a career move for example, where everything looked right at the time, but it doesn't work out, or you make a business decision for all the right reasons and it ends up being the wrong one. We all fail at times, and having failures is fine as long as you can learn from them. There is, in fact, a lot we can learn from failure. Unfortunately, one often sees mistakes being made repeatedly by some people who never seem to learn.

In any organisation, we have to actually allow for failure. For senior people, especially someone that achieves a lot, it can sometimes be difficult to recognise when there has been a mistake, and it's easier to just brush it under the carpet and move on (it can take a brave team to sit down and dissect that!). So the first thing that you have to do is recognise that something has gone wrong, and that it may need to be completely unpicked, unravelled and done again. You then need to be honest and resolve why the failure happened, what to do differently next time and what needs to be put in place to prevent it from happening again. But, one should not spend too much time overanalysing the failure or scrutinising *why* it happened. It's more important to work on what has been learned, and what processes and procedures need to change.

Sometimes, market forces can work against you. No matter how good you are, how hard you work, however good your team may be, if you are a CEO during a recession or a bear market (which can last a long time), it can be very difficult to avoid the perception of a lack of success. One can't easily buck a declining market, and as CEO, you still have to carry the can for your company's performance. Sometimes you see a CEO depart, a new person steps in and then the markets turn around, and away they go on the upswing.

We all need a bit of good luck sometimes and a fair wind. You occasionally need to be in the right place at the right time, but this is where I believe hard work pays off – because if you're not in the right place now, eventually you will be, if you work hard. 'Making your own luck' in this way, however, also has a lot to do with judgement. It's about deciding when to say 'yes' and when to say 'no' – when you should seize an opportunity and when you shouldn't take a risk. It's about judgement, and only *you* can judge. You can have the best advice around you and the best mentors in the world, but you are always the one that has to make the call.

Working hard while maintaining a healthy family life . . .

When I look back over my career, one constant throughout has been my commitment to work. I have never taken what would be considered an 'easy' CEO role (if one exists!) – I enjoy tackling challenges, whether strategic or operational. I have never cruised my way through anything and have always worked hard. Anyone who has ever worked with me would probably ask, 'Why is she so driven?' But I'm actually kind of driven by the work itself, by making a difference. I'm not driven to 'have more' or to move up all the time – I just want to do really well and be able to enjoy what I'm doing.

But once again, in order to find success at anything, *you have to work really, really hard!* This is something that young people can find difficult to grasp at first. As parents, we're all role models, and I like the fact that my children see me working hard. It helps them to appreciate and understand the importance of hard work, and how fulfilling it can be.

I am very family-oriented and ensure I'm a very 'present' parent. But, I'm also on call and 'at work' all of the time, even when I'm at home. When I was at easyJet, the international nature of the aviation industry meant that I had to be available, at the end of the phone, day or night. In all of the years that I was there, my phone was always charged and never switched off, even when I was sleeping. Technology is a fantastic enabler to me being able to find the right equilibrium between work and family. I will often work late at night after seeing my kids.

Some people might ask how it is possible to maintain a demanding career, work very hard, and yet have time to raise a family, with teenage children, and still find time to relax. To be honest, sometimes I think I'm a good mother because they're good kids and everyone is happy, no one has fallen out and no one is screaming! But there are other mornings when I think, 'My goodness! It's just so frenetic!' But to me, it's also a natural thing – everywhere around the world, people are working and raising a family. It's not easy, of course, and it can sometimes be a real juggling act. But I think that when you have a busy career, you have to be hyper-organised. When everything is organised and flowing smoothly, at work and at home, I do in fact find it very easy to switch off and also find time for myself to relax.

Sir Keith Mills GBE DL

A leading British entrepreneur, Sir Keith Mills was the creator and founder of the Air Miles and Nectar Card customer loyalty programmes. He has also established several other businesses, both in the UK and overseas. He is widely acclaimed for his role in bringing the Olympic and Paralympic Games to London in 2012, as international president and CEO of London 2012, and subsequently overseeing the games as part of the organising committee, the LOCOG. Sir Keith has won numerous awards for his business activities over the years, and in 2006 was knighted for his services to sport. He was appointed chairman of the Royal Foundation in 2016.

'I do think that opportunities come along all the time for all of us, and you have got to be ready to seize them when they do. If you want to become successful at something, you must be prepared to have a go, be brave and sometimes take a risk.'

'To be successful in anything you do, it definitely requires hard work. I know very few successful people that have reached the top without a huge amount of effort. So the need to work hard is a *really* important principle for young people to understand.'

'Money isn't everything. You can have a successful, fulfilling life doing something that you really enjoy without needing to earn a fortune.'

'I think it's very important for parents to give their children the permission to dream, to give them the confidence to pursue their passions and help them tangibly where you can.'

On success . . .

For me, success is about being happy with your life and being able to do the things that bring you the most pleasure. That's not to say, 'Go out and play golf every day,' because you can be happy doing lots of interesting things and still play golf.

Whatever success means, it is very personal to you. In my case, it's a *challenge*, and whenever I can, I like to make an impact, both for me personally and for the world in which we live. I have therefore always been attracted to things that can either make an impact, make a difference *or* make some money, or preferably all three.

I have met quite a few people over the years that have made a lot of money but are really not fulfilled. I also know a lot of people that have not made any money but are still very happy with their lives and who feel that they have been successful in ways that are important to them.

My sister was a very successful junior school teacher. That's all she did, and she was brilliant at it. The kids loved her – they got a lot out of her teaching and she got a lot out of it too. She didn't earn a lot of money, didn't receive any public acclaim, but still enjoyed a very fulfilling life and is now happily retired. Given what she aspired to do, she has certainly had a very successful life.

Making the right choices and knowing where you want to go . . .

I come from very humble beginnings. I was brought up in a council house – my dad was a factory worker and he had very low aspirations for what success might look like. After I was asked to leave school at fifteen, with nothing more than a swimming certificate, my career options were naturally somewhat limited. Most traditional careers were out of reach for me. But I do remember thinking then, how I wanted more than anything else to have the freedom to be able to choose what I wanted to do, where to live, what car to drive and where to go in the world . . . I concluded at that time, quite intelligently, really, given my youth and my lack of experience, that in order to achieve this freedom I would probably need to make quite a lot of money. I believed that being financially independent would ultimately give me much more freedom of choice.

I also recalled at that time, what my history master (who doubled up as a careers master) had once told me, 'You've got two choices, Mills; you can either work in an office or you can work in a factory. What do you want to do?' So I chose to work in an office, and my career started off as an office boy making tea and running errands. This was my first really important choice and decision. Throughout life, you will be regularly presented with choices and decisions to make. You can either go left or you can go right, so knowing broadly where it is that you want to get to is pretty important.

I'm a bit of a sailor, and I often tell a story about when I first learned to sail. I had spent the day out on the Solent, where we were learning about navigation. We got back to the marina and my instructor asked me, 'So, what's the most important thing that you've learned today about navigation?' I replied enthusiastically, 'How to read a GPS so you know where you are.' He said, 'No, that's not it . . .' I then said, 'How to read a chart so you can see where you're going?' He replied, 'No, it's not that either . . .' After venturing a few answers, I finally said, 'I don't know, what *is* the most important thing I have learned today?' And that's when he told me something I would never forget; 'Knowing where you want to go.' For me, this is fundamental, and has become a guiding principle throughout my life.

Deciding where you want to go and what you want to do is often difficult for a young person. It is important, however, to focus on those things that you most enjoy doing and avoid taking a job or pursuing a career in something that you really don't believe in or don't believe you can contribute to.

If you're not sure what you want to do, start narrowing down your options by thinking about all the things you absolutely don't want to do or have no interest in, and take them off the table. That leaves you with 'what's left', and that's effectively your first decision. If you continue to refine your options and keep refining them, you will eventually get to a space where you have better choices. Once you know broadly where you are going, you will be far more likely to find fulfilment in life and success in whatever you do.

Find your motivation and meet those challenges . . .

People can be motivated in different ways. Personally, I'm a 'challenge junkie', and I feel very uncomfortable if I don't have a challenge. Sometimes I wish I were not that way, because it can make life really difficult both for me and also for those around me! But I've always been a sucker for a challenge . . .

In my younger days, although I had a really great job at *The Economist* magazine, it still wasn't enough for me. At the age of twenty-three, I decided that I wanted to set up on my own, and I challenged myself to start a new business. So I left a very comfortable job and company car behind to start a small advertising agency. I managed to keep the business going for eighteen months or so, but then my biggest client, representing over 80 per cent of my business, went bust, leaving me with £100,000 of debt – and that was the end of my first venture. It was also my first big lesson in business: never put all of your eggs in one basket!

It took me a few years to recover from that disaster, so I had to find a job. Later, I was working for another company and trying to acquire the London office of a New York advertising agency for them. My boss at the time decided to back out of the deal, but the Americans I was negotiating with then approached me and said, 'Look, if your company doesn't want to do it, will you?' Another huge challenge! I subsequently borrowed the money to buy the London agency, and that was the first proper business that I owned, with staff, revenues and Mayfair offices.

When taking on a challenge, you obviously have no idea whether it's going to be successful or not, but it will still motivate me. When I first thought up the concept of Air Miles it was something completely new and I had no idea if it would work, but it became a huge challenge for me. It was a very successful business in the end, of course, and I made a significant amount of money from it, and it was similar with Nectar

Card some years later. The point is, neither of these businesses would have existed if I had not *challenged* myself to make them happen.

When you master the art of creating choices and making the right decisions, it's extraordinary where life can take you.

In the late 1990s, I sold one of my Air Miles companies for a great deal of money. For the following year, I was clearly becoming a complete pain at home, trying to work out what to do next. So my wife suggested that perhaps I should go and do something completely outside of my comfort zone. By chance, I happened to read an article in *The Sunday Times* about sailing around the globe in a yacht race. So I applied, and I met the legendary sailor Sir Robin Knox-Johnston, and ended up competing in a serious round-the-world yacht race as part of an amateur team.

This was to become a profound and extraordinary experience for me. I quickly learned during my time on the boat how it simply didn't matter if you were rich or poor, young or old, fit or fat – we were all part of a team and on a level playing field. You could also lose your life very easily! I soon concluded on this trip that there was more to life than just making money, and I came away with a clear goal to 'do something big in sport'. It was a conscious decision and something I would become very passionate about.

During the race, I took a small book with me about the life of Sir Thomas Lipton, an industrialist in the 1920s and 30s who had tried to win the America's Cup for Britain for over thirty years. He was the businessman behind the team, and I was intrigued and inspired by this book because I just could not understand why he had failed and why so many others had failed before him.

I began to think that it would be an amazing challenge if, after 160 years of the America's Cup, I could somehow help Britain to win a trophy that we created in 1851 and have never since won! I knew nothing really about the event, so I started to ask lots of questions and met a lot of people who knew the sport. I then watched the 2003 America's Cup take place in New Zealand, where we failed miserably once again . . .

After watching that, I decided that this was something I really wanted to do. So I approached the British team principal soon afterwards to see if I could buy the team.

I was in the middle of negotiating to buy the assets and the boats, when completely out of left field, I was asked if I would run Britain's bid to host the Olympic Games in 2012.

Just like the America's Cup, I knew very little about the Olympic Games either, as I had only ever seen it on TV. This was a bidding contest, with nine countries seeking the rights to be host, and the person who asked me to do the job persuaded me that if I won the bid, my chances of raising the money to pursue the America's Cup would be a lot easier. So after giving it some thought, I stopped negotiating for the America's Cup assets and took on the bid for the Olympic and Paralympic Games instead, pulled together a great team, and ultimately, we won the bid.

I mentioned earlier that I love a challenge. When running the Olympic bid, I didn't at first really know what I was taking on, but in the end, we had hundreds of millions of people watching us on TV make our presentation in Singapore, waiting to see whether we had succeeded or failed – incredibly high pressure, an amazing challenge, and once again precisely what motivates me. I knew that if we were successful, it would also have a huge impact on everyone in the UK and on millions of people around the world. It was, in the end, one of the most highly acclaimed and successful Olympic Games in history, and I am proud to have played the part that I did to make it happen.

Once the Games had finished, I turned my attention back once again to the America's Cup. I teamed up with Sir Ben Ainslie to help him create a team and raise investment for the UK to seriously challenge for the 35th America's Cup in Bermuda in 2017. This was to be a huge project, with the development and technologies required similar to those in a Formula One team. Unfortunately, we were knocked out of the cup in the semi-finals, but the current team now has its vision firmly set on winning the competition in the future and has a great chance of doing so next time.

When I talk to young people, I will often say that if you are not prepared to take some risks in life, your horizons will always be very narrow. Unfortunately, too many young people these days seem to be risk-averse, and fear of failure is often a big problem for them. I do think that opportunities come along all the time for all of us, and you have got to be ready to seize them when they do. If you want to become successful at something, you must be prepared to have a go, be brave and sometimes take a risk.

It is also important to keep your eyes and ears open all the time for opportunities, and when they come along, you've got to be positive and make a decision. This goes back to my earlier point about the binary decisions we must all make – 'Do I turn left or do I turn right?', 'Do I want to work in a factory or in an office?'

Be receptive and ask lots of questions . . .

Being receptive and inquisitive are really important traits. I also believe that this is how you can make your own luck. Throughout life, we all come across individuals who are both inspirational and smart, people we can learn from and who can help us. Whenever I have had the opportunity to meet such people, I've always been very inquisitive and asked lots and lots of questions.

When I was working at *The Economist*, we had a marketing director who was super-bright and who was someone I really admired. I used to regularly put him through the 'Spanish Inquisition' and ask lots of questions about how he did things. I also remember how incredibly helpful Sir Colin Marshall was to me many years ago. He was the CEO of British Airways when it was successfully taken public from State ownership. A hugely inspirational individual and super-smart, he was the man that I took the Air Miles idea to in the early days.

So I think throughout my life, and indeed throughout most people's lives, you will come across individuals who for all sorts of reasons have the wisdom that can be really helpful to you.

If you also open your eyes, listen carefully and ask lots of questions, you can pick up a huge amount around you from those who can help. There's a very old saying that I've always believed in: 'You were given two ears and one mouth and that's the proportion in which they should be used.' In other words, listen twice as much as you speak.

I love children, as they are naturally inquisitive and always asking questions like 'Why?' It not only helps them to learn things, but is also a useful way to engage with those around them. This is actually quite a powerful tool that adults often forget to use. It's also a very useful tool for young people as they develop their careers.

I try to use this approach a lot in my working life. When I assess a business opportunity, for example (I get approached regularly with propositions), I will usually ask those that are presenting their case questions like: 'Why is this business different?', 'Why do you think it's going to make a difference to the world?' and 'Why do people need this product or service?'

Asking for advice while using the 'why' question can also be a very powerful way to involve and get people on your side. My most important role when bidding for the 2012 Olympic Games for London was to win the votes of the International Olympic Committee (IOC). We needed at least fifty-five members to vote for London. When I met these IOC members, I would never ask any of them to vote for us, but I did ask questions like, 'You're the experts, why do you think the Olympic Games will be successful if they're held in London?'

Although we wanted to win their votes, I was actually asking for their advice – by getting them to respond positively to our questions, it was also encouraging them to think favourably about our proposition and, hopefully, to vote for us. This is a very useful tool for any young person to remember. When making a presentation to someone, try also asking them for advice and remember to use the question, 'Why?'

Hurdles, self-doubt and making mistakes . . .

While I have had a number of successes, I've made some big mistakes too and also had some disastrous failures. I don't think anyone goes through life without facing hurdles, and I don't think anyone can deal with failure and tell you honestly that it didn't affect their confidence, because every time you get a knock-back, you do lose some confidence. What is important is how you deal with your mistakes and failures, and what you can learn from them.

Whenever I fail at something, two things are always particularly important for me. The first is to never think of it as a waste of time. Whatever it is that has gone wrong, you can always learn from it and hopefully, you will not make the same mistake again. Second, I always look ahead and not back. When something goes wrong, put it behind you and move forward. Even the 2012 Olympic Games, which absorbed ten years of my life, were fraught with challenges along the way, but in the end, they were a great success. I still don't dwell on the good bits or the bad bits. They're over, and I'm much more focused on what I'm doing now.

How parents can help . . .

For most young people, the role of their parents is obviously key. Although I came from very humble beginnings, my mum encouraged us all to be ambitious in our thinking. I remember her telling me when I was thirteen or fourteen that I could be prime minister one day if I really wanted to be. She used to say to us, 'You can do anything you want to do if you put your mind to it,' and I always say that now to the young people I meet.

I think it's very important for parents to give their children the permission to dream, to give them the confidence to pursue their passions and help them tangibly where you can. I helped my kids as much as I possibly could, even encouraging them to rule out the things they did not want to do. I managed to get my son work in an accounting firm – after the experience, he said: 'I don't *ever* want to do accountancy!' I also got my daughter a position in a law firm and she decided that she *absolutely* did not want to pursue a career in law! So, parents can help their children narrow down their options and help them move in the right direction. This can be hugely valuable.

I also think it's wrong for parents to be prescriptive by saying you should do *this* or *that*. I remember a relative of mine – her father was a doctor and desperately wanted his daughter to become one too. He wanted her to study medicine at university so much so that she rebelled and went on to study music. Ironically, once she got her music degree she decided that she wanted to be a doctor after all and had to start again at med school, eventually qualifying as a doctor. I suspect that had her father not pushed her so hard, she would have got there a lot faster.

Through my involvement with the charity *Speakers for Schools*, I meet a lot of young people. The saddest thing for me is to hear so many of them saying, 'I have no idea what I want to do.'

I will often refer them to my experience when I was learning to sail and trying to understand navigation. My sailing instructor would say, 'If you don't know where you're going, you'll go around in circles,' and that's a good analogy for life I think. Even if you want to 'head north, south, east or west', well, that's at least a start . . . But if you start going north, and then change your mind and head south, you will just end up going around in circles. You have to plot a path and know approximately in which direction you want to go. This is where parents can be very helpful and provide a guiding hand, rather than just leaving their children to work it all out for themselves.

Sometimes it's difficult when the parents of a young person are successful individuals. While their experience can help them to guide their children, their success can also seem very intimidating.

It can be very difficult for their children if they feel that they have to meet certain expectations or have to try to emulate their parents' success. The worst thing is for them to think, 'I'll never be able to do that.' Successful parents must be really mindful of this, while encouraging their children to find their own path.

It is also very important for parents to give their children enough time. With all of the pressures and demands of life today, parents are usually very busy, and they often don't dedicate enough time to their kids. It's therefore essential to put time aside for them, even if it's just spending a while talking to them about their future, their aspirations and their concerns.

Goals . . .

For me, goals are really important. I'm definitely a goal setter, and if I don't have a challenge I can become pretty unbearable! Whether it's a big project or a small project, a charity, sport or a business, I need to have real targets – virtually everything I do revolves around goals, and that's what motivates me. I am also a list maker. I might have fifteen things that I've written down that I must do today, and getting them all done is a goal.

I like to set goals for other people too – 'By this date, we're going to do this!' When I have a meeting, I want to be clear right at the beginning: 'What is the goal? When we leave this room, what have we decided to do? What was the outcome of this meeting?' So I'm definitely at the goal-oriented end of the spectrum. I think it's a very good, fulfilling place to be, and I'd encourage young people to be the same, although I do accept it's not for everyone.

Attitude and being positive . . .

There's an old question that defines attitude: 'Is the glass half empty or half full?' I lived in the US for four years, where without question the glass is always half full. They are much more positive than we are in the UK. I have always been very optimistic, some would say overly optimistic. That's not to say that in business you can close your eyes to the dangers and the risks, but, on balance, I'm definitely a glass-half-full person.

For young people just starting out in life, it is challenging and difficult out there – finding a job or choosing a career is never easy. However, if you are a glass-half-full person, if you're positive about what you're pursuing, and positive about life and the world, you are far more likely to succeed. Another important thing to remember is that people prefer to associate themselves with positive individuals. You are more likely to attract those that can help you if you're a positive person.

Work hard . . .

To be successful in anything you do, it definitely requires hard work. I know very few successful people that have reached the top without a huge amount of effort. So the need to work hard is a *really* important principle for young people to understand.

You also do need to be smart. I am classically uneducated, but I think I'm quite smart – you can become smart by learning as you go, which is essentially what I've done in my life. You can also learn to be smart, of course, by getting educated and even going to university. Common sense and a good work ethic are key as well.

Today, I still work hard, but I play hard too. I have an incredibly full working life, primarily because I'm involved with lots of different projects, and I also have a very full social life. I've got my family that I like to spend time with, I race yachts, and I try to find time to do and see amazing things. However, earlier in my life when I was building my businesses, I did work really hard and was perhaps a bit of a workaholic.

There are naturally times during your life – and especially when you are young and embarking on a new career – when you need to be focused and completely absorbed in what you're doing, especially if you want to be very successful at it. You need at that early stage to build momentum, and that can only come from focus and hard work.

When I talk to young people, an impression I get from many of them is that they think success should come fast and easy, because that's what they've read about. That rarely happens, of course. Unfortunately, what young people may read in the media and online about multi-millionaire popstars and footballers aged twenty-three earning £100,000 a week can give a false impression and lead to unrealistic expectations. This is especially true of Western economies, where young people often underestimate the time it takes, and the amount of effort required to be successful in life. We must all remember that life is short, and we are only here once, so work hard, work smart, have fun and enjoy what you're doing. Finally, money isn't everything. You can have a successful, fulfilling life doing something that you really enjoy without needing to earn a fortune.

Well-being and thinking about others . . .

Having a healthy mind in a healthy body is also very important in a young person's journey. Being physically and mentally fit is essential if you want to succeed in life. Self-awareness of your mind and body, and knowing how to nurture good health, are therefore *really* important. If you don't look after both, then you will struggle to succeed in whatever it is that you're doing.

I also believe that it's very important to have a real purpose in life. We are only here once, so what is it that we're here to contribute? I personally get a lot of pleasure out of what I can give to and do for others.

I am also genuinely optimistic about young people. The vast majority of young people that I meet are sincere, hardworking, good people trying to do the right thing. Unfortunately, that is contrary to what we read about a lot of the time in the media. It is, I believe, very important to give young people encouragement and support, and to help them find their way to become successful in life at whatever they want to do. The next generation will, I hope, leave the world in a much better place.

Vin Murria OBE

Born in India, Vin Murria came to the UK with her family when she was just three years old. After helping with the family business while she was still at school, Vin would use this experience as a springboard to an extraordinary career, becoming one of the UK's most successful female entrepreneurs. After successfully helping to expand Kewill Systems, the first company she worked for after university, she later went on to create two substantial enterprises: Computer Software Group and then Advanced Computer Software. Vin has a host of awards to her name, including Entrepreneur of the Year at the 2012 AIM Awards and an OBE in 2018. Today, she is a serial investor, sits on numerous boards and advises many large corporations. In 2007 Vin created the PS Foundation, which helps educate young women in India.

'Throughout my life, I have lived by the fundamental principle that one should always do the right thing. It's a very simple value, but in my book, it's a hugely important one. If that sits at the heart of whatever you do, how can you go wrong?'

'Some people are afraid of failing because of what others may think, so they end up avoiding taking risks. Ironically, that's far more likely to limit their chances of finding success than failure itself.'

'While most people have a tendency to automatically say 'no' to things that might stretch or challenge them, those of us who prefer to say 'yes' to everything will end up enhancing the good fortune we have been given.'

'When I look back at what my mother did for me, she obviously did something right! She raised her children in a positive way to have great confidence in themselves. She gave us that, and she didn't hold us back.'

What success means to me . . .

On a personal level, success for me is about feeling totally comfortable in my own skin. It's also being able to stand my ground, and having the belief that I've earned the right to express my point of view and the commentary that I make to anyone, to ask questions of my peers, and to be heard. Success is also feeling incredibly grateful for where I am today and feeling truly blessed. When I think back to the start of my journey, I would never have believed then, exactly where I was going to end up and just how my life was destined to unfold.

Success on a practical level is also having the ability to do whatever I want, without having to worry about funds, and simply being able to do what I think is right, without any restriction.

Finding your success should never be just about you. And it should not be about 'the money' either. When I started my journey In business, I never thought about creating wealth. There would always be other reasons that drove me; it might be wanting to beat somebody else at something, or perhaps trying to prove a point to myself and others, or simply fear of failure.

From a slightly different perspective, do I think that success can be defined by growing great businesses? No. Success for me is more about helping people within those enterprises to become successful in their own right. It's about helping to build individuals who can eventually feel confident enough in their own abilities, and what they've learned, to start their own ventures, or to actively support others in theirs.

So for me, success in my professional life is more about growing fabulous teams and creating something fantastic with them, and we have certainly been incredibly lucky to have been able to do that for many people over the years.

If you want to become an entrepreneur, get some experience under your belt first . . .

Today, there's a real buzz around start-ups and creating your own business. I see a lot of graduates wanting to leap into becoming an entrepreneur straight from university, before having any idea of what they want to build a business around. Personally, I think that is the wrong approach, and it's also very risky. The problem is, you only ever hear about successful start-ups; you don't hear about the traumas that those behind the unsuccessful ones have to go through. There's a real learning curve that one *has* to go through first.

So my first piece of advice for any young person that may have aspirations to become an entrepreneur is to get a solid grounding in your education. Once you have done that, it is vital that you then spend time developing your networking skills and capabilities, while obtaining a wider view of the world. You also need to build some financial structure and security around you initially, before leaping into the relatively unknown. This normally means working for others to begin with, so that you can build your experience, skills and resources, while also getting to grips with some of the fundamentals of business – understanding how marketing, sales, finance and accounting work, for example. It takes time, normally at least two to three years, to get the grounding you will need. But after that, before you even think about taking the risk of building a business, you need to be *really* passionate about what it is that you want to do, what you want to create and why.

Talk to good people . . .

What most people like to refer to as 'networking', I prefer to call 'talking to good people'. It's all about getting to know as many individuals as you can from within an environment that can really help you. The problem is that most young people are naturally apprehensive about engaging with someone they would like to talk to but don't yet know. It's actually very easy! The trick is simply *knowing* that all you have to do is to *show* that you're really interested in them. When you approach someone, you need only to express interest in who they are and what they do, or ask about what their business does. Most people are delighted to talk about themselves and genuinely appreciate people who ask about them. It will also leave them with a positive impression of you. And one of the best things of all? You will also *learn* something from them every time too. Going to events, functions, seminars and even networking events is a great way to meet new people, add them to your network and learn new things that will help you.

When you are young, excited and enthusiastic, people will happily engage with you if you approach them – it's such a huge advantage, so use it! But while learning how to engage with someone directly and how to network more generally with other people may push you outside of your normal comfort zone, it's a practice that will ultimately prove invaluable for you in the future. It is actually a hugely important life skill and an essential part of anyone's journey towards success.

Choosing a career . . .

Whatever happens, don't just pursue the first thing that you can think of as a career. There are so many different careers out there that young people can explore – certainly far more than they can possibly even know about. There are also plenty of resources that can be used to investigate such opportunities, in which you can hear from different role models about what they do and what they have done. With video streaming and the internet, it has never been easier for a young person to get a real flavour of what different jobs and professions may have to offer.

Women need to stand up for themselves more . . .

Within the work environment there is still definitely a tendency for women to prefer to remain in the background and say nothing at all, rather than stepping up to be heard. Even when women may have something important or significant to say, they often prefer to stay quiet. And if challenged or questioned about something, they often seem disinclined to stand their ground. For me, it's almost as though women (one often sees this in the City) still feel reluctant to step forward in what remains often a male-dominated environment. I sometimes get asked about what it's like to be a 'successful woman', and I always find this quite funny really, because I've never really thought of myself as a 'woman' in the workplace – I'm just an individual who wants to get on with things and do something positive.

In my professional life now and in the teams I work with, we really value the contribution that women can make and the capabilities they have, once given the chance, and we will actively support them. We don't do so *because* they're women, it's simply that they have a huge amount to offer as individuals but might not always put themselves forward for a role or ensure that they're *not* overlooked. Women just need to have more confidence in their abilities, while being prepared to promote themselves far more positively, in my view.

To parents . . .

I believe that most parents want to do the right thing by their children, but they don't always know what that means. I think that good parenting is all about good guidance. But first, you must behave in the same way that you want your children to behave. It's that old adage – 'Don't smoke if you don't want your children to smoke.' If you behave like an angry person around the house, don't be surprised when your teenager turns into an angry young person too.

For me, the *number one thing* that any parent can give to their children is continuous, unlimited, unconditional love. No matter what happens, your child is always the best thing that could ever happen to you, and they are always a superhuman being in their own right. That doesn't mean you have to totally mollycoddle them, of course. One needs to be protective, but they must also develop a sense about the environment around them because unfortunately, the harsh reality is that the world out there is nowhere near as nice as you think it is when you are a child.

I believe it's important to give your children an opportunity to get a taste of the commercial world quite early on. Whether they are selling lemonade from your front doorstep so they can get used to dealing with people, or they get a part-time job at the weekend, they will have a chance to experience the outside world beyond the comfort of their home.

When I look back at what my mother did for me, she obviously did something right! She raised her children in a positive way to have great confidence in themselves. She gave us that, and she didn't hold us back. She had an expectation for us that we were all going on to do great things, while giving us a massive opportunity to get a decent education. For me, if you can provide that foundation for your child, then you are already doing a fabulous job as a parent, because *everything* grows from that. Children can then learn to become resilient, to feel comfortable in their own skins and to feel genuinely good about themselves. They can naturally acquire a positive view of the world and what it means to do the right thing within that world – that if they always aim to do good, then good things will also come back to them.

Sometimes children can be influenced in an adverse way by keeping company with others who end up having a negative effect on them. Parents can usually help if their child is associating with the wrong person, because they can see it from a higher level. The problem is, however, that if they try to 'tell' their child not to do something, they're probably going to want to do it even more! They have to *induce* the right attitude instead, which is more about *coaching* them than *telling* them what to do. But that also means it's really got to be *part of them* in the first place. Because when parents have a good attitude themselves, they can more easily inspire their children to have one too.

The importance of education . . .

Your education is one of the most crucial things of all. It doesn't necessarily have to be a university degree, but you do need to have *something* that you can always fall back on. It's also about the confidence you gain from having actually done it. Even if you never use your degree or a particular qualification, simply doing it can still act like a trigger for you. To draw a parallel – if, like me, you love walking, there may be times when you challenge yourself with a hugely demanding hike (perhaps climbing up a mountain somewhere). When you first look at what lies ahead you think, 'How the hell am I ever going to do that?' But in the end, you do it. And it's the confidence that it gives you afterwards that's key – knowing what you've done and, more importantly perhaps, what you are actually capable of doing. And that's exactly what your education does for you too.

While your schooling will provide a solid foundation, your education doesn't end when you leave school. Once you start your career, that's the point when your self-education takes over – and it should always be a process of continuous learning. For example, you might see yourself heading towards a career in business management or you may have aspirations to become an entrepreneur. You should then be asking yourself, 'What do I need to learn now? What would give me a really massive confidence boost and a great head start?' For some, it might be to pursue an MBA, but for others (who may not be ready yet to do an MBA), there are many really helpful modules that they can take, such as marketing, contract law or accounting, which are not necessarily full-blown courses. These three subjects alone can transform one's understanding of business. And while you don't have to become a fully qualified accountant to read a set of accounts, it would be really helpful for you to learn at least *some* of the basics. When someone in the future talks about EBITDA or PE multiples, you will then have at least a reasonable understanding of what they're talking about . . .

How saying 'yes' more, creates opportunities . . .

I certainly believe we are all blessed to some degree, and it's when we remember that we are that things usually turn out well for us. But I also think there is an element of good fortune that shines a light on the brave. Because while most people have a tendency to automatically say 'no' to things that might stretch or challenge them, those of us who prefer to say 'yes' to everything will end up enhancing the good fortune we have been given. Simply by saying 'yes' more often, we increase our access to opportunities and we end up meeting amazing people – and *that's* when things really happen! Even today, I still regularly say 'yes' to invitations to various functions and events. But each time I go somewhere, I will always think afterwards, 'What did I get out of it? What did I learn? What am I going to do with it?' So it's not just about trying to put yourself in 'the right place at the right time', it's also about taking advantage of opportunities when they're presented to you, which is something I have always tried to do.

Having a positive outlook and a great attitude . . .

In order to find success in life, your attitude is probably more important to you than anything else. It is often said, 'You can always skill somebody up, but you cannot train the right attitude into them.' I would go further and say that if somebody has a really positive approach to life, they will always end up becoming a success. And even when they occasionally go through times when success eludes them or they fail at something, they will invariably seek the positives *out of it* and move on to find their next great success. Because, when most positive people fail, they think of it as just another part of their learning curve – they learn from it and they move on. Some will also look at failure as being a really positive thing.

So I always have a positive attitude and approach to life, and I try to make sure that the people around me have the same attitude too. I also expect everyone to work really hard, give it their all, do everything with passion and with energy, and always want to do the right thing – I believe that all of this is a very important part of a great attitude as well.

It's easy for a young person to get disrupted on their journey, especially with all the noise around them that they have to deal with and the fact that there's just so much coming at them all the time (one can appreciate the issues around mental health that so many young people seem to be facing at the moment). This is where one's attitude and self-motivation become so important. Something that I have always found to be a very useful and inspiring way to help keep on track is to read biographies of people who have done great things with their lives. When you read their stories, you realise that nobody has ever had a straightforward journey. There is really no such thing as a 'straight line' up. There will always be distractions or obstacles on the way, and it's how someone dealt with their challenges at the time that has made them the person they are today. For most young people, a combination of self-belief and an element of coaching yourself will help you to cultivate a positive frame of mind.

If you have people around you that are habitually negative, they will drag you down. Get away from them! If they tell you that you 'can't do something' all the time, simply avoid them. You really *don't* need those kinds of people in your life. There are enough challenges out there to face without having someone with a negative attitude tell you that you are not good enough to do something. You have got to learn to step away and seek out more positive influences.

How mentors can help you think . . .

Having a mentor can be extremely helpful to you. They can guide you to look carefully at *how* you think about things. A good mentor is a person you can simply bounce ideas off – 'I really need to do this, but I'm not quite sure what's the best way . . .' A mentor can also give you good, sensible advice, not necessarily about what you should do but perhaps to suggest, 'Here are the options that you might want to consider.'

A mentor doesn't necessarily need to be a high-flyer; they just need to be someone that you trust, someone that can be a really grounded and sensible coach for you. They can be a relative, a close family friend or an accomplished person that you happen to know, who also takes a real interest in you.

Finding a mentor is something that has to be done naturally. You can't chase them down. The desire for a relationship has to be mutual and it has to be synergistic. Good mentoring is not about teaching someone the right way forward, and it's *not* about helping you to climb the ladder of corporate life while opening lots of doors for you either (if you actually find someone who does that for you, then you're very lucky! But it's also extremely rare). What you really want is someone who can provide good guidance, who can support your thinking and who can rub off some of those rough edges, so that when you address things, you do so in the right way. It's not someone who will tell you what to do but a person who will listen to you, and ask you questions about your approach and how you might think about doing something. Good guidance means helping you to become the best, most fully rounded, intelligent-thinking, wonderful human being that you can possibly be, and to become excellent in whatever field you pursue.

Failure is good for you! . . .

Failure is important and is actually good for you. We all have to fail. But the risk today is that a lot of young kids don't fail enough because they're simply protected too much. When they do eventually fail, they fail badly, and it can have a highly negative effect on them. Failure actually helps young people to build resilience, and they can learn so much from it too.

The fear of failure, in my mind, is one of the biggest things that drives the individual. When I think of the times I have failed – as we all do from time-to-time – they have ended up being triggers for me to work even harder and smarter, and wanting to succeed even more. The time and energy you invest in failing at something is probably *the* best learning curve you can ever have.

Some people are afraid of failing because of what others may think, so they end up avoiding taking risks. Ironically, that's far more likely to limit their chances of finding success than failure itself. Who cares what people think? Does it really matter? Nobody will remember anyway. The stories in last week's newspapers are already last week's news – they've already been forgotten. While you might see your failure as a big thing, in the wider world it simply isn't. You might think that you have failed, but others will think that you have tried. In the US, it's widely held that fortunes can only be made once an individual has experienced failure a few times first.

Ultimately, failure also makes your eventual success taste that much better too. If you have only ever had success in your life, you're never really going to be as grateful for it.

Listening to your gut instinct . . .

There have been times in my life where circumstances or events might have seemed quite positive at first sight, and yet my gut instinct has told me that something was not quite right. Over the years, I have also been tempted by lots of people to get involved in numerous projects and have been offered all sorts of opportunities. But very often, where my gut instinct has told me that something didn't feel right, I've decided not to pursue it, and in most cases, hindsight would later prove I was correct.

So today, whenever I assess an opportunity professionally – it might be a company to invest in or to buy – I normally rely on my gut instinct to tell me if anything seems wrong, although it's never normally to tell me to do A rather than to do B. That is when I do my numbers, I work through my thinking and work through my logic. I might say, 'I like this project because of this . . .' – and then it will be just down to whether a valuation is sensible or not – or, 'I don't like this because of that . . .' But it's when the decision is unclear or marginal, that I will rely more on my gut instinct to tell me whether to do it, or not do it.

And sometimes, it may be that everyone is expressing positive things about a company, but for me, something just doesn't seem to add up. It could be that the accounts simply don't quite look right, or it might be that I sense that someone isn't telling the truth or the whole story about something when I'm talking to them. Occasionally you can sense it in a room, and you don't feel comfortable about what you're hearing, or perhaps the behaviour of the people in there seems wrong and you come away feeling, 'Something else is going on – it just doesn't feel right . . .'

So even though it can be hard to rationalise sometimes, one should always pay attention to one's gut instinct since it can often detect when things are wrong at a subconscious level. In my experience, one's gut instinct usually ends up being right.

Being grateful . . .

We would not be human if we didn't have self-doubt from time to time. This is when you have to 'coach' yourself, and remind yourself that you *are* good enough and that you *can* do this. Self-motivational books and resources can be very useful here.

When you are having moments of self-doubt, it's easy to forget all the amazing things you have done that have led up to you becoming the extraordinary person you are today. But it's also about being grateful for where you are now and keeping yourself grounded.

So you need to understand what you want your life to look like, while being grateful for where you already are – and then not to lack ambition about where you want to get to. It keeps you focused on what you need to do as well, since people only really feel good about themselves when they are progressing. It also helps if you can keep company with people who care about you, and always remember to surround yourself with those who are positive too.

If you can maintain a feeling of gratitude for all the big things that you have already achieved in your life, then everything will feel and taste that much better for you too.

Delayed gratification . . .

A lot of people tend to spend more than they earn, from day one, and they never get into the situation where they are ahead of the game. My philosophy has always been that you spend a lot less than you earn, you put some of it aside and you invest. Over a period of time, your investments become self-generating. Eventually, they will give you the support you need and enable you to take advantage of those key opportunities when they present themselves.

Build physical exercise, space and fresh air into your routine . . .

When you are young, before you have any family commitments, your life is more likely to be skewed heavily in favour of work, while you are building your career. It's easier to manage work and social demands then too, because you have got the amazing ability to burn the candle at both ends. But it is very important, I believe, to still build in some downtime away from everything else, when you can do something completely different and have a change of scene.

If that activity can also be physically beneficial, then that's even better still, because keeping yourself physically healthy will naturally support your emotional strength. So it could be that you like running, yoga or perhaps playing football – but whatever it is, you have got to make time for it.

Do the right thing and pass it forward . . .

Throughout my life, I have lived by the fundamental principle that one should always do the right thing. It's a very simple value, but in my book, it's a hugely important one. If that sits at the heart of whatever you do, how can you go wrong?

Another principle that means a lot to me is what I call 'pass it forward'. It's a simple idea that helps to propagate goodwill, while actively inspiring a culture of generosity towards others. It starts with you or me performing a good deed for an individual who needs our help, but *without* having any expectation of being recompensed, or indeed receiving anything else back from them in return. What you ask instead from the person you are helping is that they simply perform one good deed themselves for three other people in turn. This essentially gives momentum to the good you have done for that individual in the first place, which then carries it forward to others who may also need help from time to time.

It's an extraordinary thing ... If you follow this principle and do something that's supportive to those around you in the same way, the people you help usually end up doing some amazing things for other individuals. It should never really be a precondition, however, for helping someone in need – you simply provide them with the help they require but express clearly how you would like to see them *respond* in turn. Inevitably, they will feel a natural obligation to do so, and will then *pass on* the same goodwill and generosity that you have shown towards them.

Danielle de Niese

After winning Australian TV's *Young Talent Time* at nine years old, Danielle de Niese made her operatic debut in Los Angeles at fifteen. A year later she won an Emmy Award for her presenting work on TV, and at nineteen she became the youngest singer ever to debut for the Young Artist Development Program at the Metropolitan Opera in New York. After critical acclaim in 2005, playing Cleopatra in *Giulio Cesare* at Glyndebourne, she is today one of the most sought-after lyric sopranos, performing regularly at the world's leading opera houses. Through her live performances, recordings and TV exposure, Danielle has won widespread recognition as a popular classical artist, tearing up the classical rulebook with what's been called her 'unique combination of artistic credibility, 21st-century allure, and the ability to communicate on every level'.

'I am a great believer in patience, to *never* take shortcuts, and that 'slow and steady wins the race'. It's like the story about the tortoise and the hare, where the hare runs ahead fast, but the tortoise ends up winning the race.'

'Education doesn't stop when you leave school. I still have a teacher now, and I'll still have a teacher in twenty years' time. If you are professional and dedicated to your art, and want to be the best you can be, you never want to stop learning or improving.'

'I *really* do believe in the value of hard work, of dedication and grafting. For me, having the right work ethic is hugely important if you want to find success in life.'

'My biggest advice to parents is to really look at your children when they are young, take notice of them, truly observe and engage with them, and see what they respond to. If you do nothing, your child will still grow up, but if you nurture and love your child, the rewards for both you and for them can be so much greater.'

Success and fulfilment . . .

When I consider what success means to me, it's really about achieving a successful career, while at the same time enjoying fulfilment in my family life, and having both working harmoniously together.

Success in my professional career is like a moving target. It's almost a vision that seems so far away sometimes, because there's so much more that I still want to achieve in my life. But, at the same time, I do feel successful, having enjoyed a number of significant achievements during my life so far.

Maintaining a loving and stable family life, where I can be the complete mother for my child, who is getting everything from me, while being a giving partner to my husband and our marriage, and at the same time, being able to dedicate myself to my career, is a hugely important goal me. If I were unable to prioritise these things, no amount of success in my professional life could ever be fulfilling enough.

Conversely, if I had to give up my singing career in order to manage just my family life, I would probably not be a happy person either, since I would be unable to pursue my passion for what God has given me.

So, for me, success is being able to have the best of two worlds – and finding joy and fulfilment in both.

An early start . . .

My journey started whilst I was still tiny. My mother would sing to me as a baby, and when I was less than two years of age, I was able to mimic her with near-perfect intonation. She came from a musical background, took singing and piano lessons, and was able to recognise in me the early signs of a special musical talent. She was soon doing everything possible to nurture my ability and became my first teacher. My mum was ultimately to become the single-most influential person in the whole of my future career.

We were living in Australia, and by the time I was eight, I was singing, dancing, acting, performing in musical theatre, doing voice-overs, kids' songbooks and recordings, and also TV commercials. I was working at so many different things – and I absolutely loved it! But my parents soon felt that while my voice showed real potential – everyone was pulling at me and I was doing so much – I shouldn't just rely on natural ability and singing on *feeling* alone. They believed that I should have some sort of formal training, so that I could learn a proper technique – 'Let's give her some tools to work with,' they said. I am still totally amazed, when I look back, at the extraordinary foresight my parents had at that time.

So, my mum started looking for a classical music teacher who could help me. But nobody wanted to take me on – everyone thought I was just too young. Many thought that it was actually quite preposterous of my parents at the time and that they should really wait until I was much older. But in the end, she did manage to find someone who agreed to give me a few lessons. The lady was a singer in the Victorian State Opera and she also taught. So I had my first classical lessons, and this was to be my first pivotal moment. I was just eight when I realised, after taking those lessons, that I really wanted to sing opera. I couldn't quite articulate it well enough at the time, but I remember drawing a picture for my mother of a small girl in a poufy dress, standing in front of two big curtains, and telling her, 'This is what I want, Mum – I want to become an opera singer.'

Both of my parents have been hugely supportive and have remained totally invested in me throughout my career. I feel very lucky to have enjoyed such a great relationship with both of them. They were prepared to give up everything for me when I was still very young, purely out of love and devotion. We even moved as a family to the US when I was ten, so I could continue to get the best development and training. They wanted to ensure that I had *every* opportunity to succeed; but it wasn't about my career, it was about *me*. If I had decided at some stage that singing and music were not really for me, they would doubtless have said, 'If that's what you really want, then fine. We will always love you, and we've got no regrets.'

My mother used to tell me that one of my greatest talents was that I was a good listener – I would absorb things, and that's how I learned and grew. She also taught me the difference between singing and interpreting, and what it is to make music *live* off the page. I learned to appreciate the idea, early on, that music should never be viewed as simply a two-dimensional thing – it's not just a series of written musical notes to be followed. Of course, once the ink has dried on the manuscript, the music is 'there', but it's how you actually interpret the notes, what *you* bring to the music and how you make it your own that's most important. It becomes *your* personal imprint on the music, and I learned that completely from my mother. And once I had absorbed from her what that really meant, I was able to apply it to all the different types of music that I've performed ever since, and especially where there's a particularly interpretive aspect to it.

While I was still young, my parents continually searched for doors to open for me, to help me find what I might love and also to build my experience. During the summers, I didn't just while my time away at home. My parents managed to get me an audition for the Tanglewood Festival in Massachusetts – I was accepted into the festival programme when I was just thirteen (the youngest person ever to perform there), and I sang at the music festival in Santa Barbara at fifteen. I also participated at many other musical events that they sought out for me.

It was while I was performing in *Les Misérables* on Broadway that my mother managed to secure me a half-hour appointment with Ruth Falcon, a very well-known voice teacher in New York, with the hope that I might even complete my graduate studies with her. I had already been accepted to go to university on the West Coast, but my mum had researched her and felt that this was absolutely the right thing for me to explore. She gave me a cheque for $75 and I remember her saying, 'Take this cheque, and I'll call this teacher and see if I can get you an appointment.' She was a brilliant teacher, of course, but also expensive, so we thought that if I could spend just half an hour with her, that should be enough time for me to sing a couple of pieces and for her to assess me.

So I travelled to New York to meet her. She listened to me sing, and I recall after a few moments she said, 'You *can't* go to university on the West Coast. You *have* to come here to New York! Tomorrow, you are going to sing in an audition for my conservatory, and if they accept you and let you in, you've got to come here *now* – I can't let anyone else touch your voice!'

It was really quite heart-breaking for me, however, thinking about having to move away from my family. I remember telling my parents, 'I don't really want to go . . .', but they said to me, 'Look, this is *such* a major opportunity for you. If this teacher *really* wants you there, then you must go.' So I moved to the East Coast and enrolled with the Mannes College of Music in Manhattan, while also studying privately with Ruth, which was to become another hugely pivotal time for me. It was while I was singing the leading role during a performance of *The Marriage of Figaro* for my university (it was also rare for a freshman to be given a leading role) that a scout, Peter Russell, from the Metropolitan Opera of New York saw me. I was invited to sing in front of James Levine and subsequently joined the world-famous Lindemann Young Artists Development Program, debuting as Barbarina in *The Marriage of Figaro*, in my first full professional performance at the Met with the 'Dream Team' of superstar singers. I was just nineteen at the time.

Although I have been known over the years for performing in a variety of things, while singing, acting and dancing on the stage, film and TV, what is key for me is that I am today defined as an opera singer, but one who also performs in other disciplines. Classical music has become such a deep part of my identity, and has its roots in the formal training and coaching that I received when I was young.

It was when I debuted at the Glyndebourne Festival that my career reached another milestone. *Giulio Cesare* is an opera by Handel in which I played the role of Cleopatra, and it turned into a *hugely* successful production. It was a game-changer, really, for how people used choreography in an operatic performance because I was singing classically rigorous coloratura but dancing at the same time. Normally the singer sings while the dancers dance around the singer . . . but I became both singer *and* lead dancer (a bit like Beyoncé in her famous 'Single Ladies' video!). I put a huge amount of time into perfecting my own interpretation of the role and the performance itself, which in the end really paid off enormously for me. It was a defining moment for me in my career and led to me being courted by five major record companies who wanted to sign me up. It was a time that certainly helped to elevate my profile internationally as an opera singer and performer.

Be patient and work hard . . .

I am a great believer in patience, to *never* take shortcuts, and that 'slow and steady wins the race'. It's like the story about the tortoise and the hare, where the hare runs ahead fast, but the tortoise ends up winning the race – I am definitely the tortoise in that story! It doesn't seem like that sometimes when you look at my whole career on paper, because I did so much when I was so young. But I did have time on my side and I was always able to make my choices wisely, otherwise, I might have burned out a long time ago.

I have never looked for a quick route for anything. The reason why is simple; I really *love* singing, and when you love something that much from the age of eight, you just want to cradle it and protect it, and you don't ever want to lose it or let it slip through your fingers. And so I was always very cautious in making decisions, but most importantly, I would also work *really* hard at everything I chose to do.

For the first opera I performed in at music college (the performance in which I was scouted by the Metropolitan Opera), I knew just a few Italian words. But I made it my mission to know *every* part of that opera, *every* single scene, even the ones I wasn't in. I was determined that this was the right thing to do, so that I could learn my character and its context within the opera completely, and in turn, perform my role to the best of my ability. So I literally translated 481 pages of Italian script, using a dictionary, and studied every single one of them. It was very hard work and took a long time, but it was essential for me.

I really believe that being successful as a performer is not about showing what you know, it's about how much you can absorb. Not everything that you learn in your research will 'show', but it can still be taken in and somehow stay *within you*. It will then help naturally to add dimension and depth to what you bring to the character you are portraying, and to your performance as a whole.

I passionately believe in that process and I know that it can yield great rewards, even if the hours of work I put in are not immediately apparent to my audience. But I also know that in doing so, I will have given *everything* to the discovery of that piece or that role, and will have created my own unique interpretation of it as an artist. So, at the risk of sounding like one of those old clichés, I *really* do believe in the value of hard work, of dedication and grafting. For me, having the right work ethic is hugely important if you want to find success in life.

I see a lot of young adults, only a few years younger than me, especially those that grew up around the time of the internet bubble, who have seen other people come up with just one good idea and made themselves a fortune. And they think it's easy, that's all they have to do – come up with just *one* good idea. The notion that you may have to work hard for a decade first to get somewhere is completely foreign to them . . . I even heard a bunch of young guys talking recently about setting up and running a bar: 'Yeah! What a great idea. You can manage your own hours, have loads of fun. How can you lose?' It seems naïve, of course, but there is also that underlying desire to take a shortcut, avoid the need to graft your way to something and simply look to hit the jackpot. But I always say that there is no career I know of that doesn't have some aspects of it that are really boring, tedious or laborious. There is always a *grafting aspect* to knowing your métier and learning your art.

I also meet people in my own industry that have reached a certain level of success and who feel that they no longer have to put the work in. All they have to do now is 'perform'. That is not my school of thinking at all! I just cannot connect with people like that, and somehow feel their lack of dedication to their art will eventually catch them out. I believe in that kind of karma – when you put in the work, the rewards will come through in time. And the rewards are not always the ones that other people will give you. It's also knowing in yourself that you have totally prepared for your role, squeezed every piece of information out of something you needed to perfect and, because of your professional dedication and preparation, that you performed it really well and made it your own. Just knowing this can be as rewarding as any applause or accolades you may receive from your audience on the night.

Developing attitude . . .

Having a good attitude is naturally very important. But when everything is going well for someone, it's quite easy for them to have – and to be seen to have – a great attitude. But at times when things are more difficult or challenging, that's when one's attitude really shows. It's interesting to consider the questions, 'At what stage in life does someone acquire a good attitude?' and 'How does one actually develop a good attitude?' While it can be difficult to learn something like a good attitude from reading a manual, it is certainly possible to cultivate one in later life by having good role models around you and even good mentors. They can help you to foster a sense of self-belief, which, in turn, can help to develop your attitude.

But I personally believe that the seeds are sown much earlier in life. Like so many things that we have to learn as we grow up, I think 'attitude' is something we have to be *shown*, and it starts with the guiding hand of our parents – they naturally play a crucial role in how a young person learns to face the world, and from this, to acquire a 'healthy' attitude later in life.

How parents can help young children to grow . . .

Having children is such an amazing experience because you see for yourself just how much influence parents can have on their kids, especially when they are very young.

As a parent, we hold completely in our hands this responsibility of knowing that what our children perceive in the world is based largely on how *we* help them to perceive it. A simple example of this is watching TV with our kids when they're small, which we all do. You can either just sit and watch something with them or you can use it as an opportunity to help them learn – to correlate and perceive things far more profoundly than leaving them to work it out by themselves: 'Look, that's what you saw outside yesterday, do you remember?' or 'Why has he got a smile on his face?'

I remember once watching a *Jungle Book* film with my son when he was around two. It was one of the original films with less dialogue but lots of expressions used to portray the characters. It was such a great opportunity to help him to understand the 'coding' of those expressions – what does a young child really know about categorising expressions unless we get involved and help them a little? And I would say, 'Oh! He looks really worried now' or 'Do you think he heard something?' The next time he would see those expressions, he would understand what they meant. It's like learning a new language, but faster, because I was helping him to learn it.

Young children have a great capacity to absorb things, and that's how they learn and how they grow. I would always encourage my son to talk, to look for things and even see patterns in things. And by introducing him to lots of different interesting things, I was stimulating him and helping him to think. Some parents might have looked at me and said that I was being too involved: 'Just let him be, he'll be fine . . .' But that's how my parents raised me, and all I know about parenting is what my parents successfully did for me.

Children also like to watch and listen to their parents. It's a huge opportunity for parents to show, explain and practise things with their kids, even when they're very small. It's also a completely natural process – in the wild, a mother bird doesn't say to its babies, 'Look, that's where the bugs are, go eat.' She'll say, 'Watch me. Look at what I do. Now you try. OK, watch me again. Now you try again.'

So for me, it's about that level of dedication you give to your child, and taking the time to understand their temperament and nature. And I really could not show any less than that level of dedication to my child, because that is what I learned from my parents. That's all I know. They were always there to hold me, and yet they let me be 'free' all the time. It's a combination of nurturing and flying with your children, but at the same time, letting *them* fly.

I have always believed in a patient approach to most things, and so I would always try to help my son to be patient too. Like most toddlers, he used to get really frustrated sometimes. Parents will often call this time 'the terrible twos', but in reality, I don't believe they're *terrible* at all. In most cases, they simply get frustrated because they want to communicate something – they know exactly what they want to express, but they are still just around the corner from being able to say it properly. When my son used to get like that, I would say to him quietly, 'Be calm, you're like Wilbur [from *Charlotte's Web*], you can talk.' I would then guide him if he still had a difficult time expressing himself by saying, 'Is it this?' or 'Is it that?', to which he could reply simply *yes* or *no* – it was a sort of workaround for him.

Learning how to handle challenges and fears is a capacity that parents can help instil while their child is still young. It starts in the garden, the playground or the sandpit: 'OK, I know it's hard to climb that rope, but don't worry, *you can do it!*' And you show them, guiding them a little as to how it's done. And when they're facing something scary and have to be brave, it's not about saying, 'Don't be scared,' it should be, 'It's OK to be a little scared, but if you can do it, you will be *so* brave, and I'll be *so* proud of you!' When my son was a toddler, whenever I used to say that I was really proud of him, I have no idea really what he thought it meant, but I know he detected then, an emotional satisfaction in his mother's voice, and he always responded very positively to that.

So there are lots of values and concepts that we as parents can foster in our children when they're really young, that can help them become much better prepared for the world later on. And if they start to learn such things at an early age, it also becomes a lot easier for them to develop a good attitude when they are much older.

Opening doors for your kids . . .

Unless they're extremely fortunate, most kids will never be able to find what they're good at entirely on their own. It's really up to parents to help them to discover what it might be – it's almost a divine responsibility. I feel so lucky that my parents were like that. They did everything with me, opened lots of doors for me to peek through. I know many adults who never had that from their parents and they are still trying to figure out what they're good at today . . .

So parents should try everything with their kids – take them to football, pottery classes, try the piano or anything that can stimulate them – and see what they respond to. Parents have the keys – we speak the language, we do the influencing, we drive the car to take them to places – so it's in our hands to help our children to explore, watch out for clues and find what they might like.

But once we open doors for our kids, we cannot force them through. They have to be interested to walk through by themselves, and all we can do is encourage them. Every child is unique and will respond in different ways, so we have to be balanced in our approach and be sensitive to how they react. Parents have to learn how to read their kids and understand their nature. Once a child finds something that they like, it then becomes a combination of encouragement and nudging by their parents. And as with anything else in life, there will always be the boring or tedious aspects of an activity that a child may *not* enjoy. If a parent sees that a child is good at something and that they enjoy it, they may still need to encourage them to stick with it and persevere through the boring times, the training or studying and so on – it's a bit like homework.

My biggest advice to parents is to really look at your children when they are young, take notice of them, truly observe and engage with them, and see what they respond to. If you do nothing, your child will still grow up, but if you nurture and love your child, the rewards for both you and for them can be so much greater.

Self-doubt and conquering your fears . . .

I think a lot of people might be quite surprised to learn that I am actually a person who experiences a lot of self-doubt. It's a curious thing for me, because while I frequently have self-doubt, I have a lot of self-belief in myself at the same time. I also think that any performer who gets up on stage, however much self-doubt they may have, simply wouldn't be able to face the crowds at all if they didn't have *some* degree of self-belief.

Even when I'm feeling nervous on stage, apparently it doesn't show. One of the reasons for this is that I'm able to 'wear my nerves' on the inside. But I also believe that my performance is a service – I'm telling a story, playing a character, and I have a real duty to the audience *not* to be selfish enough to allow any of my nerves to come to the surface and affect my performance.

Singing on stage is one of the worst things for having nerves! It's a bit like playing in a tennis match; you make one little fault and it starts to nag you, and then you become distracted by worrying that you might make the same mistake again. When you are performing, you only have to think about that *one time* when a note didn't come out well, and you can suddenly become flooded with nerves. And then it's so easy for one part of your vocal technique to go out of sync. Either your breath gets a little stiff or your throat muscles start to *think*, 'I'll have to manage that, because I'm nervous.' Even the desire to fight against nerves when you're thinking, 'I've *got* to get this next note right,' can make you even more tense... It's a problem that compounds itself. There are actually so many things that come from within, from your brain, that can end up stymieing your efforts. Being able to manage your nerves becomes a hugely technical aspect of singing – knowing how to control certain muscles, how and when to engage them, and when to release them. It takes practice and a lot of experience to manage.

So a large part of self-doubt for any performer is caused by simply knowing how nerves can undermine you. And by far the best way to anticipate these moments of self-doubt and to reduce your nerves is to spend as much time as you possibly can on preparation and practice. The harder you are prepared to work at it, the more resilient you will become.

Another aspect of this, which I have often thought long and hard about, is that I can become nervous simply because I really *care* about how I perform. I always want the audience to see and hear my very best performance – I owe them that – but the fear that I might not be able to sing *that* note perfectly, for whatever reason, can in itself make me feel nervous.

One of the most challenging times in my career, but also another hugely pivotal moment for me, was the first time I sang a bel canto role. Aficionados of opera often like to put people in boxes: 'She only does baroque and Mozart', or 'She sang Semele and Susanna in *The Marriage of Figaro.*' I wanted to show that I could change repertoire and still perform at the highest level. But this was to place a huge amount of pressure and expectation on me, albeit self-inflicted. I was determined but terrified at the same time. I remember being incredibly nervous before the first act of my debut performance, and I knew that I couldn't let *one single note* go even slightly wrong. If I gave them just one little thing to pick up on, they would doubtless say, 'She's not quite ready for this – she should really stick to what she knows.' But, despite the tremendous nerves and the frequent moments of self-doubt, I managed to nail it!

I vividly recall walking back to my dressing room after the performance and feeling like Wonder Woman. I looked at myself in the mirror and felt a huge sense of accomplishment. I had managed to find the mental strength to fight my own doubts and fears, and I felt *so* strong at that moment, because it was a capability that I knew I had within me, although I had to *fight* to achieve it. I had not seen those levels in myself before. So I had this feeling of exhilaration, but at the same time a quiet sense of pride in having 'won the war with myself'. Today, whenever I feel nervous about an upcoming performance or have moments of self-doubt, I will often think back to what I had to face then, what I managed to conquer and how I felt afterwards. It remains a great source of strength for me.

Getting the right help around you . . .

I strongly believe that once you have found what you want to do, and as you start to pursue your career path, you shouldn't just forge ahead completely on your own. It's imperative to have good people around you whom you can listen to, really trust 100 per cent, and who are able to offer you qualified help and advice. I have always found help from others hugely beneficial to me.

I was, of course, very fortunate to have the support of my parents when I was really young, who were really helpful in the early stages, as well as later on – and their commitment continues today. Both of them come to all of my rehearsals. My mum makes detailed notes and my dad films each one so that I can study them. For me, they are like my ears and eyes 'outside' of myself.

My mother has also been a great sounding board for me throughout my career. After every rehearsal, she critiques my performance. I can ask her, 'Did I sing that piece OK?', and she might say, 'There was one place where it sounded a bit strange.' We talk through my singing, my acting and the whole performance in a completely honest way. I know that anything she says is genuinely meant to help me, because she loves me so much.

Whether or not your own parents are able to help you with your career, you will meet people along the way who can also help you. My parents were my mentors, but I also encountered some wonderful individuals who helped me enormously in my vocal and musical development. Dame Kiri Te Kanawa had been an idol and a role model for me for years. She made it to the very top of opera, but she also came from the Southern Hemisphere and had a mixed background like me. My parents used to say, 'If Kiri can do it, *you can do it!*'

I first met her in 2008, and she is not only one of the very finest singers anywhere but a wonderful person too. She gave me a tremendous amount of advice, as well as some of the 'bravest' voice lessons I have ever had in my life. Voice lessons are usually a very intimate and naked process. You have to expose yourself completely and literally *make* mistakes in order to become better. Kiri helped me to unravel a whole part of my voice and then rebuild it. She was incredibly patient and enormously helpful, and it was such an amazing experience for me to have been so exposed in front of someone I had always respected so much. It made me idolise her even more, after knowing her and studying with her.

Other people have also been enormously helpful to me during my journey. William Christie, in particular, was an early mentor of mine, with whom I debuted in French baroque music in 2003. We collaborated on a lot of projects together, and he is someone who has consistently believed in me and I have learned so much from him. Another person who has been brilliant for me in the last decade is Gerald Martin Moore, my main voice teacher – it's just so rare to find a teacher like him that you can feel completely safe with.

And so we all need to have support from others. But when looking for a teacher or a mentor that can help you, either for a short time or for a more significant part of your life, it's always important to *know* whether this is an individual who really believes in you, loves you and is genuinely willing to invest in you as a person. They must be prepared to put the time in to help you to succeed.

Education . . .

I think that education is very important. I went to a private high school in Los Angeles called Crossroads School, where we addressed our teachers, even our headmaster, by their first names. It was a relaxed learning environment that was intended to be conducive to 'feeling happy' about being at school, with classes of fifteen and La-Z-Boy sofas, as well as desks to work from. With Robert Frost's poem 'The Road Not Taken' as its mantra, my school was certainly less conventional and much less traditional than most others. But I always felt that its aspirations were all about raising the whole individual, and not just focusing on academic subjects.

Another thing I really appreciated about my school was the values it sought to instil. Community service and giving were an important part of our school's ethos. This sat well with what my parents had already been telling us as children – 'No matter how successful you are, you must always give back.'

I was very lucky because I had great teachers. I enjoyed learning and found it quite easy to do well. My teachers wanted to know me, and I felt valued as a person and not 'just another pupil', where obtaining grades was thought more important for the school than the student. But I also know people who didn't have good teachers, which has clearly impacted their view of school. How can anyone enjoy schooling if they don't like their teachers? So although it can be very difficult to achieve, finding the right school for your children is really important.

Young singers who ask for my advice will often tell me that they feel ready for the stage. They'll typically say to me, 'Danni, you know what it's like because you sang on stage at eighteen. So what should I do?' I usually end up telling them the opposite of what they want to hear – they naturally hope that I'll encourage them to follow their dream and take to the stage as soon as they can. But the reality is that I started my music studies at the age of seven, so I had already completed more than ten years of 'schooling' by the time I was ready for the stage. I will usually tell them to be patient, and if they have a teacher that they can trust, to listen to them and continue to work hard at their studies until they are ready. I sometimes feel awkward because I don't want to say, 'Well, I sang on stage at eighteen but I'm the exception to the rule,' but people often forget just how much time and effort I put in beforehand.

Education doesn't stop when you leave school. I still have a teacher now, and I will still have a teacher in twenty years' time. If you are professional and dedicated to your art, and want to be the best you can be, you never want to stop learning or improving.

Goals . . .

When I was ten, I set myself a goal to have learned three new languages by the time I was twenty-one. I knew that I wanted to be a singer and have a global career, which would mean working around the world in foreign countries, so I was determined to learn French, German and Italian in order to really understand the melody and natural cadence of a language, not only for singing, but also for living and feeling at home in a country. This became a firm goal, which I subsequently achieved.

So I think it's hugely important to set goals. But it can be difficult for young people to think about goals if they don't yet really know what they want to do. It can also put them under a lot of pressure if they're asked to do so when they don't even know what the future looks like. Short-term goals are also just as important, even if it's just one step away, so why not set a goal for tomorrow? When a young person starts thinking about these short-term goals, it helps them to think about the future.

Work-life balance . . .

When I first started out, I used to think, 'I want to have it all – I work *very* hard, so why shouldn't I?' And now I have a young child, which has added such a huge dimension to my life, I realise that while I can still probably have it all, I just cannot do every single thing that I want, when I want to and at the pace I want. Sometimes there are simply not enough hours in one day to get everything done, and so I have to keep carrying things forward in my planner and live another day.

Having a big career with lots of travels, and often performing evenings and at weekends, means that I have to be very skilled at balancing everything so that I can still be a good mother and wife. But a great joy in my life is when I look at my son and I can see my influence *in* him as his mother, and I can see that he feels loved. And this is because I'm still able to give him the quality time and love that he needs.

While I feel that my life has been a success on many levels, I certainly wouldn't feel as successful if for any reason my son was unhappy or not excelling, or if my marriage was under pressure. I'm very fortunate to have a strong, loving marriage that's deeply rooted in mutual love and support of our individual and shared passions. My husband and I don't like to be apart for a long time, so he makes huge efforts to visit me when I'm away performing, not only to be there with me on my opening nights, but also so that our family life can continue to thrive even when we're away from our home base. To have a life partner who is supportive of my career in the same way that I support his is an amazing gift, and makes me feel that I can fly even higher. I treasure my family more than anything in the world, so getting the balance right between my career and my home life has always been my goal, and being able to achieve that is a tremendous source of happiness and satisfaction for me.

And finally, there is a part of me that really believes that if I do something good, even when I'm very short on time, it's always the right thing to do. So I will always try to make the time during my busy schedule to do good things – it might be outreach activities, bringing music to kids or schools that don't have fiscal budgets for music programmes, or accepting to be an ambassador for various charities or programmes. I know it makes a difference and I always feel good doing it. There's a certain karmic element here, and I often think that when we give unselfishly to the earth, without any expectations of getting anything back, we will naturally receive something back in some way, as it comes around again in time . . .

Rabbi Lord Jonathan Sacks

As a religious leader, philosopher, theologian and award-winning author, Rabbi Sacks is one of the most respected intellectuals and inspiring moral voices of our time. From 1991 until 2013, he held the position of Chief Rabbi of the United Kingdom and Commonwealth. Among the thirty books he has published to date, several have become widely acclaimed for the significant intellectual contribution they have made to Judaism and beyond. Rabbi Sacks was knighted by Her Majesty the Queen in 2005 and made a life peer, taking his seat in the House of Lords in 2009. He currently holds professorships at several academic institutions, and has been the recipient of seventeen honorary doctorates and a number of prestigious international awards, including the 2016 Templeton Prize.

'It's your failures that really make you grow up, grow strong and grow to be the person you *could* be. None of us would like to relive our failures, of course, but we couldn't be the person we are today without those failures. But if you do not have the courage to fail, then you do not have the courage to succeed – full stop!'

'Self-doubt is the fuel that keeps the engine running. You say to yourself, 'Maybe I'll get it right next time,' which then forces you to *do* a next time, and a next time. It means that you never quite stop growing, because you are never quite satisfied, and with it, your resilience grows too.'

'What is true about the mind is what is true about the body – use it or lose it. You just have to keep stretching yourself mentally, and don't even think of coasting.'

'It's always important for parents to share the passion of their children and support them in the pursuit of their dreams. But I think parents have to take a step back as well, and empower them to find their own way. Just applaud every success and be very, very forgiving of every failure.'

On success . . .

For me, at the simplest level, I think success means having lived a life that you feel has given you a sense of satisfaction in knowing that you have made a positive difference to other people's lives. But, I would not wish to be held back by a narrow definition of success. There was a great statesman and President of Israel, Shimon Peres, who at the age of ninety-one was asked, 'How do you stay young?' And he replied, 'Well, what you have to do is count up your dreams and count up your achievements, and then work out which is the more numerous. If your achievements exceed your dreams, then you are already old, but if your dreams outnumber your achievements you are still young.'

So I would say, don't be too preoccupied by 'success'. Just stick to your dreams, and a life that is guided by your dreams will be a life that you can surely look back on as a success.

Follow your dreams and be persistent . . .

One of the most practical things you can ever do is dream. I'm constantly puzzled by the fact that people can take a month or even a year planning a holiday, but they don't even take one day to plan a life. The most important thing you can do when planning your life is to dream.

Explore the world of possibilities and see *which one* really speaks to you, that's the first thing. The second is to be persistent. This is a quality you may not believe you have, but persistence is something that you will eventually discover you do have because, surely to goodness, when you are inspired by a dream and you follow it, you are also going to fail many times along the way!

From an early age, my great dream was to write a book. I tried so hard and devoted every spare minute I had from the age of twenty until forty to this, but I consistently failed, failed and failed again! I used to have this enormous filing cabinet full of books I had started and never finished . . . And so for twenty years I had tried and failed, and then, as I was approaching my fortieth birthday, I happened by pure chance to be reading George Bernard Shaw's preface to *Plays, Pleasant and Unpleasant*, in which he says, 'If you are going to write a book, write it by the time you're forty.' I remember thinking, 'He's talking to me and he's not even alive!' It was for me one of those life-changing moments. I suddenly realised that I had to do it *now or never*, and it was at the age of forty that I completed my first book. I have written pretty much a book every year since, and that is really down to sheer persistence.

If you have a dream and you are persistent, you have the ability to do great things, and you will.

Taking the initiative and opening doors . . .

When I was a teenage student, I developed a thing that in Jewish circles we call 'chutzpah', which basically means nerve, cheek or audacity. My chutzpah was to find people that I admired, whose books I had read or whose lives really inspired me, and then go off to meet them. At twenty years of age, I travelled around the US to meet all the people I most admired who lived in that part of the world. I bought a Greyhound bus ticket that allowed me unlimited travel, and I would either phone them or knock on their door and say, 'I've travelled 5,000 miles to meet you, could you please spare me a few moments?'

However famous you are, it's always fun to meet someone who really admires you, and so they would invariably give me their time. It was audacious, but I got to meet some very great people in this way and most of my heroes – truly inspirational individuals, who became role models for me and who made a huge difference to me at an early age. I have continued to meet people in this way ever since.

When I was in New York I met with a very famous rabbi. As a philosophy student, I was full of questions about religious faith and had already met several rabbis, and they all told me that the greatest one of them all was this man who lived in Brooklyn, Rabbi Menachem Mendel Schneerson, known as the Lubavitcher Rebbe. Eventually, I got to meet him. I asked him my questions, he gave me his answers – which was all quite straightforward – and then he did an extraordinary thing. He performed a complete role reversal and started asking *me* questions: 'What was I doing for Jewish life?', 'What was I doing to lead kids of my generation?', all of which caught me absolutely by surprise because the last thing I ever thought of doing was to become a leader, let alone a religious leader. It was certainly not on my life agenda at that time, and yet he had *charged* me to lead. There is no doubt, although it didn't happen instantly and took several years to work its way through, that this extraordinary encounter was to completely change my life.

Looking back on it, many years later, I have often said, 'Everyone saw this man as a great leader, with a great number of followers, but they have all missed the most important thing about him: a good leader creates followers, but a *great* leader creates other leaders.' And that is what he did for me.

So this significant event in my life started with my initiative as a young person, to explore and meet with great people that I could learn from. I literally went out to find the doors that I could open.

Choosing your path in life . . .

For a young person, knowing what they should pursue in life is challenging and difficult. If there were a formula to follow, the closest one I can think of is to recognise when 'what you want to do meets what needs to be done', since that is where you ought to be. So, it's a kind of coming together of two worlds: your inner world of ambitions or aspirations and that outer world which is crying out for certain things. It's where these two worlds meet that something magical happens, and you can never predict what that's going to be.

Who would have thought you could change the world by coming up with a better search engine? When Larry Page and Sergey Brin sat down together at Stanford to construct what was eventually to become Google, we were certainly not short of search engines. I had twenty of them on my computer and I wasn't even computer literate. So the idea that you could change the world through a search engine was a very insightful one. Did anyone ever think that you could change the world by creating a 'bookshop' in cyberspace where you couldn't even take the book off a shelf to feel its cover and open it first? No, but Jeff Bezos did when he founded Amazon, and he too changed the world.

So it's somehow that meeting of these two worlds – a sense of what you may be passionate about doing and your ability to perceive a gap out there in the world, a need that perhaps no one else has seen or notices except you. That, once again, is where *what you want to do* meets and connects with *what needs to be done*, and that's the place where you should be.

The importance of a mentor . . .

There is no doubt in my mind, no matter how talented you are, you cannot succeed to the full in life without having a mentor. I have known people with enormous natural talents which they just have not been able to hone, refine or focus simply because they lacked a mentor. A mentor is someone who tells you what you *need* to hear in such a way that you can hear it. That means they care about you and your future so much that they are prepared to tell you what you are doing wrong and not just talk about what you are doing right.

Even great sportspeople who are able to succeed through sheer talent, at some stage, they will realise that they need to find or hire somebody who can point out what they do wrong. For most of us, however, when you find somebody who believes in you more than you believe in yourself, or who sees in you a talent that you don't fully see in yourself – *that's* the person who should be your mentor.

For parents – empowering your children . . .

My father came over to Britain as a refugee and had to leave school at fourteen because his parents were poor. He helped his family to make a living, so he never had time for a formal education and had to educate himself. We used to go to the synagogue together, and I remember, when I was around five years old, we would walk back and I would ask him lots of questions – 'Dad, why did we do this?' and 'How do we do that?' – and he would always give me the same answer: 'Jonathan, I didn't have an education so I can't answer your questions, but one day you will have the education that I didn't have, and when that happens, you will teach me the answers to those questions.'

Now, if you want your son to be a chief rabbi or a chief of anything, that's how you do it! To empower your children to go ahead of you and then to take *you* with them – that is an extraordinary and challenging thing for any parent, but there is nothing a parent can do that's more powerful than this. And now, of course, I'm getting it from my grandchildren! When he was just six years old, one of my grandchildren had been teaching himself about astronomy from the internet and decided to induct me into the mysteries of space. He said, 'Grandpa, I'm now going to ask you a question. But don't worry, I'm going to make it easy for you.' I remember thinking, 'That's it! Now I've got my *grandchildren* to be my educators!' If you can give your children that space to go where you haven't been and then to help you accompany them on the way – that's the most empowering thing that a parent can do.

I think, without needing to say anything, kids quietly learn from their parents. Wordsworth put it so well in his great work *The Prelude*: 'What we have loved, others will love, and we will teach them how.'

I did not necessarily want our three children to go down the same road I chose for myself – I was working out a highly personal thing in my own journey. We are not a traditional rabbinic family and I had not intended to be a rabbi when I was young, but our children just naturally picked up from my wife Elaine and me some good habits, such as reading a lot and working hard. They also learned about 'hanging in there', because when you have a very public life, you can also have some very difficult public moments. Seeing you negotiate and survive these difficult times helps to build their inner strength, and I think kids do this without us having to be explicit at all.

I was the eldest of four boys and first in our family to go to university. In the end, we all went to Cambridge, and have each gone on to do reasonably well in our lives. In a sense, we had all been given every chance at the time, but I remember thinking, before our kids were even born, 'What chance are we giving them?' It was very clear to me that they would need a certain strength of character that was never asked of me or my brothers, to go out, find their own way and do something that we never had to do. In the end, each of them did just that, and I'm so incredibly proud of them now and I learned a lot from them too – they were able to find the strength to choose their own direction, and not simply try to repeat or be intimidated by what their parents had done.

It is always important for parents to share the passion of their children and support them in the pursuit of their dreams. But I think parents have to take a step back as well, and empower them to find their own way. Just applaud every success and be very, very forgiving of every failure. I have enormous problems with parents trying to dictate their children's lives – the saddest thing would be for their child to spend a whole lifetime thinking, 'If only I'd been able to pursue *my own* idea of the future me.'

The importance of education . . .

Education, and self-education too, are really important for young people to take seriously, I feel, and they were certainly both important for me. But then, I do belong to a faith that has always put education at the very heart of its existence. Judaism is a religion whose heroes are teachers, whose citadels are schools and whose passion *is* education and the life of the mind.

Going to university was a kind of epiphany for me, since no one had done it before in my family. From grammar school, I went to Cambridge, and then on to Oxford. For me, this was the next best thing to heaven! It was a just wondrous time, but I do believe that my education really started for me when I ceased being a student at university. I began studying for the rabbinate, and soon realised that however demanding Oxbridge was, the traditional Jewish academy was a whole lot more demanding – and that's what made me into a scholar. Jewish scholarship is predominantly text-based and really, really intellectually demanding. Although, at twenty-five, I had started my studies for the rabbinate quite late, I also had a teacher, Rabbi Nachum Eliezer Rabinovitch, who believed in me and who did a very clever thing (which also took some courage). He realised that, as a student, I had a great deal to learn very quickly and since the fastest way to learn a subject is to teach it, he also took me on as a teacher. On the same day I became a student, I also became a lecturer at the Rabbinical College, teaching certain secondary disciplines that I needed to learn too. This really forced me to take my self-education very seriously.

Failure, self-doubt and resilience . . .

Some will reflect on their successes and believe they have been blessed with good fortune – and that may be so – but I prefer to take a slightly more religious view. In any given situation, I ask, 'What does God want of me here and now?', 'What have I found myself in this situation in order to achieve?', and that for me is a daily discipline.

My being here and in these circumstances is not an accident. I have always treated this as providence, and as life asking certain questions. For me, it's a call to do something, and that's really how I have responded to things. This is also how the late Viktor Frankl saw it (the great psychotherapist, whose works were famously based on his personal experiences in Auschwitz). He would say, 'Don't ask what I need from life, ask what life needs from me.'

I mentioned earlier that when you are inspired by a dream, you are still going to experience failure many times along your journey. I have had many failures on mine. Some of them have been spectacular, some my own fault, some just tripping over a banana skin. In the end, one has to decide, *this is not about me*. There is *something* that needs to be done and you have been chosen to do it. So just get on and *do it*, and stop worrying about whether you believe in yourself, stop worrying about the number of failures you have, just keep going because if you don't, you will betray anyone who has ever put their faith in you. And in the end, it was other people's faith in me that kept me going, not my own faith in myself.

In Carol Dweck's book *Mindset*, she encapsulated everything that needs to be said about failure; 'people who really achieve things are the ones who actually *enjoy* failure, because they learn so much more from it than from success.' I have certainly found that to be the case for me – at the very lowest points in my life, those were the moments that really put the steel in my soul.

Another person who expressed the very same thing, and in a way that I felt most powerfully and with almost a sense of kinship after I discovered what she had said, was J. K. Rowling. After her first Harry Potter book was turned down by the twelfth publisher in a row, as a single mum living off welfare she had reached absolute rock bottom, and that's when everything else ceased to matter and she just *had* to keep going. When you throw away all of the incidentals, all that's left is *you*, and what you have to do.

It's your failures that really make you grow up, grow strong and grow to be the person you *could* be. None of us would like to relive our failures, of course, but we couldn't be the person we are today without those failures. But if you do not have the courage to fail, then you do not have the courage to succeed – full stop!

We will all experience self-doubt on our journeys – I've lived with it since I was a kid, I haven't grown out of it yet and I still continually doubt myself. Self-doubt is the fuel that keeps the engine running. You say to yourself, 'Maybe I'll get it right next time,' which then forces you to *do* a next time, and a next time. It means that you never quite stop growing, because you are never quite satisfied, and with it, your resilience grows too. You often discover that you have the resilience you didn't know you had, and it's almost entirely a property of doing the things you feel passionate about.

Beethoven is a wonderful example of true resilience. You can feel it when you listen to his music. Here is a man during his 'middle' period, who has written many of the works that we remember him for, including the Emperor Concerto and the Fifth Symphony, but who still needs to write more to keep himself going, to support his nephew and to pay his bills. In the meantime, he has also gone profoundly deaf and yet there is something in him that keeps saying, 'No, that wasn't good enough, I can do it better.' And that produces late Beethoven – the 9th symphony, those incredible late piano sonatas and, most spiritual of all, his late string quartets. If anyone ever reached up there to heaven with the angels, it's Beethoven. And you can feel that restlessness in him that is continually chipping away, honing, refining, saying, 'I haven't got there yet.' Ultimately, this was an enormous source of creativity for him.

Look forward, never back . . .

Learning from your mistakes may require a degree of reflection. Hindsight, on the other hand, is a total waste of time. Really strong and driven people are those who relentlessly and with iron self-control only look forward, not back. I learned this from survivors of the Holocaust. At first, I did not know how they could survive, having seen what they saw and knowing what they knew. They had lost their families and virtually everything else, and now as strangers in a strange land, they became focused on building a career, building a family, a home and a new life. Maybe fifty years on, they might allow themselves just a moment to look back. That is why hindsight to me is the most uninteresting of all human endeavours. Never waste a minute looking back, just look forward.

Setting your goals . . .

When I became Chief Rabbi, I would often go away – sometimes with my team and sometimes on my own – to work on my goals and to establish what I really wanted to achieve within five years, ten years, and twenty years from now. In those days, long before the arrival of smartphones, we had something called a 'Filofax'. The first thing that I saw when I opened my Filofax, on the first page, were my goals – and this made sure that I never lost sight of them.

Now, the knowledge that you have set these goals allows you to make the most important distinction that anyone can ever really face, which is to know the difference between an opportunity to be seized and a temptation to be resisted. Because unless you know exactly where you want to be, you cannot tell the difference between those two things. Life has a tendency, however, to regularly throw out new opportunities (the right kind of opportunities) that you never anticipated, which does require an element of pragmatism. So I used to have a rolling five-year plan as part of my goals that I would review every three months. This worked well for me then, and I still do it today.

Goals need, however, to be set at a level that challenges you. In his book *Flow*, the famous Hungarian psychologist (with an almost unpronounceable name) Mihaly Csikszentmihalyi presents a graph that depicts the relationship between aspiration and ability. It demonstrates how, if you set the bar too low you will get bored and if you set it too high you will get anxious. So goals that are achievable but *only* by stretching yourself to the limit – *those* are the goals that you should set yourself.

I once had a great mentor in the art of hope and it was called my satellite navigation system. For the twenty-two years that I was Chief Rabbi I had a professional driver, and I recall the time when sat-nav systems were first introduced. He would key in our destination, and this very polite woman would then tell us to 'turn right in three hundred yards'. I was thrilled by this, but also intrigued that whoever designed this system had never met a Jewish driver – 'What does *she* know?! I've been driving for fifty years and I *know* you have to go three hundred yards and then turn left!' I was also fascinated by what would happen when my driver completely ignored her instructions – because he, of course, *knew better* than the computer – and ended up making a wrong turn. But the computer never lost its cool. After going very quiet for a few seconds, the polite woman would calmly say, 'Your route is being recalculated,' and lo and behold, the sat-nav would then show you a new route from where you got lost to where you wanted to be.

I learned many things from this computer. I learned about patience and self-control, but I also learned that once you know where your destination is, however lost you get, there is always a route from *here* to *there*. This, to me, was a great signal of hope.

Maintaining a healthy mind and a time for rest . . .

What is true about the mind is what is true about the body – use it or lose it. You just have to keep stretching yourself mentally, and don't even think of coasting. If you continue to read the books or watch the films or listen to the music that make you feel comfortable, you will eventually go to sleep mentally. I would not advise anyone to do that. Stay young, which means stay open, which means, keep challenging yourself mentally.

It is important to balance working hard with a time for rest. Judaism brought the concept of the Sabbath into the world, and indeed we all owe the seven-day week to it, because a week doesn't exist in nature. The *month* comes from the lunar calendar and the *year* from the solar calendar, so they are both embedded in nature, but the *week* is a creation of Abrahamic monotheism, which says that we must *rest* for one day in seven to spend time with our family, with our community, and give thanks.

Through the Sabbath, this 'work-life balance' has kept the Jewish people going for a very long time. The Greeks and the Romans didn't understand this at all – they thought Jews kept the Sabbath because they were lazy, and so they had to rest one day in seven. The end result is that the great Greece of Athens lasted maybe four centuries from the time of Solon until its decline, and was burned out by the second century BCE. Rome eventually burned out too, of course. But Jews and Judaism never burned out, because of the Sabbath. A great Jewish scholar once said, 'More than the Jews have kept the Sabbath, the Sabbath has kept the Jews,' and it's true. I couldn't imagine living a life without the Sabbath, because you will eventually either burn out or burn up – there will be something very unbalanced about you.

Following your disciplines . . .

It can be tough to remain disciplined, but habits and rituals are hugely important. Anyone who has ever tried to write a book knows how impossible it is to do unless you are absolutely firm with yourself. A classic example of this was the novelist Anthony Trollope, who despite having to maintain a full-time job working for the Post Office, became a prolific writer, producing up to nine books a year. He famously – and for the princely sum of £1 a year – hired a young man to wake him at five o'clock every morning. He would then write against the clock, 250 words every fifteen minutes, for three hours each day until eight-thirty, when he would finally put his pen down and set off for work. Few people would do it the way Anthony Trollope did, but any successful writer, from J. K. Rowling to Stephen King, will probably tell a similar story.

So, the first discipline that I would commend to any young person is to establish habits that break the universal tendency to procrastinate. That's number one.

Number two is to keep reading and to keep stretching yourself. If you are intensely dedicated to one discipline, make sure you read other disciplines and expose yourself to perspectives different from your own. If you want to be creative, you have to think outside of your speciality. Many of history's greatest creative thinkers are people that have done just that.

And number three, make sure that your personal life is full of joy and thanksgiving. It's a great privilege to be able to find what you really enjoy working at, but it's a life necessity to find joy and happiness at home. For me personally, this means a happy marriage and a happy family, and to take the Sabbath off to express a sense of gratitude for all the wonderful things we have been blessed with in our lives.

The greatness in all of us . . .

And finally, just know that some little seed of greatness exists in all of us, and it does not necessarily have to be greatness in the eyes of the world. Sometimes one single act of kindness can redeem a life. Sometimes a single smile can rescue a person from loneliness and despair. You never know what the consequences of your next act may be, but people never forget a good or kind or encouraging word or deed. That greatness is there for each of us, and all we have to do is have the courage to respond and let it express itself in a way that only we can do, and that's true for every single one of us.

Shriti Vadera

Following a distinguished career in investment banking, Shriti Vadera became widely respected for her expertise on international debt restructuring and debt relief, and advising governments around the world. She was a member of the Council of Economic Advisers at the Treasury, a government minister, and one of Gordon Brown's most trusted policy advisers and chief negotiator on financial issues when he was prime minister. She was a central architect of both the UK's unprecedented banking rescue package during the international financial crisis in 2008, inspiring governments worldwide to adopt similar strategies, and of the 2009 G20 London Summit, which was described by the IMF as 'breaking the fall in the global economy'. She is today a member of the House of Lords, on leave of absence since 2011. In 2015 she became chair of Santander UK and in 2020, it was announced that she will become chair of Prudential plc from January 2021 (stepping down as chair of Santander UK in October 2020).

'People who are really successful are the ones who are actually *doing* what they really want to do. They have found what they love and what they have a talent for, they become good at it because of their passion, and they also work very hard at it.'

'If you define your goals in terms of the things you want to create, the things you want to change and the things that you really want to spend your time on, how can you possibly fail?'

'When you are truly passionate about something that you are doing, it gets noticed and you are more likely to attract opportunities through being 'open'. People will offer things to those who they think are open, and simply won't offer them to people who are not.'

'I think the most important thing a parent can do is to see their child as an individual person, not as an extension of themselves, which is what I see many parents wanting to do.'

On success . . .

I think of success almost exclusively in terms of *outcome*. What changes have I made? What good did I achieve? Personally, it has never been about money, status, honours, job titles, size of office or anything else like that – I think it's really pointless thinking about those things. For me, success means simply, 'Did I do something to make the world a better place?' It's all about making a difference in the outcome of what you do.

It's not all about 'you'. . .

I think one of the most important things a young person needs to understand is that it is not about what you need to achieve or become, it's about what you *want to do*. If you follow your passion and end up doing something that you really care about, what is the worst thing in life that can happen to you? You might end up spending your time on something that you really love doing! In the end, you may or may not succeed in doing exactly what you set out to do, but if you have really *loved* doing something you enjoy, what else is better than that?

Of course, for a young person starting out, it can be difficult to identify what it is that they want to do in life. A good place to start is simply to ask, 'What do I really care about?' Because actually, everyone cares about *something*. For me, it's all about finding how you can live your life through being connected to the things you care about. Whether you are writing, painting or singing, or being a nurse, a teacher or even a business person (creating a product or a service that you care about), it has to be about something *other than you*. For example, if you want to be a pop star and become rich and famous, that is all about *you*. On the other hand, if your dream is to make lots of people happy through your music, and are passionate about playing it and love performing so others can enjoy it, that is now about the thing you are *doing* rather than just about you. It's caring about how you and your music are able to touch people's lives, how you can connect with them and make them happy.

Once you find what you care about, and you develop a passion for and a focus on what you are doing, you have then got to work really hard at it. There's no magic here – you still have to add *commitment* to your passion in order to find success. The notion that everything will come easy just because you have found your passion for something is a false one, unless you are extremely lucky, of course.

Discovering what you really care about...

There were two significant episodes when I was young that helped me to discover what I would really care about and want to do later on in my life.

When I grew up as a child in Uganda, it was a country that had a lot of divisions. I had an *'ayah'* or nanny to look after me. She was black, although as a kid you don't really see colour, and her family was poor. It was difficult for me to understand that while this person had brought me up, she was not actually part of my family and that she also didn't have any money. There was one occasion when I found her looking desperate and crying, and I recall her telling me that she couldn't afford to send her children to school. I was only four at the time, but it really moved me, maybe because her kids were also my friends – I used to regularly sneak out and play with them at the back of the house (even though I was forbidden from doing so!).

I was unable to grasp why they couldn't go to school like me, just because of 'money'. But I had already acquired a basic understanding of economics at my young age – I knew my grandmother had money, and that if you needed some, that's where you'd go! I can remember demanding, 'What's wrong with giving them money if they need it for school?' I then had to deal with this whole complicated explanation about how my *ayah*'s partner would drink and gamble the money away, but my grandmother did listen to me and agreed that we would help. If she paid the money directly to the school, this would naturally solve a major part of the problem.

So my granny and I would go to the school with my *ayah* to pay the school fees. But I also remember having this feeling that something was still wrong. I was too young to articulate matters in my head, of course, but I clearly had this emotional response at the time that something was not fair, and it just wasn't right.

When I was eight, my family left Uganda and we moved to India. I still recall the impact that seeing the poverty in India for the first time had on me. I arrived on the streets and saw all these kids, many of my own age, who were starving. Quite a lot of them were maimed or disabled, but I didn't know why at the time (we know today that these injuries were often deliberately inflicted). And I remember feeling like I could easily become lost in this big hole, disappear into a mass of people. I was in a new country on a new continent, and there were all these desperate children. They had no parents, and no one was looking after them. It was one of the most destabilising things for me at that time.

The sense of injustice I felt, in both Uganda and India, was to remain with me for a long time and would ultimately drive me to want to do something about it. It was also something I really cared about, and I remember often thinking, 'If you want to justify your existence, you have to do something to fix this.'

Years later, I would go back to Uganda as an adviser. After university, I had pursued a career in banking, specialising in international government advisory and debt restructuring, and I was asked to advise the government of Uganda on its external debt. It was a tricky time for the country, just a couple of years after their civil war had ended, with political and economic instability. My task was to try to piece together all the money that the country owed and determine how its debt could be restructured. There was inevitably a high level of corruption to deal with as well, which was also dangerous for us. Some officials were repaying the debt of whoever bribed them, as opposed to repaying the people that really ought to be repaid first. And, because they were not repaying everyone they should, all of their exports were also being impounded at the ports, which of course meant they couldn't get much-needed money back into the country. It was a vicious circle, and everything became gridlocked. For a time, we had to have a system where nobody would get paid unless I signed off on it. This helped to eliminate the existing level of corruption, but it also made me a target. I had to face death threats routinely and often menacing calls in the middle of the night – it was, needless to say, a very difficult time.

We returned back home after a while, and there was quite a big discussion in the firm about whether or not to carry on, because of the risks to us personally. After receiving assurances from the governor of the central bank (the man who had originally hired us) that he would assign his personal bodyguards to protect us, I decided to go back, although my colleague chose not to. It was an amazing thing for me to be able to finish off that job. We got to the point where we had done all we could to restructure the country's debt, but under the rules for international finance at the time, Uganda would still be forced to pay back more than it was able to bring in from its exports. The rules were simply stacked against the country, and it was crazy to ask it to commit to something that it couldn't possibly repay. So I started to work with Oxfam and many other organisations on a campaign for debt relief.

Later on, I was to move from international banking into government. Gordon Brown – the then chancellor of the exchequer and future prime minister – invited me to become a member of the Council of Economic Advisers at the Treasury, after becoming aware of my banking experience and my commitment to international development. I started working on the international debt relief programme, and, coincidentally, Uganda was the first country on the list. This was mainly due to its debt records being the most organised following all the restructuring work we had been involved in when I was in the country, together with the work that others carried forward after us.

A natural consequence of debt relief is an improved balance of payments position and, consequently, more widely available resources. The next problem is, how to deploy these funds wisely to directly benefit the country and its people. So, the international donors had to negotiate. I remember being sent urgently to meet the Ugandans in Washington to engage with them on how they would spend the money. We wanted to announce something soon, to kick-start the process for all countries. Two months earlier, the Ugandans were forced to lay off a lot of teachers because they could not afford to pay their salaries. So we agreed that they should use the funds to re-hire all of the teachers and promise free education for every child at school.

I remember the following morning, standing at the back of the hall of the IMF, when it was announced that every child in Uganda would now receive free education, funded out of the debt relief that I had first started working on over a decade before. It was a very powerful moment for me. I remember crying while listening to the announcement, as I vividly recalled my four-year-old self and my *ayah* and her children when I grew up in Uganda, and the commitment I made to do something about the injustices that I saw when I was young. It can take a long time sometimes, but it all comes around. When you really care about something, you simply have to keep pushing and never give up.

The importance of education . . .

When I was much younger, it seemed I was destined for a different life altogether. I was facing the usual traditional cultural pressures for a girl. I was expected to have an arranged marriage and to have lots of kids while I was young. My family loved me, of course, and only wanted the best for me, but they also *knew* (or thought they knew) what the right thing was for me. My father wanted me to be a lawyer, my grandfather felt that I should study pharmacy, and it was all about pursuing that well-trodden path of 'having a profession'. I was often told by my family that this would be my big insurance policy or a backstop just in case anything went wrong with my marriage! I really needed to escape, and education was my route out.

But I also wanted a different, more broadening education that did not necessarily point me towards any particular profession. I set my sights on Oxford University, and because very few students from my school would normally get to go there, I had to push my teachers to allow me to sit the exams. I didn't tell my parents about my intentions and relied mostly on the deputy headmistress, who was very supportive. It was difficult for her to justify and commit the time required for tutoring only me to sit the exam, so I managed somehow to persuade a few other students to participate (who all dropped out over the course of time). By then, my teacher had already committed herself and it was too late to stop. So I carried on being tutored to sit the entrance exam for Oxford, and managed to get a place, which was something that would completely change my life.

I had a wonderful time at university, discovered amazing things and the most amazing people. I was allowed the space and the time to learn about a whole new world from my contemporaries, and no one was judging me on what I was doing. I also was to find out at that time what I really wanted to do. My education was not just important for me – it was, in fact, *the* most significant facilitator for me in what I have been able to achieve later on in my life.

Mentors . . .

I didn't have a mentor when I was younger, but I do think it can be very helpful for a young person to have one. If I had a mentor, my life would probably have been a little more balanced, and I might have done things better and not made as many mistakes. It was difficult, however, because I was breaking so many cultural taboos when I was young and, as a slightly 'errant' child in the eyes of my family, it would have been hard for me to find someone close that didn't simply try to rein me in. I was never very good with barriers, and in a way, it was helpful being able to think independently, because I could be defiant about things more easily.

But I do think it's helpful to have someone adult to talk to who is *not* your parent or family. Having a mentor can also be a bit of a safety valve for you, and a safe place to explore the future *you* outside of that space in which your parents and family see you. You can then talk as the person you *want to be*, rather than the person you are now. You can test anything from 'Am I allowed to be the person I want to be?' and 'Am I going to be encouraged to be that person?' to 'Can I pull it off?'

Finding a mentor need not be difficult. Just be cheeky, and ask somebody you respect and like. Most people would be happy to say 'yes'.

To parents . . .

I think the most important thing a parent can do is to see their child as an individual person, not as an extension of themselves, which is what I see many parents wanting to do. They should be very careful not to impose expectations on their children that make them feel in any way constrained. Kids usually want to make their parents happy, especially when the relationship is good. But it can be difficult for children who have to reconcile doing what they want to do with not wanting to let their parents down.

I seem to have acquired several godchildren over the years, and whenever one of them comes to me with an issue they want to talk about, it is more often than not to do with some form of expectation they are dealing with from their parents, often at quite a subtle level.

Instead of living their lives through their children, which some parents are not even conscious of doing, they should be prepared to let go.

Fortune . . .

Everyone has to accept that there *is* real serendipity in life. People who are successful and claim that serendipity played no part in their journey are just kidding themselves and others. But while you do have to be in the right place and at the right time, there is no question in my mind that you also have to have the right attitude, the right approach and the right capabilities in order to seize the moment.

Quite often, an opportunity can be presented fairly broadly, where you are not the only person that it's going to be offered to. You might even be in a crowd of people when something comes up. In such moments you have to have 'something' in you that enables you to attract it and seize it, but you also have to *be* there first – and that's luck.

When you are truly passionate about something that you are doing, it gets noticed and you are more likely to attract opportunities through being 'open'. People will offer things to those who they think are open, and simply won't offer them to people who are not. When you are the person presenting the opportunity, you can normally sense who's open. When you ask someone to take on a project, you already sense or know that you are asking the person that would want to do it – your intuition tells you that they're interested and that they're keen, passionate and committed around the area that the project relates to.

You also have to *seize* the opportunity that's being offered, and that may mean taking a risk. But it's not that much of a risk, really, if you are still just following your passion and it's something you really care about. That is exactly what happened to me when I moved into government.

I first met Gordon Brown when I was part of a delegation of NGOs during a discussion about international development. I remember him asking me, 'What's an investment banker doing here?' and I said, 'Well, I'm here to show you why this actually makes financial sense . . .' Years later, I was introduced to Tony Blair. The Labour Party were in opposition, and I wrote a paper for him on the reform of the IMF and World Bank that I felt the party could propose, but he said it was too technical for him! And so I was reintroduced to Gordon. I wrote a few more papers on other issues, and carried on doing some bits and pieces for him, mainly because I wanted to – I felt that Labour were doing some important things and I wanted to help. I then started working in South Africa for a while on behalf of my firm, and in the meantime New Labour – as they were then known – got into power. Almost two years later, I received a telephone call from Gordon Brown's office (he was now chancellor of the exchequer) asking me to come and see him. The

Treasury had lost a minister, who had been a businessman, and I was told that this left 'a bit of a gap' and that they were looking for someone with commercial experience who could help.

I remember Gordon mentioning a few particular projects to me that he was dealing with at the time, including the Royal Mail and transport financing, and asking me whether I'd consider helping. I assumed that this would involve doing more of what I had already done – writing the odd paper on something – so I said, 'Yes, sure!' He also added, 'I can't pay you very much,' and I said, 'Oh, you don't have to pay me!' After the meeting, I bumped into two of his advisers and was immediately asked, 'So, did you take the job?' I said, 'What job? Nobody offered me a job! He didn't say it was a job!' They said, 'Of course it was a job! You can't say "no" now!' I only thought about it for a brief moment and then said, 'OK. Sure, why not?'

I was to take a 90 per cent pay cut, and it *was* a real job. But I actually thought at the time, 'This will be fun!' I had always cared about international development and I knew that Gordon Brown really cared about it too (from the days when I first met him with NGOs). I remember thinking, 'I can definitely do this. I can help. I will get to do many really worthwhile things here.'

This naturally led me on a new journey, in an area that I had always cared about – and into new areas as well. It would eventually become an incredibly fulfilling and worthwhile part of my life. Was it serendipity? Was it luck? *Of course it was!* But I was also *open* to an opportunity. People realised that, they offered it to me, and I seized it with both hands.

Failures are inevitable . . .

Failure is tough, yet it's also completely inevitable – you *will* fail from time to time. We all do. But when you do, time, in the end, will help you. Your friends and family can also help you, and it's also important to ask those involved around you, 'I need you to help me *not* to do that again.' Asking for forgiveness from those that you have let down is important too.

Anyone who is on a journey will usually experience periods, even long periods, of not succeeding. This can be dispiriting and very hard, and can lead to self-doubt.

One of the most difficult things to deal with in life – if not *the* most difficult – is having to confront your own failures. It's when you say to yourself, 'I didn't succeed in doing that because I totally messed up.'

It's much easier if something goes wrong that's external to you. When you have to stand up and admit it's *your* fault, when you acknowledge it was actually *you* and that you must never do it again – this is particularly hard. As you grow older, however, it does become a bit easier when you realise that everyone actually messes up from time to time and you are not on your own.

I think most women find it harder to accept when they have made a mistake compared with men, and they will beat themselves up over it more easily too.

It's often said that failure makes you stronger, but that's not always the case. Some people just can't take failure. For a young person, how they deal with their first failure is key. I think it's extremely important to be truthful to kids – one thing that they despise is when adults are not honest with them. They need support in dealing with their first failure, and they need to understand from us that this is what growing up is all about. So although failures are completely inevitable, it's how we deal with them that's most important.

Another interesting view is that when everything is going really well, and someone's apparently highly successful, that's really the right time to ask the question 'Why?', as opposed to waiting for their next failure before posing the same question. Asking it at this point helps to identify whether their success is real or not. A lot of success may be transient or temporary, which is why it's important to understand what is actually happening and whether it's sustainable. Is it just luck? Is it just catching the market cycle? Are they *really* doing everything right? Unfortunately, these questions are not often asked. Success will usually be attributed to the brilliance of the individual, and failure is because 'something else' happened . . .

Looking back . . .

I look back all the time and think about how I could have done things better, not in a highly analytical way, but more emotionally and in a slightly self-critical way – 'I wish I could have handled that differently,' 'I wish I had done that better.'

When looking back over a period of time, one can sometimes see a pattern of things that one might be consistently doing wrong. Something I have identified, for example, is that when I'm working on a particular task and can see a solution, I will often tend to forge ahead to get the job done without necessarily carrying people with me. But if something is going to last, you have got to get other people on board as well, to help sustain the solution. This is something I have often thought about.

It's only when you look back and think about what you have done that you can see these things, but it's sometimes very painful to do.

Your attitude – don't anticipate limitations . . .

First, nobody likes people who moan all the time, who are negative and need to be continually supported because of their attitude.

People around you are normally busy, and they have to take you at face value. Your employer or your teacher doesn't necessarily have the time to discover who you really are. Your attitude is therefore what they see, and you have got to carry that and provide them with an opportunity to see the real you. I sometimes say to young people, especially young women, 'Don't let your inner demons be the ceiling.' If you continually think about your limitations and what you are *not* good at, then others are going to perceive that in you too, because it becomes part of your attitude and how you carry yourself. The important thing here is that until we explore what we might be good at, we won't know what our limitations actually are. It's *far* better to discover what your limitations and failings might be by *trying* something, and then saying, 'Well, OK, I now know that I'm actually not really good at that,' rather than to think beforehand, 'I'm not going to be good enough to do that and so I'm not going to try.' Don't set your limits before you know what they actually are, and be prepared to push them and stretch yourself.

One of my own strengths has always been that I push limits – a lot. I push or break boundaries, barriers or ceilings, and the reason for this is that I don't see them very clearly, and I don't look for them. This is not a strength that I have cultivated in some way. It is just an attitude I have always had that enables me to approach anything challenging without thinking, 'This is not going to be possible.' Instead, I will think, 'Well, this is what's happening. What do I need to do to change it?' You can sometimes be overwhelmed by a particular challenge and think, 'I'll never be able to do this,' before even trying, and it then becomes a barrier. Or it can be about what I need to do to get a specific thing done (without looking for any limitations), and then not giving up until I get there. It might be easier for me because I was born with the sort of character that does not give up easily, but if you can develop this attitude, it really works.

Setting your goals . . .

Your goals should be connected to following your passion and what you care about, and *not* be about, 'I want to be a pop star and become rich and famous' or 'I want to be a banker to earn lots of money' or 'I want to be an athlete and win that medal.' *Your goals should reflect what you really, really want to do.* 'I want to sing because that's what makes me happy,' 'I want to do this job because I think it's really amazing and interesting,' 'I want to run because I love running and want to be the best I can be.'

If you define your goals in terms of the things you want to create, the things you want to change and the things that you really want to spend your time on, how can you possibly fail?

People who are really successful are the ones who are actually *doing* what they really want to do. They have found what they love and what they have a talent for, they become good at it because of their passion, and they also work very hard at it. Success then becomes a natural consequence of working hard at what they love.

Success itself should never be the goal. So set your goals around *doing* what you really love and care about, and you are far more likely to find your happiness and success in the future.

Sir Clive Woodward OBE

Originally intending to pursue a career in football, Clive Woodward would learn rugby instead at his boarding school in Wales. He eventually excelled at the game, enjoying spells at Harlequins and Leicester, and playing for the England national team. Following his playing career, Clive became a highly regarded rugby coach. After training the England Under-21s, he was appointed as the England coach in 1997, building a hugely successful team using his unique coaching methodology. From 2000 to 2003, the England team won 41 out of 46 matches, and famously won the Rugby World Cup in 2003. Clive is a successful business speaker and coach, a TV commentator, and media columnist, and was director of sport for Team GB at the Beijing 2008, Vancouver 2010 and London 2012 Olympics. He is currently director of sport for the Apex2100 International Ski Academy in Tignes, France.

'If you think a particular role or career makes real sense and you are able to do it, just follow your dreams, follow your passion, throw everything at it and work really hard. The worst thing that you can possibly do is to have a dream but not pursue it, and then look back years later with regret and say, "I really wish I had made the effort to try that".'

'Someone with a good attitude will always push themselves to become even better at something, and they will make the time, as part of their discipline, for additional learning and self-improvement.'

'I will often say to young people: "OK, so your parents are doing that for you . . . your school and your teachers do that for you . . . or your employer does that for you. So what, then, are *you* doing?" '

'It is important for parents, in my view, to not only encourage their kids to enjoy their education, but to help them respect their teachers and to understand what they are trying to do for them. Teaching is not an easy profession, and parents have a role to play in helping teachers too, through encouraging their children to show good behaviour, respect and appreciation.'

About success . . .

On a completely practical level, success for me is really about happiness, and especially being happy at home. I feel very fortunate because I have a lovely wife and three wonderful kids (who are now adults). One of the great strengths of my family has always been that while I have had to work very hard at my career, they have been willing to work *with me* on this and have always been completely supportive of what I have had to do.

I have never thought about a working life as being somehow separate from my home life – the two have naturally gelled perfectly together. My family would always understand the times when I have been exceptionally busy, and when I have had to make sacrifices or big decisions that would sometimes affect them too. But we have a saying in our family – 'The upsides far outweigh the downsides.' During difficult times, such as when I've been away for long periods or have had to endure negative press on occasions, these have all been far outweighed by all the positive things that have happened for us as a family, because aligned with success at home, there has, of course, been financial success. Being able to enjoy a great standard of living and a wonderful lifestyle that has been fun and enormously rewarding for my family is, perhaps, the most important measure of success for me.

A difficult start . . .

I was eleven when the England football team won the World Cup in 1966. I was totally inspired by the success that the national side achieved; and because it was also a win for our country, I had a taste of what it felt like to be part of winning something really big. I fell in love with the sport, and playing football became a passion for me. I would rarely go anywhere without a ball at my feet and I soon built a strong desire to become *the very best* I could be at playing the game. I dreamed of becoming a professional footballer one day and to follow in the footsteps of those World Cup heroes of mine, especially Martin Peters, whom I had idolised. I excelled at the game and by the time I was thirteen, I was already playing for my school as part of the under-15 team.

Professional football in those days was, of course, completely different to today. It was more of an adventure, really, than a realistic career opportunity for most, especially for a young lad of my age. My father at first appreciated the abilities that I was clearly developing and the success I enjoyed as a player for my school, but he was also becoming increasingly concerned about the impact that this might have on my education. It was rare and quite hard for kids to get into university in those days. My sister had done it, and my father hoped that I would do the same. He was eventually swayed, however, by my grammar school headmaster, who persuaded him that I *did* have the potential to do well at school, and that if I applied myself properly to my academic studies, I could quite easily win a place at university . . . If only I were able to get past this 'unfortunate obsession' with football.

My father was a highly respected Royal Air Force officer and he was a good man too, who only wanted the best for his family. He was aware that I dreamed of becoming a professional football player one day, but for him, this was really just a pipedream. He knew, of course, that very few individuals would ever be good enough to play professionally. So he decided to discuss the dilemma he had with his commanding officer at the base where he was stationed, RAF Linton-on-Ouse. He suggested to my father (as I learned years later) that I would probably do a lot better if I were sent away to the same naval boarding school that he had attended when he was my age – HMS *Conway*, based in Anglesey in North Wales. There, I could concentrate on my studies but most importantly, they played *no* football at all – only rugby.

I will never forget that day when my world really began to fall apart . . . I was playing for my school in a very important match. I had an excellent game and was simply unstoppable in midfield. Everton FC had sent a scout down to have a look at me (a number of professional clubs were already taking an interest in me as a young player). I got home, feeling on top of the world and really excited about my performance that day and the implications this might have for my burgeoning football career. But sadly, my father had a totally different view. The Everton scout had obviously spoken to him at the match and tried to convince him about my potential. My father remained unmoved – he had already made up his mind about my future. He called me into the living room and immediately told me that I was going to be leaving Easingwold Grammar School at the end of the term and would be sent away instead to board at HMS *Conway*. I remember my father was unusually serious and he dealt with me more in a *military* manner than in a fatherly way. I recall the Everton scout phoning again later that evening and speaking with him, but it was a very brief conversation. I then realised that my dreams and my passion for something that was so completely central to my young world were probably never going to come true. It was a truly devastating time for me as a thirteen-year-old – I couldn't care less about university, I just wanted to play football . . .

So I moved from North Yorkshire to North Wales, and for a very long while it was to be the most depressing time of my life. In desperation, I ran away from HMS *Conway* three times, and on each occasion my father just sent me straight back. But I was still determined to get the message through to my parents that *all* I wanted was to pursue football. After my third escape, I was summarily beaten by a senior cadet when I was finally returned to the school. But even after that, I still wasn't ready to give up.

I was outdoors with one of my teachers one day and by chance we began messing around with a football. After a casual kickabout with him, he quickly became aware of my footballing skills. He was so impressed, in fact, with my control of the ball that he invited me to trial for his local club, where he coached boys of my age. Buoyed with the enthusiasm that he expressed about my abilities, I thought it would be a good idea to approach the headmaster and try once more to convince him about my desire to pursue football. But he was completely unimpressed. He threatened to beat me himself and told me quite clearly to 'forget this ridiculous nonsense' about football. It was then that I realised my resistance was probably futile. I was forced to give in, and began to resign myself to the fact that if I were to survive, I would have to accept that my dream of becoming a professional footballer one day was finally over . . .

I am sure that my father's intentions for me were sound, based on his conviction that I would be far better off pursuing academic study than risking a career in professional football, where the odds of becoming a top player were naturally very slim. But on the other hand, I do still feel that it was completely wrong for him to have denied me a chance to at least explore how far I could go in the pursuit of something that I was truly passionate about. It was *my* life, not his, but I don't think that he really understood that. I clearly had a talent for football, and it was quite possible that I was good enough to pursue the sport as a career, if only I were allowed an opportunity to find out. It was something that would haunt me for decades to come.

As in many traditional boarding school environments of the time, bullying was quite normal, and at HMS *Conway* the younger students had to deal routinely with physical intimidation from the senior cadets. The best way to survive was to play sport and to become good at it. The entire sporting tradition of the school revolved around rugby. I was soon excelling at the game, and in my first season, I was made captain of the under-14s. Although I was playing rugby because I was forced to, not because I loved it, I did start to enjoy winning – and this was ultimately to really help me put my past dreams behind me and to concentrate on doing well at the game.

I did eventually reconcile with my father some years ago, before he died, which is something I will always be thankful for. When I look back at my time at that naval school, however, it was undoubtedly formative and character-building, but certainly not enjoyable. While I eventually grew to like rugby, it was also tremendously sad for me to see my abilities and my passion for football just go to waste. As a young boy, I had a dream and a path, but I simply was not allowed to follow them. The implications of this were to have a profound effect on my life. I certainly became fiercely independent and learned how to look after myself from a young age. I also became, without knowing it at the time, a very driven and determined person. One thing I did learn – and it's something that still drives me to this day – is not to listen to anyone who tells me, 'You can't do that.' Deep down, I think that there's also a part of me that always wants to prove *those* people wrong and to show them what I really can do. The rest, as they say, is history . . .

Choosing what you want to be . . .

The key to choosing what it is that you want to do with your life and as a career is to pick something that you *really* enjoy doing. Some people say, 'It's only a short life,' but I believe that we have a long life and that we owe it to ourselves to find something that is really enjoyable, since we will end up spending a huge part of our lives doing it.

I have never quite understood the concept of a 'work-life balance', where people separate their work time in their minds from their home and leisure time, as though the latter were always somehow a much better place to be. Even early on in my career, when I was working for a company, I can honestly say that there was never a day when I woke up and thought, 'Oh no . . . I'm going to have to go to work today.' Your work life, if you really enjoy it, should just blend together nicely with your non-work life. Even working hard is enjoyable if it is something that you enjoy doing.

However, should you ever find yourself working at something that's a bit mundane (either a mundane role or a mundane job), then just do your best to enjoy it for what it is, but use the resources it provides to pursue something else worthwhile that you can really love outside of your work. This could be a sport, charity work or perhaps something creative. Quite often, it can actually lead to new opportunities for work and result in a positive change of direction.

Enjoyment is always top of the list for me. In sport – although the same applies to other occupations – there's real enjoyment to be found in working on *improvement* and getting better at what you do. When I became a coach, I would tell my players, 'The number one thing I want you to know is that when you *play* for your career, it's going to be *hard work*, but it's going to be fun as well.' I have also never known anyone to become successful in life without a strong work ethic and a continuous desire to improve.

So once you can actually find that *something* you love doing, that you *really* enjoy, then just go for it! If you think a particular role or career makes real sense and you are able to do it, just follow your dreams, follow your passion, throw everything at it and work really hard. The worst thing that you can possibly do is to have a dream but not pursue it, and then look back years later with regret and say, 'I really wish I had made the effort to try that.'

And whatever your chosen opportunity may be, just ignore all those people who try to tell you, 'You can't do that' or 'You'll never be successful at that,' because if for any reason it doesn't work out for you, the worst thing that can happen is that you may have to change direction later on. But at least you will have given yourself a chance to *find out* if you could have been really good at it.

Attracting opportunities . . .

While I was so passionate about playing football when I was young, I was, of course, forced to give it up and had to pursue rugby instead. But as my abilities improved and my obsession with *winning* began to emerge, I would eventually embrace the game as my new sport and worked very hard to be my very best at it.

Many amateur sportsmen make time for the sport they are passionate about and use their work to fund what they love doing. Many years later I was to build up a successful IT leasing business, and this provided me the opportunity to pursue rugby more seriously and further develop my passion for the game. As an amateur player, I eventually found myself competing at the highest levels and ultimately, I would play for my country – I typically represented England on a Saturday afternoon in front of 75,000 fans at Twickenham and then on Monday morning, I would be hard at work in the sales office doing my forecasts. Looking back now, it's hard to imagine how rugby at that level was actually still a totally amateur game – we didn't get paid a penny to represent club or country!

After sixteen years of playing competitive rugby, I eventually moved into coaching but again, strictly for fun. From coaching Henley, and for a short while London Irish, I was then invited to coach the England Under-21 team. This was a wonderful opportunity for me, and one I believe I attracted because I was so conspicuously immersed in the game and had worked very hard at developing my coaching skills. I also had my own vision for how to get the best out of players. It goes right back to what I was saying earlier – if you follow your passion and you work really hard at it, opportunities will naturally cross your path.

By the mid-1990s, there was a tectonic change in the world of rugby union. The International Rugby Board declared the sport 'open', which meant that previous restrictions on clubs being allowed to pay their players were lifted. After well over a century since the sport had been created, rugby was to transform from being a strictly amateur game into a professional sport. None of us had any clue that this was coming or what the implications might be . . .

The people who ran English rugby from Twickenham decided that they now needed to appoint a professional England coach. There were many highly experienced coaches around the country to select from, all of whom had excelled in the game, so I was really surprised to get a telephone call out of the blue from Don Rutherford, who was employed by Twickenham at the time, asking if he could come and see me. I met him at my home, and it was to be the first of a few truly bizarre discussions I was to have with him and the Rugby Football Union (RFU).

The first thing he told me was that the RFU had unanimously decided that I should be appointed to manage the England team. The way he presented the decision to me was almost like being anointed: '*You* are now the England coach.' I remember telling Don that I was delighted to have been considered for the job, but I was also hugely busy at the moment, so I wouldn't be able to do it. 'What do you mean, you can't do it?' he said. I then explained to him how I was running a small business with ten employees, and besides which, he hadn't even told me how much the board were willing to pay me for doing the job! I recall him saying, 'Well, we haven't discussed that yet . . .' It was actually quite extraordinary. I suggested to him that he could come back later if he wanted, perhaps with something a bit more constructive.

After a short while he was indeed back. He then handed me a folded piece of paper that had my proposed salary written on it. 'This is what the job will be worth', he said. I took one look at it, shook my head in disbelief and sighed, 'Look, we're just wasting our time here . . .' I then pointed out that the proposed annual salary was significantly less than what I was earning *every month* from my business. I said sarcastically, 'OK, I'll tell my family that I'm now the England rugby coach, but the bad news is that we'll have to sell the house and change schools, because Daddy can't do it otherwise.' I then showed him one of my PAYE income statements to prove what I earned each month (before bonuses). I remember Don immediately saying, 'But that's just ridiculous!' I then politely reminded him that I had not actually applied for this job – it was the RFU that had contacted me. I tactfully sent him on his way again.

It was a couple of weeks later that the chairman of the RFU then came over to see me at the house. He was a banker, and immediately apologised for the unfortunate 'confusion' over my proposed salary. We got into discussions straightaway, and ended up agreeing a respectable package for doing the job.

While taking on the England coaching role was a great opportunity, it was also a huge risk for me and my family. I was running a successful business, which already demanded a lot of my time, and this new role was also a full-time position. It would mean having to undergo some serious rearranging of my affairs. Anne, my business partner, was truly brilliant, and she agreed to manage our IT leasing business without me for a year (I told the RFU that I would give the role twelve months initially). My family were also fully on board and hugely supportive, despite the disruption that this would inevitably cause for all of us. I remember my wife Jane saying to me early in my discussions with the RFU that if I didn't say 'yes', I would probably never get the chance at something this big in rugby again. But it was still a massive undertaking – and because the role was so new, I didn't even really know what to expect. I was appointed in 1997, and thankfully enjoyed an incredibly exciting time managing and developing the team, culminating in England winning the Rugby World Cup in 2003. This was naturally the highlight of my career.

Once again, I believe the key point here for any young person is simple – if you can find something you really enjoy, and work exceptionally hard on it and excel at it, people will then notice you and will want you to be part of their team. I developed a passion for playing rugby and for coaching. I ended up playing for my country and then coaching the England Under-21s. I was always very positive and totally committed, and when the opportunity arose for *someone* to take on the role of England coach, the RFU came knocking at my door. It was an opportunity that I seized with both hands in the end and made the most of.

To parents . . .

There is no doubt that being a parent is a hugely challenging responsibility. All parents want the best for their child, but precisely what that 'best' is can sometimes be a little bit grey. I believe the number one role for any parent is to make sure that their child is healthy and happy, while supporting them in whatever it is that they are trying to do.

Parents should never be too prescriptive about what *they* think their child should become. If a child happens to find something that they are good at and enjoy, no matter what it is, just support, encourage and make sure that they have every opportunity open to them to pursue it.

Sometimes, it may not be obvious what a child might be good at. Parents must then help their children to explore different things. If a child is good at sport, this is something that will usually be fairly obvious quite early on. Parents should then encourage their child to try a range of different sporting activities until they can find what they like and may be good at. Once they find something, just allow them to *go for it* if they really want to.

Parents must be careful, however, not to become *too* involved themselves in their child's sporting activities and development. Some can get so embroiled that they end up inadvertently holding their children back. I've seen this many times in football, especially parents that have talented kids, where they often end up becoming almost an embarrassment for their child. This is something that has been well documented, of course – I've seen many astonishing videos of parents' behaviour and their reactions from the touchline!

Education is certainly hugely important for our children, but in order for them to embrace it fully at a young age, they must also enjoy it. Parents should therefore take care to help their children find the right school – it doesn't have to be a posh private school either, but simply one that their child will enjoy going to. Enjoyment is everything.

It is important for parents, in my view, to not only encourage their kids to enjoy their education, but to help them respect their teachers and to understand what they are trying to do for them. Teaching is not an easy profession, and parents have a role to play in helping teachers too, through encouraging their children to show good behaviour, respect and appreciation.

Parents should also take a keen interest in their children's schoolwork, and in the school itself. It shouldn't be just about going once a term to a parents' evening. Help them with their homework. Take a regular interest in the subjects they're learning and get involved. It's about being a good parent. It's also priceless, and can really help your child to enjoy their schooling and encourage them to do well.

Empowerment – helping children to adopt the right values . . .

I see many parallels between coaching a team, trying to get individuals to adopt the right values and raising children to do the same. For me, these are not things you can simply impose. You cannot just tell someone what they must do – it has to come from within. They have to understand the real meaning of good values and acceptable behaviour, and *want* to adopt these for themselves. It's a mixture of empowerment and getting someone to take responsibility for their actions. When I was coaching the England rugby team, one thing I got them to do was discuss and set their own rules. Rather than lecturing them on time-keeping, for example, I would get them to discuss the importance of always being on time and what the consequences should be for being late. In the end, it became a value that they all conceived, took seriously and adopted in a *cultural* way. The same approach can apply to kids. You have to get them to understand and appreciate the importance of values, and, in a way, bring them to life.

When I visit companies, I often notice the way in which they try to promote their corporate values internally – it might be a plaque on a wall that says something like 'The Customer always comes first.' One sees different versions of such values, typically using words like 'trust', 'respect', 'reliability' and so on. But when you ask any one of their employees what these values actually mean, they either find it difficult to explain or they haven't got a clue.

In a similar way to seeing corporate values displayed in companies, whenever you go into sports clubs or changing rooms, you typically see lots of *motivational* posters on the walls to help inspire or stimulate positive thinking. I have recently become involved in a major sports project, building a new ski academy (in the resort of Tignes in the French Alps) to help develop young skiing talent. Rather than simply putting up regular posters everywhere to *tell* kids what they should be inspired by, we are now getting the kids to create their own. When they sit down and think about what a poster should be saying, based on what *they* believe it should say and mean, it's bringing the message to life for them while also *delivering* it. They are more likely to understand values in this way – and adopt them – rather than when they're just being told. When these kids look at the posters later on, they will actually *mean* something to them.

I have also done this with my own kids — rather than just introducing them to the right values, I have always tried to get them to think about them and express them so that these values can become *their* ideas. They can then own them, and they are not simply *my* ideas imposed upon them.

So for me, whether it's a team or an individual I'm coaching, or my kids, it's about creating a culture that embraces values and that sees the virtue of being led by them, rather than just rules to be followed as a matter of discipline. It can apply to things like acceptable behaviour, time-keeping, dress, language or whatever, but you actually want children to *think* about the actions they are taking and how these actually represent those values.

Role models and mentors . . .

There are several people I have worked with over the years, especially on the rugby side, who I developed an enormous amount of respect for — people who coached me, and when looking back, from whom I learned a huge amount. I wouldn't necessarily call them 'mentors', because they didn't know that they were mentoring me at the time, but they were all excellent role models for me. It was really helpful to observe what they were doing as a player or as a coach.

Because of the difficulties I faced when growing up, I became very independent in my thinking and was determined to make my own way. I therefore never really had a formal mentor to guide me, and I can't really say whether that's been a good or a bad thing. I just got on and did what I had to do. But I do think it can be very helpful for a young person to have a mentor at some stage who can be a bit more than just a role model — someone whom they can engage with and build a relationship with, who can act as a sounding board and from whom they can seek advice. It's something I often advise young people to look out for today. And when children are young, a sufficiently experienced and enlightened parent can be a good early mentor for them too. I would love to think that my kids saw me as a mentor to them.

Later in life, when young people start working at a career or pursuing an opportunity, a mentor can be very useful to help them chart a good path. If they can find someone who works in their industry or business area, they can then bounce ideas off them and discuss their options. A good mentor can also help them to make good decisions.

When a child has a talent for a particular sport, it can be a very difficult thing to manage. I have actually seen it from all sides; I've seen it from me as a kid, I've seen it as a parent of three kids and also from coaching kids in rugby. Today, I can see it at the Ski Academy, where we have some enormously talented kids – brilliant skiers, amazing athletes, some as young as twelve. But occasionally, the younger ones can have real difficulties fitting in with a team of people and coping with boarding away from home. Some of them might even risk losing their place at the academy because of their behaviour, which would be a real shame, given their level of talent.

In such cases, we always do our best to help them directly, of course, but we also now encourage them to find someone independent (not necessarily one of their parents) who can help them in a mentorial way. That person needs to be someone that the child respects, can look up to and listen to, who can sit them down when necessary in a nice way and say, 'Come on, you've really got to start thinking about what you are doing.' They have to be interested in the child or young person, and want to help them to do the right thing and find the right way. But they must also be available for them to speak to regularly – not just once a term but perhaps once a week, either in person or on the phone.

How to shine and get lucky . . .

I do believe in luck, but it can work both ways, of course. You may go down a path, make some decisions, take some risks and everything works out well, which is great. But you could also be unlucky and choose the wrong path, and it doesn't work out for you. Then the cost to you personally can be high. What I do believe is that if you work really hard and you try many things, then you can *get* lucky. It's as simple as that, and it's about numbers and opportunities. As already mentioned, the harder you work and the more you do, the more opportunities will naturally fall across your path. If you do very little – or just wait for things to happen – you are far less likely to 'get lucky'.

The secret is also in being able to spot those opportunities when they do arise, choose the right ones to pursue and make the most of them. That also requires hard work.

There is a saying that 'the grass is always greener on the other side.' If you pursue an opportunity and it's not working out for you, be careful about simply changing direction, especially within the same industry – if you cannot be successful at something, there's no logical reason why there should automatically be another goldmine for you somewhere else in the same area. But sometimes it can just be very hard, and you need persistence and to stay on track. This is the time when a good mentor can help, of course – someone with experience in your industry who can help you to chart a clear path forward and make some fresh decisions.

Employers are always interested in people who work hard and come up with ideas. One of the businesses I am currently involved in is a small software company. We employ around fifty people now. They are all young, mostly in their early to mid-twenties, and incredibly clever at computers, software and programming. Most of them are ambitious and looking for a big career, but for now, they need a job and to make a living while they are finding their way. But I am always looking out for those individuals within the company that genuinely shine. They tend to be the ones that get in early, who get on with their work, who love what they're doing and who also enjoy the whole thought process of innovation and creating new ideas. These are the individuals that I will try to get totally involved with the business because I know that most of the good ideas for the company will ultimately come from them.

I also encourage our employees to speak up when they think they have an idea. They shouldn't just sit there and keep it to themselves – I urge them to stand up, bang the table if they have to, and say, 'I think we should take a look at this!' If they're not confident enough to express an idea openly or to stand up in a group, they should at least find someone they can present their idea to one on one. People will always listen. I ask all of my people to keep thinking, keep working hard, and *'Please! We need lots and lots of new ideas!'* That's invariably how businesses push the envelope and move forward. It's also how individuals excel in their careers and create opportunities for themselves. When you shine, you get noticed – and good things will naturally come to you.

Education and learning . . .

When it comes to learning and acquiring knowledge, I will often say to young people: 'OK, so your parents are doing that for you . . . your school and your teachers do that for you . . . or your employer does that for you. So what, then, are *you* doing?' There is only so much that we can receive from others, and if everything is given to us on a plate, I don't think that ever works either. It has to be self-education and it has to come from within – you have to find that inner drive to *want* to study and *want* to learn more.

The equation is simple: the more you study a particular subject or area of interest, the better you can become at it. But you cannot just rely on other people to simply *give* you all the information that you need. You have to go out there and find it, study it (and I mean *really* study it) and learn it. Go and talk to as many people as you can who are involved in that subject, if you have to. And, with the internet today, there are simply *no* excuses at all for not acquiring knowledge.

I have a saying that I like to use – 'You have to be a sponge, not a rock.' That space between your ears should be a sponge for new information, new ideas and further knowledge. But then you must also be organised and know how to store it, since there's a limit to how much we can retain in our heads. You need to create a 'bank' where you can safely keep that wealth of knowledge. Fortunately, we have great technology these days to store everything securely, while being able to access it whenever we want.

If you are serious about sport, there's the play and the practice and training sessions you can participate in, but there's also *far* more you can study from books, videos, courses and resources on the internet. When you are passionate about it, you will also *enjoy learning* more about it.

Planning for failure . . .

As sure as night follows day, everyone will have ups and downs along their journey. My career path has certainly never been straight. I've been all over the place, with some wonderful highs but many serious lows on my way to where I am today. But that's the real world.

The problem is, when serious challenges do come along, how are you going to deal with them? If you are completely unprepared, are you going to simply choke up or 'lose your bottle'? Will you just freeze like a rabbit in the headlights? Many people do, of course. In my view, the solution is quite straightforward: you must *prepare yourself for failure*.

Several years ago, I devised a strategy specifically for sports coaching that can help both teams and individual players to positively anticipate possible failures. It was a key part of the England rugby team's preparation during our successful campaign for the 2003 Rugby World Cup, and I now use it regularly, applying it successfully to my own business career and regularly speaking about it during corporate presentations and talks. I call this strategy 'T-CUP' – or *Thinking Correctly Under Pressure.*

It's about planning for future events and virtually *planning* for pressure situations. As a coach, I probably spent more time in a training room with my players than any other coach I have seen. We would go meticulously through every possible different scenario and 'what if's: 'What if *this* were to happen?', 'What if *that* were to happen?', 'We're four points down with twenty minutes to go and *this* happens – what should we do?' We would explore every single possibility, anticipate everything that could go wrong, and then plan for how we would deal with those situations if or when they arose.

The biggest problems in life usually occur when someone is faced with a serious issue that they are not familiar with or that they have not anticipated. In these circumstances, the chances of thinking correctly under pressure are definitely very slim. But if you have prepared for the issue carefully, even if it's just discussing it in the training room, your chances of knowing how to deal with it, when it arises, are hugely improved. From a coaching standpoint, your players will learn how to be *far more likely* to make the right decisions when they need to, and when they are under pressure.

The same applies to business. Most people get into trouble because they haven't planned for something when it goes wrong. If you plan for the downtimes, for when things do go wrong, if you discuss them and visualise what you will do, then you will be much better placed to handle them and far less likely to be caught out. Another benefit of planning for downtimes is, of course, that you start to think, 'I never ever want to go through that. What can we do now to *avoid* that from happening in the future?'

'I never lose – I either win or I learn' . . .

This is one of my favourite sayings. You can certainly gain and learn a lot from winning, but you can learn a massive amount from losing too. Understanding that you are *going to fail* at some stage is vitally important. It goes right back to the T-CUP principle: planning for every possible eventuality and then, when it happens, knowing how to deal with it – and how to learn from it too. That whole approach helps to toughen you up, while building your resilience and confidence.

After winning an important game, most teams will celebrate, perhaps going down the pub for a few drinks. When they lose, it's often, 'Let's all get together first thing on Monday morning for a serious talk about what went wrong.' I actually believe it should be the other way around.

When you win, *that's* the best time to get together to thoroughly analyse why you won and how you can do even better next time. Even when you win, improvements can still be made. To understand and analyse these can help to make the win even stronger next time.

You can have really great meetings when you win, and you can also be a lot harder on your players too! When you lose, rather than having an intense and critical session, which can sometimes demoralise and therefore compound the problem for some players, that's the time to get together for a pint and just chill and quietly contemplate – especially where you *have* planned for failure, thought about it beforehand, but it still went wrong. One can then have a more positive and constructive session later to analyse and to plan effectively for the next time. It's a balance, really – never underestimate the importance of winning, but don't overreact to failure. You can certainly learn hugely from both.

Most highly successful people will have had big failures along their journey. No one at the top has a perfect CV. In fact, as a rule, I will never normally employ someone with a perfect CV because it will make me wonder, 'What have you been doing all this time if you've never failed at something?' I actually want to find failures on your CV. I want to find out what happened – how did you get through it and how did you get out of it? – because that for me is the real world!

Working on and working in . . .

The same applies whether you have your own business, a job in a company, or in a large organisation. You can work *in it* and you can also work *on it*. Most high achievers work really hard, they are driven and spend 100 per cent of their working time *in* their work or business. The *really* high achievers, however, will spend 95 per cent of their time in their work and 5 per cent of their time *on* it. In other words, they will always take a couple of hours a week to sit back and reflect, write down their thoughts, talk their ideas through with others, and think about what they are doing and why: 'What are the risks currently? Where are the opportunities? Where are we going?

Goals, visualisation and discipline . . .

When I think about goals, I prefer to use the term 'blue-sky thinking', and from that, to break everything all the way down into what needs to be done in order to get to where you want to be. So it's never just about striving towards one major goal, but more to do with, 'What are the component parts to that goal?', and then studying each of those areas deeply, while identifying what 'key points' (as I call them) need to be worked on specifically.

For example, when I used to play at Twickenham, it was mostly a dull and boring place for both players and spectators. When I took over managing the England rugby team, it became my dream to change all of that – I literally wanted to get 85,000 people jumping up and down with excitement at Twickenham. So that was to become my blue-sky plan, and it was all to do with playing far more exciting rugby. To achieve that, we identified seven main areas of the game to work on, each of which revolved around winning the ball quicker and playing much faster. From the mass of information that we considered as a team, we broke it all down into smaller chunks and then into the relevant key points. My role as coach was to make sure that *every* player knew these key points inside out (based on deep and careful study, not just gut instinct), and achieving *that* was to become my primary goal. In the end, we got the whole of Twickenham on their feet and going nuts, which is, of course, exactly what we wanted to achieve.

Attitude and discipline . . .

Everyone talks about the importance of having a good *attitude* when pursuing success in life, but when asked to define what 'attitude' actually means or how one can measure it, most people don't know where to begin.

Attitude always says a lot to me about *the person* and whether they are *fit for purpose*. For most individuals, a good attitude is a product of their background, upbringing and schooling, and it naturally becomes part of their basic values. But it can also be developed further through self-discipline.

As a coach, I talk about attitude a lot, and, when working with a high-performing team, you can actually take it up to a whole new level. When you think about the conventional 'annual staff appraisal', it's really a complete nonsense! For me, the best way to appraise an individual is to measure their attitude on a *continuous basis*. First, however, you have to break attitude down into its different areas or components, each of which can then be analysed and measured for every individual. I normally work with a list of *ten* specific components, which I can then use to measure each team member's personal performance. The list is not completely cast in stone and can be varied, depending on the team scenario. One of the best things is that all of these components can be coached, so that every individual can be helped to improve in each area.

It is important, however, for all members of the team to completely buy into this whole process from the outset and agree a collective definition for each component. They then need to understand what I will be looking out for as their coach, and what I will be measuring. But I also encourage my team to measure my performance as well, so that they can see that I'm also delivering on each component. It is therefore a fully transparent process that applies to everyone, me included.

For young people, embarking on their life journey, the most important areas of attitude (and discipline) that they should focus on to begin with, are probably these:

Time-keeping and punctuality – If you speak to anyone who has worked for me, they will say, 'Don't ever be late. Clive is *always* on time!' In fact, there has to be a major incident for me to be late for anyone . . . Punctuality says more to me about an individual than practically anything else. But it's not just about being on time. I will always plan to get to an appointment *early*, as a discipline, to make sure that I am never late. One should also respect the amount of time that people actually give you for an appointment – don't waste it, and always try to end the meeting on time. And, when someone makes an appointment to see you, always allow them enough time to cover what they want to discuss with you as well.

Presentation – Your appearance and the way you present yourself to others are absolutely key. How you dress (this may sound a little old-school, but it isn't) and even small things like your handshake when you first meet someone are all important reflections of your attitude. You really have got to look and act the part, and you have to really understand what *that* can represent.

Confidence – Communication skills and building your confidence for when you interact with other people are vital. Learning how to feel comfortable when you are standing up in front of others and talking is also very important. These are pretty big skills to learn; they take practice but also require an element of pushing yourself outside of your comfort zone.

Be prepared and assume nothing – Anything can change, and things sometimes do go wrong. It's back to the T-Cup principle – you should learn to anticipate all possible scenarios and be prepared for them. Make this part of your mindset, and think about all the challenges that could possibly arise and how you would deal with them.

Take responsibility – Whatever you decide to do, or are tasked to do, take full ownership and responsibility for it. Throw everything at it, and work at it positively and to the best of your abilities. Recognise that if something really stretches you, then it will always be good for you.

Enjoyment – People generally really appreciate someone that enjoys their work, when they see them working hard and putting everything into it. Enjoyment is also a measure of positivity – your colleagues will then naturally enjoy working with you too, and they will want to help you or involve you more in what they're doing. Opportunities also come to those who are seen to enjoy what they do, because it's simply another reflection of a good attitude.

Work hard – Perhaps the most important component of attitude is being totally committed to working hard at whatever you choose to do. As mentioned earlier, I have never seen anyone being successful in life without having worked really hard for it.

Relentless learning – You should always strive to learn and acquire knowledge that can help you to improve. Don't just rely on what you have been taught during your normal education. Someone with a good attitude will always push themselves to become even better at something, and they will make the time, as part of their discipline, for additional learning and self-improvement. When you are part of a team, it's especially important to share useful knowledge and ideas with your colleagues so that everyone else can benefit as well.

All of these points are applicable to whatever you may be pursuing in life, but even if you are not yet sure about your direction, applying them as principles will help you to prepare yourself for your future. For those who may already be thinking about a career in sport, the two following qualities are important components of a good attitude (they can also apply more generally in other fields):

Obsession – Part of the DNA of a true sports champion is being absolutely obsessive about winning, beating the person or people you are competing against and improving your game. It is also about having a total obsession for the *detail*, and understanding *everything* you can learn about your opponent in *real* depth. I call it 'having the obsessive gene'! You can actually be a completely normal person and enjoy a normal family life, but anyone at the top level in sport will also be 24/7/365 obsessed about the detail, what they are doing and doing it better.

Trust and teamwork – It is absolutely vital that all of your teammates trust and respect you completely for the commitment and dedication you are showing to *all* of them. I very often get asked as a coach, 'How do you motivate your team?' But actually, I *never* think like that . . . For me, it's not about *motivating*, it's all about having every single member of our team trusting completely that we all know exactly what we're doing, that everyone is working really hard and that every individual is throwing absolutely everything at it, to be the best and to win.

At the Ski Academy in Tignes, we now run a programme called 'personal performance', where we focus on nutrition, sleep, strength conditioning, and developing personal skills and discipline. It's all about getting youngsters prepared for life, how they conduct themselves, what they prioritise, and developing those essential communication skills. It's quite military-sounding, but these disciplines are an essential part of their personal development as young athletes.

The same applies in broader life – if you come to work late, you look a mess, you've not had enough sleep, you've not eaten properly, you will then be no good to me, as your employer. You will not be fit for purpose. However, if you apply yourself to these disciplines, understand and appreciate their value to you as an individual, you will be far more able to deal with all of the challenges that you will have to face in life and be far more likely to succeed!

ACKNOWLEDGEMENTS

A Few Wise Words would simply not have happened without the help and encouragement of a great number of wonderful people, to whom I will always be indebted.

I am especially grateful to Lord Mervyn Davies, whose support, friendship and involvement throughout this project have been hugely positive and completely invaluable to me.

Our amazing contributors have of course been absolutely brilliant – it has been a real pleasure to spend time with all of them over the last few years while I have been working on this book. I am especially grateful for all of the time and input that each have so generously given, making it possible to put their extraordinary chapters together. Thank you so much to Sir Ben Ainslie, Frank Arnesen, Zak Brown, Ursula Burns, Sir Roger Carr, Sherry Coutu, Pablo Ettinger, Mikhail Fridman, Stephen Fry, Dame Katherine Grainger, Tanni, Baroness Grey-Thompson, Anya Hindmarch, Declan Kelly, Martha, Baroness Lane-Fox, Joanna Lumley, Dame Carolyn McCall, Sir Keith Mills, Vin Murria, Danielle de Niese, Rabbi Lord Jonathan Sacks, Shriti Vadera and Sir Clive Woodward. I would also like to offer my sincere thanks to all of their amazing EAs, PAs and assistants, who have been so helpful as well.

Behind every significant project sits invariably a great executive team. Mine has been completely wonderful and I am really grateful to Ben Dunn (literary agent and adviser), Laura Visick (social media manager and adviser), Amelia Knight, Anna Zanetti, Jason Bartholomew and Fiona Marsh (Midas PR), Mark Bolland (copy-editor), Laura Westcott (adviser), Matt Hicks and Claire Mugridge (Lightflows web design), Charlotte Posner and Chris Bentham (cover design), Natalie O'Brien (community manager), Belle Hinchin (Clays, printers), and Tim Russell (proof-reader).

The following individuals have also been especially helpful and generous with their time, advice, counsel and support: Christian

Angermayer, Lady Jeanne Davies, Parmjit Dhanda, Mischa Dohler, Lilly Dunn, Angela Farrugia, Martin Gent, Deborah Hilderly, Owen Lee, Tim Marlow, Tony Matharu, Sam McAlister, Robin Mukherjee, Bob Patmore, the Baroness Rebuck DBE, Caroline Stevens, David Stileman and Robert Suss.

I am also grateful for the support that all of the following have provided to help this book to transition from concept to reality: Edd Bateman, Paul Davies, Eric Dowding, Dorian Furlonger, Samantha Garrod (and the Mayfair Hotel, London), Chris Gibbons, Mark Goddard, James Guest, Robbie Hicks, Steve Lee, Andrew Murphy, Jan Noble, Nicole Patterson, Eleanor O'Rourke, Genevieve Quierin, Rebecca Schumacher and Adam Sherwin.

To anyone else that has also helped, even a little bit, thank you too.

And finally, I would like to thank my lovely family, Shareena and Sebastian, for helping with preparing material, reading and critiquing. Their unerring patience, love and support have also meant everything to me while I have been immersed in preparing this book.